The Asian Games: Modern Metaphor for 'The Middle Kingdom' Reborn

The premise of *The Asian Games: Modern Metaphor for 'The Middle Kingdom' Reborn – Political Statement, Cultural Assertion, Social Symbol* is emphatic. The Guangzhou 2010 Asian Games were a metaphor for hegemony and renaissance. China crushed the other Asian nations with the massive weight of its gold medal 'haul' and demonstrated regional self-confidence regained. The huge accumulation of gold medals emphasized that once again China stood apart, and above, other nations of Asia. China's reaction and the reactions of the other Asian nations are explored in *The Asian Games*. There is another premise in the publication that the 'Chinese' Asian Games were a harbinger of a wider dominance to come: geopolitically, politically, militarily, economically and culturally. And there is a further issue raised by the Guangzhou Asian Games – the continuing determination of the Asian nations to mount a distinctive Games that is Asian and resistant to the cumbersome gigantism of the Modern Olympic Games. Asia now has the wealth to promote, present and project a global sports mega-event with an Asian identity and in an Asian idiom. This collection is unique in focus, argument and evidence.

This book was previously published as a special issue of the *International Journal of the History of Sport*.

J.A. Mangan, Emeritus Professor, University of Strathclyde; FRHS; FRAI; FRSA; RSL; D. Litt, is Founding Editor of the *International Journal of the History of Sport* and the series *Sport in the Global Society*. Professor Mangan is the author of the globally acclaimed *Athleticism in the Victorian and Edwardian Public School, The Games Ethic and Imperialism* and *'Manufacturing' Masculinity: Making Imperial Manliness, Morality and Militarism* and author or editor of some fifty publications on politics, culture and sport.

Marcus P. Chu lectures on Chinese Politics and International Relations in the Department of Political Science, Lingnan University, Hong Kong. He obtained his PhD from the University of Auckland in May 2012. His thesis reviews the central and local inter-relations in China's bids for international events since the 1980s. He currently works on a project regarding the political preoccupations of East Asian countries at the London 2012 Olympics with Professor J.A. Mangan.

Dong Jinxia is a Professor at Peking University. She obtained her PhD from the University of Strathclyde in 2001. She was also a visiting scholar at Yale University in 2009. Her research interests include Olympic culture, gender and sport, and sports sociology. She received the 'International Max & Reet Howell Award' of NASSH in 2007.

The Asian Games: Modern Metaphor for 'The Middle Kingdom' Reborn
Political Statement, Cultural Assertion, Social Symbol

Edited by
J.A. Mangan, Marcus P. Chu and Dong Jinxia

LONDON AND NEW YORK

First published 2014
by Routledge
Published 2014 by Routledge
2 Park Square, Milton Park, Abingdon, Oxfordshire OX14 4RN

and by Routledge
711 Third Avenue, New York, NY 10017

Routledge is an imprint of the Taylor and Francis Group, an informa business

First issued in paperback 2015

© 2014 Taylor & Francis

All rights reserved. No part of this book may be reprinted or reproduced or utilised in any form or by any electronic, mechanical, or other means, now known or hereafter invented, including photocopying and recording, or in any information storage or retrieval system, without permission in writing from the publishers.

Trademark notice: Product or corporate names may be trademarks or registered trademarks, and are used only for identification and explanation without intent to infringe.

British Library Cataloguing in Publication Data
A catalogue record for this book is available from the British Library

ISBN 978-0-415-73140-9 (hbk)
ISBN 978-1-138-95466-3 (pbk)

Typeset in Times New Roman
by Taylor & Francis Books

Publisher's Note
The publisher accepts responsibility for any inconsistencies that may have arisen during the conversion of this book from journal articles to book chapters, namely the possible inclusion of journal terminology.

Disclaimer
Every effort has been made to contact copyright holders for their permission to reprint material in this book. The publishers would be grateful to hear from any copyright holder who is not here acknowledged and will undertake to rectify any errors or omissions in future editions of this book.

Contents

Series Editors' Foreword	vii
Series Pages	ix
Citation Information	xix

Preface: A Regional and Global Symbolic Proclamation
Roberta J. Park — 1

Foreword: Holding Up More Than Half the Asian Sky
Jinxia Dong — 3

1. Introduction: Marketing 'Brand China': Maintaining the Momentum –
   'The Middle Kingdom' Resurgent and Resplendent
   J.A. Mangan — 4

Part One: Chinese Motives: Realism, Rivalries and 'Reassertion'

2. *People's Daily*: An Evolutionary Narrative on Asia in Its Coverage of the
   Asian Games
   Wenting Xue and Qing Luo — 15

3. The Pursuit of Regional Geopolitical Aspirations: China's Bids for the Asian
   Games and the Asian Winter Games since the 1980s
   Marcus P. Chu — 26

4. Strict Compliance!: Chinese Careful Conformity and the Guangzhou Bid
   for the Asian Games
   Marcus P. Chu — 37

5. 'Glittering Guangzhou': The 2010 Asian Games – Local Rivalries,
   National Motives, Geopolitical Gestures
   J.A. Mangan, Jinxia Dong and Di Lu — 49

6. Chinese Desires? Olympism and Dominance, Guangzhou and Missed
   Opportunity, Major Leagues and Isolation on the Pacific Rim
   John D. Kelly — 65

CONTENTS

Part Two: Pacific Rim Reactions and Responses

7. Guangzhou 2010: Eastern Orwellian Echoes – Yang Shu-chun and a Taiwanese Patriotic Media Offensive
Chen-Li Liu, Ping-Chao Lee and J.A. Mangan   77

8. From Honeymoon to Divorce: Fragmenting Relations between China and South Korea in Politics, Economics – and Sport
J.A. Mangan, Sun-Yong Kwon and Bang-Chool Kim   91

9. Rivalries: China, Japan and South Korea – Memory, Modernity, Politics, Geopolitics – and Sport
J.A. Mangan, Hyun-Duck Kim, Angelita Cruz and Gi-Heun Kang   108

10. Guangzhou 2010: Singapore at a Global Crossroads
Peter Horton   131

11. Guangzhou: The Asian Games and the Chinese 'Gold-Fest' – Geopolitical Issues for Australia
Peter Horton   143

Part Three: The Pacific Rim and Beyond: Confrontation and Cooperation

12. The Asian Games and Diplomacy in Asia: Korea – China – Russia
Victor Cha   154

Index   167

Series Editors' Foreword

On January 1, 2010 *Sport in the Global Society*, created by Professor J.A. Mangan in 1997, was divided into two parts: *Historical Perspectives* and *Contemporary Perspectives*. These new categories involve predominant rather than exclusive emphases. The past is part of the present and the present is part of the past. The Editors of *Historical Perspectives* are Mark Dyreson and Thierry Terret.

The reasons for the division are straightforward. SGS has expanded rapidly since its creation with over one hundred publications in some twelve years. Its editorial teams will now benefit from sectional specialist interests and expertise. *Historical Perspectives* draws on *International Journal of the History of Sport* monograph reviews, themed collections and conference/ workshop collections. It is, of course, international in content.

Historical Perspectives continues the tradition established by the original incarnation of *Sport in the Global Society* by promoting the academic study of one of the most significant and dynamic forces in shaping the historical landscapes of human cultures. Sport spans the contemporary globe. It captivates vast audiences. It defines, alters, and reinforces identities for individuals, communities, nations, empires, and the world. Sport organises memories and perceptions, arouses passions and tensions, and reveals harmonies and cleavages. It builds and blurs social boundaries, animating discourses about class, gender, race, and ethnicity. Sport opens new vistas on the history of human cultures, intersecting with politics and economics, ideologies and theologies. It reveals aesthetic tastes and energises consumer markets.

By the end of the twentieth century a critical mass of scholars recognised the importance of sport in their analyses of human experiences and *Sport in the Global Society* emerged to provide an international outlet for the world's leading investigators of the subject. As Professor Mangan contended in the original series foreword: "The story of modern sport is the story of the modern world—in microcosm; a modern global tapestry permanently being woven. Furthermore, nationalist and imperialist, philosopher and politician, radical and conservative have all sought in sport a manifestation of national identity, status and superiority. Finally for countless millions sport is the personal pursuit of ambition, assertion, well-being and enjoyment."

Sport in the Global Society: Historical Perspectives continues the project, building on previous work in the series and excavating new terrain. It remains a consistent and coherent response to the attention the academic community demands for the serious study of sport.

Mark Dyreson
Thierry Terret

SPORT IN THE GLOBAL SOCIETY – HISTORICAL PERSPECTIVES

Series Editors: Mark Dyreson and Thierry Terret

THE ASIAN GAMES: MODERN METAPHOR FOR 'THE MIDDLE KINGDOM' REBORN

Political Statement, Cultural Assertion, Social Symbol

Sport in the Global Society: Historical Perspectives
Series Editors: Mark Dyreson and Thierry Terret

Titles in the Series

Encoding the Olympics
The Beijing Olympic Games and the
 Communication Impact Worldwide
Edited by Luo Qing and Giuseppe Richeri

Gymnastics, a Transatlantic Movement
From Europe to America
Edited by Gertrud Pfister

London, Europe and the Olympic Games
Historical Perspectives
Edited by Thierry Terret

'Manufactured' Masculinity
Making Imperial Manliness, Morality
 and Militarism
J.A. Mangan

Mapping an Empire of American Sport
Expansion, Assimilation, Adaptation
*Edited by Mark Dyreson, J.A. Mangan
 and Roberta J. Park*

Militarism, Hunting, Imperialism
'Blooding' The Martial Male
J.A. Mangan and Callum McKenzie

Olympic Aspirations
Realised and Unrealised
*Edited by J.A. Mangan and
 Mark Dyreson*

**Post-Beijing 2008: Geopolitics, Sport and
 the Pacific Rim**
Edited by J.A. Mangan and Fan Hong

Representing the Nation
Sport and Spectacle in
 Post-Revolutionary Mexico
Claire and Keith Brewster

**Rule Britannia: Nationalism, Identity and
 the Modern Olympic Games**
Matthew Llewellyn

Soft Power Politics – Football and Baseball in the Western Pacific Rim
Edited by Rob Hess, Peter Horton and J.A. Mangan

Sport and Emancipation of European Women
The Struggle for Self-fulfilment
Edited by Gigliola Gori and J.A. Mangan

Sport, Bodily Culture and Classical Antiquity in Modern Greece
Edited by Eleni Fournaraki and Zinon Papakonstantinou

Sport in the Cultures of the Ancient World
New Perspectives
Edited by Zinon Papakonstantinou

Sport in the Middle East
Power, Politics, Ideology and Religion
Edited by Fan Hong

Sport in the Pacific
Colonial and Postcolonial Consequencies
Edited by C. Richard King

Sport, Literature, Society
Cultural Historical Studies
Edited by Alexis Tadié, J.A. Mangan and Supriya Chaudhuri

Sport, Militarism and the Great War
Martial Manliness and Armageddon
Edited by Thierry Terret and J.A. Mangan

Sport Past and Present in South Africa
(Trans)forming the Nation
Edited by Scarlet Cornelissen and Albert Grundlingh

The Asian Games: Modern Metaphor for 'The Middle Kingdom' Reborn
Political Statement, Cultural Assertion, Social Symbol
Edited by J.A. Mangan, Marcus P. Chu and Dong Jinxia

The Balkan Games and Balkan Politics in the Interwar Years 1929-1939
Politicians in Pursuit of Peace
Penelope Kissoudi

The Beijing Olympics: Promoting China
Soft and Hard Power in Global Politics
Edited by Kevin Caffrey

The History of Motor Sport
A Case Study Analysis
Edited by David Hassan

The New Geopolitics of Sport in East Asia
Edited by William Kelly and J.A. Mangan

The Politicisation of Sport in Modern China
Communists and Champions
Fan Hong and Lu Zhouxiang

The Politics of the Male Body in Sport
The Danish Involvement
Hans Bonde

The Rise of Stadiums in the Modern United States
Cathedrals of Sport
Edited by Mark Dyreson and Robert Trumpbour

The Triple Asian Olympics
Asia Rising - the Pursuit of National Identity, International Recognition and Global Esteem
Edited by J.A. Mangan, Sandra Collins and Gwang Ok

SPORT IN THE GLOBAL SOCIETY SERIES PAGES

The Triple Asian Olympics - Asia A scendant
Media, Politics and Geopolitics
Edited by J.A. Mangan, Luo Qing and Sandra Collins

The Visual in Sport
Edited by Mike Huggins and Mike O'Mahony

Women, Sport, Society
Further Reflections, Reaffirming Mary Wollstonecraft
Edited by Roberta Park and Patricia Vertinsky

Sport in the Global Society
Past SGS publications prior to 2010

Africa, Football and FIFA
Politics, Colonialism and Resistance
Paul Darby

Amateurism in British Sport
'It Matters Not Who Won or Lost'
*Edited by Dilwyn Porter and
    Stephen Wagg*

Amateurism in Sport
An Analysis and Defence
Lincoln Allison

America's Game(s)
A Critical Anthropology of Sport
*Edited by Benjamin Eastman, Sean
    Brown and Michael Ralph*

American Sports
An Evolutionary Approach
Edited by Alan Klein

A Social History of Indian Football
Striving to Score
*Kausik Bandyopadhya and
    Boria Majumdar*

**A Social History of Swimming in
    England, 1800–1918**
Splashing in the Serpentine
Christopher Love

A Sport-Loving Society
Victorian and Edwardian Middle-Class
    England at Play
Edited by J.A. Mangan

**Athleticism in the Victorian and
    Edwardian Public School**
The Emergence and Consolidation of an
    Educational Ideology, New Edition
J.A. Mangan

Australian Beach Cultures
The History of Sun, Sand and Surf
Douglas Booth

Barbarians, Gentlemen and Players
A Sociological Study of the
    Development of Rugby Football,
    Second Edition
Eric Dunning and Kenneth Sheard

Beijing 2008: Preparing for Glory
Chinese Challenge in the 'Chinese
    Century'
Edited by J.A. Mangan and Dong Jinxia

Body and Mind
Sport in Europe from the Roman Empire
    to the Renaissance
John McClelland

British Football and Social Exclusion
Edited by Stephen Wagg

Capoeira
The History of an Afro-Brazilian
    Martial Art
Matthias Röhrig Assunção

**Crafting Patriotism for Global
    Dominance**
America at the Olympics
Mark Dyreson

SPORT IN THE GLOBAL SOCIETY SERIES PAGES

Cricket and England
A Cultural and Social History of Cricket
   in England between the Wars
Jack Williams

Cricket in Colonial India, 1780–1947
Boria Majumdar

Cricketing Cultures in Conflict
Cricketing World Cup 2003
*Edited by Boria Majumdar and
   J.A. Mangan*

Cricket, Race and the 2007 World Cup
*Edited by Boria Majumdar and
   Jon Gemmell*

Disciplining Bodies in the Gymnasium
Memory, Monument, Modernity
Sherry McKay and Patricia Vertinsky

Disreputable Pleasures
Less Virtuous Victorians at Play
*Edited by Mike Huggins and
   J.A. Mangan*

Doping in Sport
Global Ethical Issues
*Edited by Angela Schneider and
   Fan Hong*

Emigrant Players
Sport and the Irish Diaspora
Edited by Paul Darby and David Hassan

Ethnicity, Sport, Identity
Struggles for Status
*Edited by J.A. Mangan and
   Andrew Ritchie*

European Heroes
Myth, Identity, Sport
*Edited by Richard Holt, J.A. Mangan
   and Pierre Lanfranchi*

Europe, Sport, World
Shaping Global Societies
Edited by J.A. Mangan

**Flat Racing and British Society,
   1790–1914**
A Social and Economic History
Mike Huggins

**Football and Community in the
   Global Context**
Studies in Theory and Practice
*Edited by Adam Brown, Tim Crabbe and
   Gavin Mellor*

Football: From England to the World
*Edited by Dolores P. Martinez and
   Projit B. Mukharji*

Football, Europe and the Press
Liz Crolley and David Hand

Football Fans Around the World
From Supporters to Fanatics
Edited by Sean Brown

Football: The First Hundred Years
The Untold Story
Adrian Harvey

Footbinding, Feminism and Freedom
The Liberation of Women's Bodies in
   Modern China
Fan Hong

France and the 1998 World Cup
The National Impact of a World
   Sporting Event
Edited by Hugh Dauncey and Geoff Hare

Freeing the Female Body
Inspirational Icons
Edited by J.A. Mangan and Fan Hong

SPORT IN THE GLOBAL SOCIETY SERIES PAGES

Fringe Nations in Soccer
Making it Happen
Edited by Kausik Bandyopadhyay and
  Sabyasachi Malick

From Fair Sex to Feminism
Sport and the Socialization of Women in
  the Industrial and Post-Industrial Eras
Edited by J.A. Mangan and
  Roberta J. Park

Gender, Sport, Science
Selected Writings of Roberta J. Park
Edited by J.A. Mangan and
  Patricia Vertinsky

Globalised Football
Nations and Migration, the City and
  the Dream
Edited by Nina Clara Tiesler and
  João Nuno Coelho

Italian Fascism and the Female Body
Sport, Submissive Women and
  Strong Mothers
Gigliola Gori

Japan, Sport and Society
Tradition and Change in a Globalizing
  World
Edited by Joseph Maguire and
  Masayoshi Nakayama

Law and Sport in Contemporary Society
Edited by Steven Greenfield and
  Guy Osborn

Leisure and Recreation in a Victorian
  Mining Community
The Social Economy of Leisure in
  North-East England, 1820–1914
Alan Metcalfe

Lost Histories of Indian Cricket
Battles off the Pitch
Boria Majumdar

Making European Masculinities
Sport, Europe, Gender
Edited by J.A. Mangan

Making Men
Rugby and Masculine Identity
Edited by John Nauright and
  Timothy J.L. Chandler

Making the Rugby World
Race, Gender, Commerce
Edited by Timothy J.L. Chandler and
  John Nauright

Militarism, Hunting, Imperialism
'Blooding' The Martial Male
J.A. Mangan and Callum McKenzie

Militarism, Sport, Europe
War Without Weapons
Edited by J.A. Mangan

Modern Sport: The Global Obsession
Essays in Honour of J.A.Mangan
Edited by Boria Majumdar and
  Fan Hong

Muscular Christianity and the Colonial
  and Post-Colonial World
Edited by John J. MacAloon

Native Americans and Sport in North
  America
Other Peoples' Games
Edited by C. Richard King

Olympic Legacies – Intended and
  Unintended
Political, Cultural, Economic and
  Educational
Edited by J.A. Mangan and
  Mark Dyreson

Playing on the Periphery
Sport, Identity and Memory
Tara Brabazon

SPORT IN THE GLOBAL SOCIETY SERIES PAGES

Pleasure, Profit, Proselytism
British Culture and Sport at Home and
    Abroad 1700–1914
Edited by J.A. Mangan

Rain Stops Play
Cricketing Climates
Andrew Hignell

Reformers, Sport, Modernizers
Middle-Class Revolutionaries
Edited by J.A. Mangan

Rugby's Great Split
Class, Culture and the Origins of
    Rugby League Football
Tony Collins

Running Cultures
Racing in Time and Space
John Bale

Scoring for Britain
International Football and International
    Politics, 1900–1939
Peter J. Beck

Serious Sport
J.A. Mangan's Contribution to the
    History of Sport
Edited by Scott Crawford

Shaping the Superman
Fascist Body as Political Icon – Aryan
    Fascism
Edited by J.A. Mangan

Sites of Sport
Space, Place and Experience
*Edited by John Bale and
    Patricia Vertinksy*

Soccer and Disaster
International Perspectives
*Edited by Paul Darby, Martin Jones and
    Gavin Mellor*

Soccer in South Asia
Empire, Nation, Diaspora
Edited by Paul Dimeo and James Mills

Soccer's Missing Men
Schoolteachers and the Spread of
    Association Football
J.A. Mangan and Colm Hickey

Soccer, Women, Sexual Liberation
Kicking off a New Era
*Edited by Fan Hong and
    J.A. Mangan*

Sport: Race, Ethnicity and Indigenity
Building Global Understanding
Edited by Daryl Adair

Sport and American Society
Exceptionalism, Insularity, 'Imperialism'
*Edited by Mark Dyreson and
    J.A. Mangan*

**Sport and Foreign Policy in a Globalizing
    World**
*Edited by Steven J. Jackson and
    Stephen Haigh*

Sport and International Relations
An Emerging Relationship
*Edited by Roger Levermore and
    Adrian Budd*

Sport and Memory in North America
Edited by Steven Wieting

Sport, Civil Liberties and Human Rights
*Edited by Richard Giulianotti and
    David McArdle*

Sport, Culture and History
Region, Nation and Globe
Brian Stoddart

Sport in Asian Society
Past and Present
Edited by Fan Hong and J.A. Mangan

SPORT IN THE GLOBAL SOCIETY SERIES PAGES

Sport in Australasian Society
Past and Present
*Edited by J.A. Mangan and
    John Nauright*

Sport in Europe
Politics, Class, Gender
Edited by J.A. Mangan

Sport in Films
*Edited by Emma Poulton and
    Martin Roderick*

Sport in Latin American Society
Past and Present
*Edited by Lamartine DaCosta and
    J.A. Mangan*

Sport in South Asian Society
Past and Present
*Edited by Boria Majumdar and
    J.A. Mangan*

**Sport in the Cultures of the Ancient
    World**
New Perspectives
Edited by Zinon Papakonstantinou

Sport, Media, Culture
Global and Local Dimensions
Edited by Alina Bernstein and Neil Blain

Sport, Nationalism and Orientalism
The Asian Games
Edited by Fan Hong

Sport Tourism
Edited by Heather J. Gibson

Sporting Cultures
Hispanic Perspectives on Sport, Text
    and the Body
*Edited by David Wood and
    P. Louise Johnson*

Sporting Nationalisms
Identity, Ethnicity, Immigration and
    Assimilation
*Edited by Mike Cronin and
    David Mayall*

Superman Supreme
Fascist Body as Political Icon –
    Global Fascism
Edited by J.A. Mangan

Terrace Heroes
The Life and Times of the 1930s
    Professional Footballer
Graham Kelly

**The Balkan Games and Balkan Politics
    in the Interwar Years 1929-1939**
Politicians in Pursuit of Peace
Penelope Kissoudi

**The Changing Face of the Football
    Business**
Supporters Direct
*Edited by Sean Hamil, Jonathan Michie,
    Christine Oughton and Steven Warby*

The Commercialisation of Sport
Edited by Trevor Slack

The Cultural Bond
Sport, Empire, Society
Edited by J.A. Mangan

The First Black Footballer
Arthur Wharton 1865–1930: An
    Absence of Memory
Phil Vasili

The Football Manager
A History
Neil Carter

The Future of Football
Challenges for the Twenty-First Century
*Edited by Jon Garland, Dominic
    Malcolm and Mike Rowe*

SPORT IN THE GLOBAL SOCIETY SERIES PAGES

The Games Ethic and Imperialism
Aspects of the Diffusion of an Ideal
J.A. Mangan

The Global Politics of Sport
The Role of Global Institutions in Sport
Edited by Lincoln Allison

The Lady Footballers
Struggling to Play in Victorian Britain
James F. Lee

The Magic of Indian Cricket
Cricket and Society in India, Revised
  Edition
Mihir Bose

The Making of New Zealand Cricket
1832–1914
Greg Ryan

**The 1940 Tokyo Games: The Missing
  Olympics**
Japan, the Asian Olympics and the
  Olympic Movement
Sandra Collins

The Nordic World: Sport in Society
*Edited by Henrik Meinander and
  J.A. Mangan*

The Politics of South African Cricket
Jon Gemmell

The Race Game
Sport and Politics in South Africa
Douglas Booth

**The Rise of Stadiums in the Modern
  United States**
Cathedrals of Sport
*Edited by Mark Dyreson and
  Robert Trumpbour*

The Tour De France, 1903–2003
A Century of Sporting Structures,
  Meanings and Values
Edited by Hugh Dauncey and Geoff Hare

This Great Symbol
Pierre de Coubertin and the Origins of
  the Modern Olympic Games
John J. MacAloon

Tribal Identities
Nationalism, Europe, Sport
Edited by J.A. Mangan

**Women, Sport and Society in Modern
  China**
Holding up More than Half the Sky
Dong Jinxia

Citation Information

The chapters in this book were originally published in the *International Journal of the History of Sport*, volume 30, issue 10 (May 2013). When citing this material, please use the original page numbering for each article, as follows:

Preface
A Regional and Global Symbolic Proclamation
Roberta J. Park
International Journal of the History of Sport, volume 30, issue 10
(May 2013) pp. 1023–1024

Foreword
Holding Up More Than Half the Asian Sky
Jinxia Dong
International Journal of the History of Sport, volume 30, issue 10
(May 2013) pp. 1025

Chapter 1
Preamble: Marketing 'Brand China': Maintaining the Momentum – 'The Middle Kingdom' Resurgent and Resplendent
J.A. Mangan
International Journal of the History of Sport, volume 30, issue 10
(May 2013) pp. 1026–1036

Chapter 2
People's Daily*: An Evolutionary Narrative on Asia in Its Coverage of the Asian Games*
Wenting Xue and Qing Luo
International Journal of the History of Sport, volume 30, issue 10
(May 2013) pp. 1037–1047

Chapter 3
The Pursuit of Regional Geopolitical Aspirations: China's Bids for the Asian Games and the Asian Winter Games since the 1980s
Marcus P. Chu
International Journal of the History of Sport, volume 30, issue 10
(May 2013) pp. 1048–1058

CITATION INFORMATION

Chapter 4

Strict Compliance!: Chinese Careful Conformity and the Guangzhou Bid for the Asian Games
Marcus P. Chu
International Journal of the History of Sport, volume 30, issue 10 (May 2013) pp. 1059–1070

Chapter 5

'Glittering Guangzhou': The 2010 Asian Games – Local Rivalries, National Motives, Geopolitical Gestures
J.A. Mangan, Jinxia Dong and Di Lu
International Journal of the History of Sport, volume 30, issue 10 (May 2013) pp. 1071–1086

Chapter 6

Chinese Desires? Olympism and Dominance, Guangzhou and Missed Opportunity, Major Leagues and Isolation on the Pacific Rim
John D. Kelly
International Journal of the History of Sport, volume 30, issue 10 (May 2013) pp. 1087–1098

Chapter 7

Guangzhou 2010: Eastern Orwellian Echoes – Yang Shu-chun and a Taiwanese Patriotic Media Offensive
Chen-Li Liu, Ping-Chao Lee and J.A. Mangan
International Journal of the History of Sport, volume 30, issue 10 (May 2013) pp. 1099–1112

Chapter 8

From Honeymoon to Divorce: Fragmenting Relations between China and South Korea in Politics, Economics – and Sport
J.A. Mangan, Sun-Yong Kwon and Bang-Chool Kim
International Journal of the History of Sport, volume 30, issue 10 (May 2013) pp. 1113–1129

Chapter 9

Rivalries: China, Japan and South Korea – Memory, Modernity, Politics, Geopolitics – and Sport
J.A. Mangan, Hyun-Duck Kim, Angelita Cruz and Gi-Heun Kang
International Journal of the History of Sport, volume 30, issue 10 (May 2013) pp. 1130–1152

Chapter 10

Guangzhou 2010: Singapore at a Global Crossroads
Peter Horton
International Journal of the History of Sport, volume 30, issue 10 (May 2013) pp. 1153–1164

CITATION INFORMATION

Chapter 11

Guangzhou: The Asian Games and the Chinese 'Gold-Fest' –
Geopolitical Issues for Australia
Peter Horton
International Journal of the History of Sport, volume 30, issue 10
(May 2013) pp. 1165–1175

Chapter 12

The Asian Games and Diplomacy in Asia: Korea – China – Russia
Victor Cha
International Journal of the History of Sport, volume 30, issue 10
(May 2013) pp. 1176–1187

Please direct any queries you may have about the citations to
clsuk.permissions@cengage.com

PREFACE

A Regional and Global Symbolic Proclamation

The Olympic Games and their analogues are about far more than sports. They have served as ways to open to the rest of the world important aspects of the host nation and also powerful statements regarding politics and geopolitics. This fact is perceptively made in *The Asian Games: Modern Metaphor for 'The Middle Kingdom' Reborn – Political Statement, Cultural Assertion, Social Symbol*. 'Middle Kingdom' (Zhongguo), a term that China has used for centuries to assert that it is the cultural, economic and political as well as geographic centre of the world, conforms well with what China has been working diligently to make certain today.

As John MacAloon perceptively argued more than three decades ago in books such as *This Great Symbol: Pierre de Coubertin and the Origins of the Modern Olympic Games* (1981) and *Rite, Drama, Festival, Spectacle: Rehearsals Toward a Theory of Cultural Performance* (1984), the Olympic Games, typically scripted within a number of symbolic 'frames', have been powerful means for declaring messages that the organisers deem important. The Chinese hosts of the 2008 Olympic and 2010 Asian Games were well aware of this fact. They skilfully used both events to emphatically send their preferred Asian messages to the rest of the world.

Whereas Britain, the nation that 'taught the world to play', is usually credited with having been the world's economic and political power during the nineteenth century – and likewise the USA during much of the twentieth century – today a remarkable number of sources posit the emergence of China as the dominant geopolitical power of the twenty-first century. Before the 2008 Beijing Olympics took place, there had been works such as *China's Rise in Asia: Promises and Perils* (2005) and *China Inc.: How the Next Superpower Challenges America and the World* (2005). These have been impressively supplemented by writings such as *When China Rules the World: The End of the Western World and the Birth of a New Global Order* (2009) and *Modern China and the New World: The Reemergence of the Middle Kingdom in the Twenty-First Century* (2011).

The Asian Games: Modern Metaphor for 'The Middle Kingdom' Reborn deals with an event that had received nowhere near the attention that it merits – one in which 9704 athletes from all 45 member nations of the Olympic Council of Asia participated at Guangzhou, China, from November 12 to 27, 2010. Twenty-eight of the 2010 Asian Games' 42 events were Olympic sports; however, 14 (e.g. kabaddi; sepaktakraw) were activities that were popular mostly in various participating countries. The inclusion of events that have their origins and are popular in diverse Asian countries was undoubtedly used to express a distinctive Asian identity and Asian unity among the participating nations paradoxically at the same time that China's dominance in the medal count (416 total of which 199 were gold) was yet another statement of its forthcoming regional and world superiority.

Reforms that had begun in 1978 had put the People's Republic of China on the path to becoming what today is usually recognised as the world's second largest – and, many contend, soon the become largest – economy. Three decades later, the 2008 Beijing

1

Olympics, only the third Summer Games to be held in Asia since the modern Olympics were launched at Athens in 1896, would serve as a powerful means for the host nation to declare its arrival on the world scene. The nation's leaders skilfully used both the symbolic 'frames' within which the Beijing Games were carried out and contest victories (51, the highest gold medal count) to declare that China was on its way to becoming the dominant geopolitical power of the twenty-first century.

This state of affairs was not overlooked by academics in many disciplines including the history of sport. Following the IOC's announcement that the 2008 Games would take place in China, there emerged a growing number of insightful books such as *The Beijing Olympiad: The Political Economy of a Sporting Mega-Event* (2007), *Beijing's Games: What the Olympics Mean to China* (2008) and *Olympic Dreams: China and Sports, 1895– 2008* (2008). China's impressive success in carrying out the 2008 Games evoked works such as *The Olympics in East Asia: Nationalism, Regionalism, and Globalism on the Center Stage of World Sports* (2011), which continued to broaden the scope of enquiry and cast additional light upon an array of matters. As William Kelly, co-editor of this impressive collection, pointed out, a number of East Asian countries had been involved in various ways with the Olympic Movement for nearly a century. One of these was the IOC-sanctioned quadrennial Asian Games, which had held their first competitions at New Delhi in 1951.

The Asian Games: Modern Metaphor for 'The Middle Kingdom' Reborn brings forth important information regarding these formerly too little studied Games. It includes chapters dealing with how *The People's Daily* (the leading party newspaper of the PRC) covered the Asian Games beginning in 1951, how China set about bidding for the 2010 Asian Games, how local governments sought to use these Games to upgrade their development, how other countries (e.g. Japan, South Korea, Singapore and even Australia, which might be considering transforming into an 'Asian' sports nation) perceived of events – and much, much more. It also evokes important questions such as whether Asian nations are desirous of creating a distinct type of Games that conform more to their particular social and cultural perspectives than do the highly westernised and scripted modern Olympics, and what role or roles a more Asian-oriented Games (and sports) might – or might not – have in strengthening 'the geopolitical hegemonic influence of China'.

By 2000, academics, politicians and others were becoming increasingly aware that globalization and geopolitics would be major twenty-first century issues. Their tendency was to focus attention upon economic and geographical matters. However, with his typical perceptiveness, James A. (Tony) Mangan turned to analyses of the power that sport often can have. Through his efforts, there emerged books such as *Beijing 2008: Preparing for Glory – Chinese Challenge in the 'Chinese Century'*, *Post-Beijing 2008: Geopolitics and the Pacific Rim* and *The Triple Asian Olympics – Asia Rising: The Pursuit of National Identity, International Recognition, and Global Esteem*. Extending, expanding and deepening the many aspects of sport as an enormously powerful political and geopolitical power, *The Asian Games: Modern Metaphor for 'The Middle Kingdom' Reborn – Political Statement, Cultural Assertion, Social Symbol*, which Mangan also initiated and co-edited, offers yet another impressive collection needed to better understand what the future may bring.

Roberta J. Park
University of California, Berkeley, CA, USA

FOREWORD

Holding Up More Than Half the Asian Sky

At the recent London Olympics, the USA regained the premier position in the Gold Medal Table, which it had lost to China at the Beijing Olympics.

The USA had saved face – for the moment. However, the challenge from China will not go away. In the first week of the London Olympics, China held pride of place in the gold medal count. Significantly, Chinese athletes achieved their best ever results outside China in London. Systematic training, extensive institutional facilities, a streamlined organisational infrastructure, a supportive government and not least now for the athletes themselves considerable financial rewards for international success mean that the challenge to American past supremacy will only increase. To this end, Chinese athletes compete in numerous national and international competitions. They are increasingly 'battle-hardened'.

One recent competition was the Asian Games held in Guangzhou in China in 2010. The Chinese delegation consisted of 1400 members including 997 athletes. Women athletes numbered 464. China dominated the Games by winning 416 medals (199 were gold). They won many more medals than Korea and Japan (second and third, respectively, in the medal count) combined. It is worth noting, incidentally, that young Chinese athletes held up more than half the Asian sky at Guangzhou. The average age of the Chinese athletes was 24! Furthermore, some 67% were 'new faces'. The Games demonstrated their potential. The portents for future involvement in the Games seem good. A further point to note is that Chinese women athletes made a huge contribution to the success of China in Guangzhou; of the 416 medals won by Chinese athletes, 291 were won by women. In addition, the women won 112 gold medals and the men won 74! Women hold up more than half the Chinese sky – athletically.

It is reasonable to suggest, it is argued here, that these sports performances are further evidence of China's emerging status, not only in Asia, but globally.

The Chinese challenge to America, the twentieth-century superpower, is real and not only inside but outside sports stadiums. Is the Guangzhou Asian Games a harbinger of things to come? Is John Ikenberry correct in his prediction that 'The drama of China's rise will feature an increasingly powerful China and a declining United States locked in an epic battle over the leadership of the international system'? Rio de Janeiro, at least, will provide the next act of the international athletics drama.

Jinxia Dong
Department of Physical Education and Sport Science
Peking University, Beijing, P.R. China

INTRODUCTION

Marketing 'Brand China': Maintaining the Momentum – 'The Middle Kingdom' Resurgent and Resplendent

J.A. Mangan[a,b]

[a]Strathclyde University, Glasgow, UK; [b]Cairns Institute, Cairns, Qld, Australia

> The multiplicity of manoeuvres that characterise modern China's geopolitical ascendancy and ambition illustrate political ingenuity used calculatedly with the clear intention of becoming invulnerable. Past recent humiliations are not to reoccur. In addition, 'The Middle Kingdom' is to be reincarnated: invincible imperialism pursued. The strategic plurality employed in complex compositional patterns is both imperial and historic in nature: the past is to be projected into the present and the future. The once 'Great Game' is now 'The Great East Asia Game'! In the light of the Guangzhou Asian Games Triumphalism, there could be a 'double entendre' employed here of sizable significance. This essay considers the possibility.

Prelude

Power

... power at its core is not a material but a psychological force. It represents the vital desire of individuals or communities to prevail, to impose change on others while remaining unchanged and to dominate rather than be dominated, whether by violence or by the subtler arts of peace and always in the compelling contests of invidious comparison. Viewed in this manner, power is foremost a concern of human consciousness: ... All analyses of power – or all power-orientated studies of history – must therefore begin with human consciousness, whether individual or collective. Power is a matter of human perception (culturally conditioned perception, to be sure). The material aspects of power originate in the mind, in human ingenuity and in the desire to be less vulnerable.[1]

Dominance

Rather than single-minded conquerors, they were strategic pluralists who achieved widespread dominance with policies that defy easy categorisation. They relied on strategies and operations that can easily be recognised as expansive, but the geopolitical order they created was at once distinctly imperialistic and distinctly indigenous in nature.[2]

'Otherness'

A modern equation: money equals modern mega events. The West gets poorer; the East gets richer. Tokyo 1964, Seoul 1988, Beijing 2008 are metonyms for Asian economic metamorphosis. In consequence, the world has witnessed a shift in its geopolitical axis – from West to East. Asian 'Otherness' has been redefined; the mantra is no longer faded esoteric Asian promise but blooming modernistic Asian achievement. Asia is no longer the object of the complacent, but rather the apprehensive, Western gaze. Tokyo 1964, Seoul 1988, and above all, Beijing 2008 are metaphors for a deeper and wider modernity.[3]

China through Nineteenth-Century Western Eyes: Prejudice without Perception?

At the time of the infamous First Opium War (1839–1842),[4] many British merchants in Southern China were clear in their minds, certain in their prejudice and caustic in their contempt. Mostly, these

> ... buccaneering money-makers, full of mockery for the empire outside whose walls they were held, or at any rate for the unrepresentative southern fragment that they glimpsed at Canton [now Guangzhou!] ... objected to what they saw as its pompous, often venal bureaucracy; its determination to keep them and their trade at a prudent remove; its antiquity, its smells, its absence of Christianity and decent water-closets; the offensive Chinese habit of staring at foreigners; the arrogant Chinese failure to stare at foreigners; and so on.[5]

James Matheson, with William Jardine, co-founder of 'the great opium house', summed up a general view. The Chinese were,

> a people characterised by a marvellous degree of imbecility, avarice, conceit and obstinacy ... It has been the policy of this extraordinary people to shroud themselves and all belonging to them in mystery impenetrable ... [to] exhibit a spirit of exclusiveness on a grand scale.[6]

These self-assured Easterners infuriated the self-righteous Westerners.

Many Western missionaries in China empty of Christian charity and short on Christian compassion but certain of ultimate Christian conversion, subscribed to this ethnocentric prejudice. For merchant, missionary *and* diplomat, force was considered the only effective instrument to ensure respect, persuasion and influence. Attitudes in Britain were more ambivalent. Supreme confidence seeping from successful imperial endeavour and a consequent well-developed sense of racial triumphalism[7] went hand in glove with racial neurosis: 'Troubled *fin de siècle* theorists made an intellectual industry of de-generation fears'[8] and the prospect of the 'white race' in decline. Racial neuroticism was endemic. Early in the twentieth century, a Secretary of State for India speculated that Civilisation was in danger from rising Asiatic power – sinister and terrible – yellow, brown and black.[9] Prejudiced but not wholly without perception, the dominant domestic Victorian view of China was as a potential threat – a sophisticated 'sleeping lion' eager when awakened to attack its despised Western aggressors. Towards the end of the nineteenth century, British bad conscience over the Opium Wars was fusing with imperial loathing for China: the outcome was the concept of the 'Yellow Peril'. Discussed nauseously in the period's literature which reflected 'a paranoid world of European racial science',[10] this 'science' even infused children's literature. By 1905, it had become 'a staple of children's publications like Pluck and Magnet'.[11] By 1910, even the fragrant *Girls Own Annual* had warned its innocent and sheltered readers of the Chinese global conspiracy taking place around them.[12] For adults, of course, there was Sax-Rohmer's Devil-Doctor, Fu Manchu,

> At the height of Rohmer's fame [circa 1920] Fu Manchu novels occupied public libraries, cinemas and the book collections of liners carrying Westerners out the China, ensuring (in the words of one such traveller of the 1920s) that they "knew all about Chinamen: they were cruel, 'wicked people' ".[13]

In time, to the epithet 'Yellow Peril' was added the epithet 'Yellow Horror'. This brought in its 'fearsome' wake the epithet, the 'Yellow Panic'. Panic has recently reappeared in Western consciousness. Old fears have resurfaced in the form of 'new fears': old wine in new vessels!

To move pertinently, therefore, to the theme of *The Asian Games* – to what extent is the threat of Chinese domination, at least in Asia, a reality in terms of the political potential of modern sport with its magnetic attraction as a demonstration of geopolitical and political standing? Does it bring in its wake East Asian anxieties? Was East Asia discomforted by the dominance of China in Guangzhou? Was East Asia, in particular, disturbed by Chinese crushing supremacy – and its wider implications?

China through Twenty-First Century Western Eyes: Perception without Prejudice?

Times change and perceptions alter! Henry Kissinger in *On China* wrote recently,

> China can find reassurance in its own record of endurance and in the fact that no American administration during any period of Chinese history – including those in which no bilateral relations existed – has sought to alter the reality of China as one of the world's major states, economies, and civilization.[14]

And on a personal note, he declared that ' . . . I have been to China more than fifty times. Like many visitors, over the centuries, I have come to admire the Chinese people for their endurance, their subtlety, their family sense and the culture they represent.'[15] He then added, sympathetically, 'China is rightly proud of its strides in restoring its sense of national purpose following what it sees as a "century of humiliation" '.[16] For his part, the sinologist Jonathan Fenby waxes lyrical in his *Tiger Head, Snake Tails* on the subject of modern China:

> Never before has a state, whose concerns are primarily domestic, housed three of the seven most valuable companies on the planet or built up a treasure chest of foreign exchange that could buy the whole of Italy or all the sovereign debt of Portugal, Ireland, Greece and Spain (as of 2011), plus Google, Apple, IBM and Microsoft plus all the real estate in Manhattan and Washington, DC plus the world's fifty most valuable sports franchises. Never before has a country with such a mismatch between the size of its population and its relative lack of natural resources had such an effect on global commodity prices and shipping rates. Never before has the world's superpower been so dependent on funding and cheap imports from a state whose nominal per capita is wealth equivalent to that of Angola, creating a completely new monetary – political relationship.[17]

Nor does his paean of praise end there:

> Never before has a nation come back from such a long history of revolts, invasions, repression and natural disasters to awe the world. Never before, for that matter, has China been so involved with the rest of the globe: though less isolated than is often supposed, the great imperial dynasties were essentially inward-looking, content to focus on their vast domains. Never before have so many people in a single country been so focused on simultaneous material advancement. Never before has a leader who defines his goal as being simply to achieve 'moderate prosperity' for his state been selected as the most powerful figure on earth, as was Hu Jintao, by an American magazine in 2011. Never before has a country whose ruling party aims to apply 'socialism with Chinese character' adopted such a red-blooded approach to market competition and crude economic growth.[18]

Fenby is too knowledgeable, well informed and realistic to be completely carried away. To offset a litany of awe and admiration, he adds a beadroll of dismay and reproach:

> Never before has such a state possessed the ultimate weapon of mass destruction, the world's largest army and a permanent seat at the top of the major global forum. Never before has technology enabled manufacturers and traders deep in China to communicate instantly with the world of hackers to pose a security threat to foreign nations.[19]

and a savage summary of inexcusable imperfections:

> Never before has such a globally vital nation been so attacked for cheating in so much of what it does. . . . Never before has an avowedly left-wing regime been so stingy in healthcare, education, welfare and pensions – and urged others to reduce their social spending.[20]

There is more in this vein throughout his balanced assessment of modern China elsewhere in *Tiger Head, Snakes Tails*.

Patterns, Dreams and Ambitions

'We understand the new by reference to [the] known. We cannot do without comparison'. Thus comparison '... can be used not simply as a method of description ... but as a means of ... imputing patterns'.[21] In the sinologists' scrutiny of China, there is a discernable pattern. Fenby declared in *The Penguin History of Modern China: the Fall and Rise of a Great Power 1850–2008* that 'For twenty-one centuries China ... contained the oldest continuous civilization on earth and possessed a self-confidence ... which rested on a real belief that the Middle Kingdom was unique, standing apart from, and above, all other regimes.'[22] This self-confidence, however, was accompanied by

> the periodic collapse of Chinese empires [leading] to periods of warlordism and widespread disorder, until the Mandate of Heaven was passed on to another imperial dynasty which restored order. The Chinese have, therefore, always placed a very high value on the order provided by their successive empires.[23]

Past self-confidence and past preference for 'order' recently reappeared – *blatantly*.

'Chinese Dream' Is to Lead the World Again

In his inaugural address as president, and with rhetorical flourishes of which Barack Obama would be proud, Xi Jinping recently laid out his vision of the 'Chinese Dream', in which China would again lead the world. Unlike the American Dream, in which the individual can achieve success, Mr Xi's Chinese Dream is about collectivism: 'To create the Chinese Dream, we must unite all Chinese power. As long as we stay united, we will share the opportunity to make our dreams come true.'

According to commentators, Mr Xi's dream is to return China to its position in the Middle Ages, when it was the world's most advanced and civilised nation.[24]

The 'Chinese Dream' constitutes a calm and confident proclamation of global hegemonic purpose – both purposeful and transformative: a sinological *Sursum corda*.

This transparent ambition explains, explicitly and implicitly, the impressive effort put into Guangzhou 2010 and the towering domination of Chinese athletes there. Guangzhou has contributed to an Eastern uneasy perception of twenty-first century China that has replaced the nineteenth-century easy prejudice of Western imperialists.

Geopolitical momentum is well advanced. And in this advance, China recognises that modern sport

> is a ... prism through which nation states project their image to the world and to their own people ... [and] creates emotion ... not replicated by ... music, art, or even politics ... little else can inspire as much emotion and pride ... as the victory of an athlete or team.[25]

'What matters most about political ideas are the underlying emotions.'[26] This is equally true of modern sport as political ideas – particularly when nakedly nationalistic. In Guangzhou, the projection of sport as politics was brutal: harmony is seldom created out of humiliation and the magnitude of Chinese supremacy spelt humiliation, notably for Japan. It sent a majestic clarion peal echoing across East Asia: the melody – the 'Middle Kingdom' Reborn! As in Beijing 2008,[27] it was also an Assertive Anthem; this time a celebratory consolidation at a regional level of national redemption and regeneration: the nineteenth-century 'Sick Man of Asia' was now the twenty-first century 'Strong Man of Asia'.[28] In Guangzhou by means of national muscular and mental exertion, China pushed aside the other Asian nations in an obsessive propulsion upwards that attracts compulsive attention. Guangzhou was as much a demonstration of the power of modern sport as a means for the magnificent marketing of modern

China – and a declaration of its presence as the major 'player' in the region in sport – and beyond sport: raptorial in its predation.

In the twenty-first century, internationally and regionally, 'sport … is a central component of the complex architectural structure of geopolitical soft power politics'.[29] Furthermore,

> nationalism and the nation itself, far from being weakened by globalisation, have now returned with a vengeance … Instead of a new world order, the clashing interests and ambitions of the great powers are again producing the alliances and counter alliances, and the elaborate dances and shifting partnerships, that a nineteenth-century diplomat would recognise instantly. They are also producing geopolitical fault lines where the ambitions of great powers overlap and conflict and where the seismic events of the future are most likely to erupt.[30]

Consequently, in the decades ahead, sport could be the talismanic tool of soft power penetration in pursuit of influence, respect and status, while the 'athlete has become a nationalistic icon: a political talisman transmuted'.[31] In China, athletes – men and women – have become political 'Talismans' representing Patriotism pushed without concern for cost by the Party.

A note of realpolitik reality, the unsentimental 'Machiavellian genius', Henry Kissinger has warned 'with aphoristic authority that international competition is embedded in human nature … One outcome is a major geopolitical recalibration.'[32] Of China's present geopolitical 'Patriotic Push', Fenby remarks that 'China remains in a systemic time-warp: a re-emerging Middle Kingdom reverting to a self-absorbed and self-congratulatory Neo Confucian Patriotism.'[33] And, he adds 'All great historical transformation involves re-connection with the past.'[34] In the present shift of geopolitical power, China marches once more to a historical drumbeat but as yet for its own good reasons mostly modestly muted – *but not in sport!* The emphasis for the moment is on soft rather than hard power projection.[35] Domination through sport not war is the chosen projectile of political and geopolitical self-projection. Guangzhou exemplifies a present political purpose perfectly – to return China to its position in the Middle Ages! Dirigisme dogma dominant.

Metaphor, Analogy and Guangzhou

To turn again, therefore at a timely moment to 'The Asian Games: Modern Metaphor for "The Middle Kingdom" Reborn – Political Statement, Cultural Assertion, Social Symbol' and its premise, Guangzhou was a metaphor for renaissance. China crushed the other Asian nations with the massive weight of its Gold Medal 'haul': regional self-confidence regained. With its huge accumulation of gold medals, once again China stood apart, and above, the other nations of Asia. There is further premise in 'The Asian Games': the 'Chinese' Asian Games were a harbinger of a wider distance to come, geopolitically, politically, militarily, economically and culturally. After 'a century of humiliation' initially by the West aided stupidly by China itself, and later by the East aided short-sightedly by China itself, China is entering 'a century of assertion'. Categorisation is implicit in process. The World, and the West especially, but also the East, is re-categorising China: nineteenth-century prejudice is being replaced by twenty-first century perception – reflected accurately, incidentally, in the East Asian reactions in 'The Asian Games: Modern Metaphor for the "Middle Kingdom" Reborn',[36] namely, sports events in East Asia are often the projections of bitter past regional antipathy into the present and of present regional disillusion into the future. Sport, in short, is an analogue of historical hostility and contemporary fragmentation. Contextual confirmation of this is found in *Beijing 2008 – Preparing for Glory: Chinese Challenge in the 'Chinese Century'*. In a new epochal period of East Asian ever growing wealth, power and assertion-heightened confrontation is entirely possible in the future in politics, economics *and* sport. The East will confront the East; the West will be a colonialist memory! Antagonisms will escalate. There is yet a further premise in 'The Asian Games': the determination of the Asian nations to mount a distinctive games distinctly Asian and resistant to the global gigantism of the Olympic Games will grow. Asia now has the money to promote, present and project a global sports mega-event with an Asian identity and in an Asian idiom.

Metaphor operates at several levels.[37] At one level, it can be used to invoke congruity and consistency: in historical terms, the coming together of the past and present. This is one of its uses in 'The Asian Games'. Metaphor, however, is never static. It initiates new meanings and reveals new connections but *never* permanently: it matches circumstance. For this reason, it serves a temporary purpose. In contrast to metaphor, however, analogy has a special strength:

> It expresses itself by first ranging two patterns of experience alongside each other, seeking their points of identity and then using one pattern to extend the other. There is always a sense of sequence in analogy, in a way that there need not be in other forms of metaphor: the sequential story of past, present and future.[38]

Therefore analogy can replace metaphor as a preferable instrument of perception allowing hidden but real corollaries to become visible. Analogy permits crosscuts in history between time and space.[39]

Guangzhou was an analogous 'feat'. Fact and fiction were demonstrated in presentation and performance, namely Chinese glittering presentation and dazzling performance: mythological and modern 'heroism' expressed in imagery and action.[40] While analogy has its dangers, 'applicability may not survive the telling of its story because of the resurgence in memory of all excluded aspects which cannot be accounted for in the analogical process'.[41] Nevertheless, Guangzhou as a 'feat' stimulates thought, harnesses imagination and offers the possibility of illuminating veracity. Both Guangzhou 2010 and Beijing 2008 display the magnitude of Chinese endeavour ensuring that the axis of realism and fantasy was perfectly balanced: Eastern sports 'palaces' and sports 'paladins' projected as Chinese reality and romance. The new China made the old China once more meaningful! Prescience is a gift offered by analogy: past and present can be extrapolated into the future. The argument of 'The Asian Games' is that the analogous consideration of Guangzhou offers the possibility of prescience: a vision of the realisation of Chinese ascendancy in regional if not global terms: past, present and future political power in syllogistic solidarity.

'Modern Metaphor for the "Middle Kingdom" Reborn' is a carefully chosen phrase – possibly provocative and prescient. Time will tell. The name Guangzhou, for many outside China bland in its newness (Guangzhou was Canton) and lost in a Chinese vastness, conjoined, incidentally, with the supportive adjective, 'Glittering',[42] becomes vitalised: the ordinary raised to the extraordinary by the potency of language. Wealth, modernity, success and soft power become inextricably linked with terminology. Now once again, to take the longer metaphoric historical perspective,

> For one hundred years ... Chinese interests in Western sports has largely been motivated by a collective desire to establish a modern national identity ... to save the nation, to rid China of the 'sick man of East Asian label', and to make China strong ...[43]

Guangzhou 2010, with Beijing 2008, has helped achieve this via present soft-power persuasion. Both, in fact, have contributed to ensure the restoration of China's greatness 'through the erasing of the memory of a humbled, reduced and subordinate people and its replacement with a confident, risen and super-ordinate people: physical effort twisted into skeins of political action.'[44]

Guangzhou 2010 contributed to the mesmerising marketing of modern China but *not* in an emulative Western idiom: the Games promoted Eastern sports, cultures and traditions in a way that the Olympic Games under the aegis of the International Olympic Committee would never permit. Thus not only was 'Glittering Guangzhou' a Statement of Cultural Modernity, it was also a Declaration of Cultural Tradition: an analogy for a newly confident and assertive East Asia secure in its own image aided and abetted by a newly confident and assertive China secure in its own image. Guangzhou was an analogy for East Asian identity – recovery. It was also an analogy for an East Asian and Chinese accommodation of change, assertion of change, promotion of change and triumph over change. But it was more for China and the Chinese: a manifestation of change leaping out of a historic legacy: actualisation grounded in history. 'History is always "political but nowhere more so than in China." Sport in modern China is also invariably political';[45] and not just sport!

> In the post-Mao era [the] desire for recognition has manifested itself in the neo-pathological yearning for international prizes and "face" – for Nobel Prizes [when government supported!], to gain entry to the WTO, for Olympic medals, and of course, for the prestige of hosting the Games themselves.[46]

Civilisations, Cultures and Cosmologies

Guangzhou 2010 represented an East Asian Cultural Renaissance to enhance and adorn the coming East Asian Epoch.

This will be hard for some to stomach,

> ... for America to be displaced, not in the world but ... in the Western Pacific, by an Asian people long despised as decadent, feeble, corrupt and inept is emotionally very difficult to accept. The sense of cultural supremacy of the American will make ... adjustment very difficult ... Americans believe their ideas are universal – the supremacy of the individual and free, unfettered expression. But they are not – never were.[47]

Displacement involves not only America – its geopolitical vine increasingly unable to bear potent political fruit.

> Europe's assumed centrality in accounts of world history [has also] come under attack ... From the late 1970s, an intellectual movement inspired by the Palestinian – American Edward Said denounced the classics of European writing in the history, ethnography and culture of Asia (and by extension elsewhere) as 'orientalist' fantasy. According to Said, European description was fatally flawed by the crude attribution of stereotyped qualities, almost always demeaning, and the persistent attempt to portray Asian societies as the slothful, corrupt or degenerate antitheses of an energetic, masterful and progressive Europe.[48]

The implication was self-evident.

> Europeans' reportage (whether fact or fiction) ... intended to serve the ulterior aim of extending Europe's hegemony, ... even ... unconsciously, ... had no historical value except as a reflection of Europeans' own fears and obsessions. The comparative study of Europe and non-Europe was hopelessly compromised. It could even be argued ... that history itself was an alien enterprise that forced knowledge of the past into the concept and categories invented in (and for) Europe.[49]

In pursuit of reasonable perspective, however, the following should be added:

> Few intelligent people accepted the logical conclusion of this post-modern extremism – that nothing could be known and that all inquiry was hopeless.[50]

THE ASIAN GAMES: MODERN METAPHOR FOR 'THE MIDDLE KINGDOM' REBORN

Nevertheless, the general point stands up to scrutiny.

> European depictions of other parts of the world needed very careful decoding. The Saidian critique was part of a great sea change, a conscious attempt to 'decentre' Europe or even to 'provincialize' it. European accounts of other cultures and peoples should no longer be treated as the 'authorized version' ... Europe should no longer be seen as the pivot of change, or as the agent acting on the passive civilizations of the non-Western world. Above all, perhaps, the European path to the modern world should no longer be treated as natural or 'normal', the standard against which historical change in other parts of the world should always be measured. Europeans had forged their own kind of modernity, but there were other 'modernities'.[51]

Without question ' ... Europe's place in world history looks rather different from that in conventional accounts written a few decades ago'.[52] The once conventional is increasingly becoming the unconventional.

Yet once again, in pursuit of appropriate perspective,

> ... histories that aim to 'provincialize' Europe still leave a lot to explain. The European states were the main force that created the 'globalized' world of the late nineteenth century {and} the chief authors of the two great transformations that were locked together in the 'modern world' of the 1870s to the 1940s. The first was the making of a world economy {involving} the global exchange of manufactures, raw materials and foodstuffs, in huge volumes and values, with the accompanying flows of people and money. This was an economic revolution that was chiefly managed (not always well) from Europe or by Europeans, and fashioned to suit their particular interests.[53]

There is a further point to make in search of balance linked to the transformation above.

> The extension of European rule, overt and covert, across huge swathes of the non-European world – a process under way before 1800, but accelerating sharply in the nineteenth century. It was strikingly visible in the colonial partitions of Africa, South East Asia, the South Pacific and (later) the Middle East; in the great ventures of empire-building in North Asia (by Russia) and South Asia (by Britain) in the subjection of much of maritime China to foreign controls, and in the European occupation (by demographic imperialism) of the Americas, Australasia and parts of South Central Africa. In Africa, the Middle East, much of South East Asia, the Pacific, Australasia and even the Americas, it created the territorial units that provide the state structure of the contemporary world.[54]

Be that as it may, throughout East Asia, there is a new cosmological confidence – a prelude to a cultural reassertion.

> A distinction between the cosmological and material beliefs of different civilization (cultures) may be useful in explaining why one set of Western beliefs – the material – may command universal acceptance while another – the cosmological – may not. Material beliefs concern ways of making a living. As the environment in which one has to earn an income changes, these material beliefs will alter ... They are malleable. The process of modernization ... will thus change material beliefs associated with different religions ... cosmological beliefs of different cultures are difficult to change ... While the Rest may voluntarily embrace the material beliefs of the West through globalization, they do not want to embrace its cosmological beliefs. *They want to modernize but not westernise.* [emphasis added][55]

And modernisation involves a re-engagement with Eastern sport reflecting in turn a wider regional renaissance, an increasing shift in cultural balance and an increasing reduction in recent cultural dominance, and involves a deliberate de-emphasis of a recent historic emphasis. The outcome: nothing less than the revitalisation and reassertion of Eastern cultural tradition reflecting in turn a cosmological confidence. This turns recent history on its head reflecting a changing world order.

Old Eastern philosophies are revisited and revived. Metaphor is repossessed:

> Most of our expressions are metaphorical. The philosophy of our forefathers is hidden in them.[56]

11

In coming decades, such Eastern metaphors will be increasingly visible – not least, in the Asian Games. The new 'Otherness' will be the successful pursuit of power and pre-eminence – in the Asian Games – and beyond the Games!

Coda

A reminder and a recollection:

Reminder:

... thriving physical exercise cultures and sporting cultures did exist in other parts of the world long before the Europeans arrived. Chinese sports scholars can find evidence of references to physical exercise and games in the writings of Confucius and Mencius more than two thousand years ago, to take only one example ... the Korean peninsula also had its own sporting activities well before the 'West' arrived on its shores.[57]

Recollection:

The author of this Preamble has the most vivid recollection of a visit to the Chengdu University for Sport in the early 1990s and a guided inspection of shelf upon shelf of Chinese research monographs, collections and journals on the evolution of Chinese sport going back many centuries. At the time, as the Founding and Academic Executive Editor of *The International Journal of the History of Sport*, he made a promise to himself – on the spot – that he would endeavour to bring as much of this rich scholastic resource as he could to the attention of an international readership: cultural relativism as personal realisation.

Postscript

The multiplicity of manoeuvres that characterise modern China's geopolitical ascendancy reveal human ingenuity utilised cautiously with the sensible desire to be invulnerable.[58] However, the strategic plurality employed in complex compositional patterns is at once both distinctly imperial and indigenous in nature: the projection of past into present and future. Could it be timely to suggest that this is a new episodic moment for the 'Middle Kingdom' caught nicely in the expression, 'The Great East Asian Game' – to appropriate and update Kipling's ironic 'The Great Game'?[59] In the light of the Guangzhou Asian Games Triumphalism, there could a 'double entendre' employed here of sizable significance!

Notes on Contributor

J.A. Mangan is an Emeritus Professor in the University of Strathclyde and an Adjunct Professor in Cairns Research Institute, FRHS, FRAI, FRSA, RSL, D.Litt, is Founding Editor of *The International Journal of the History of Sport* and the series *Sport in the Global Society*. He is also the author of the globally acclaimed *Athleticism in the Victorian and Edwardian Public School, The Games Ethic and Imperialism* and *'Manufactured' Masculinity: Making Imperial Manliness, Morality and Militarism* and author or editor of some 50 publications on politics, culture, and sport. Recently, he has been invited to be a Fellow of the Royal Society of Arts and a member of the Royal Society of Literature.

Notes

1. Laue, *The World Revolution of Westernization*, 349.
2. Hamalainen, *The Comanche Empire*, 349.
3. Mangan, "The New Asia," 2229.
4. Lovell, *The Opium War*.
5. Ibid., 4.

THE ASIAN GAMES: MODERN METAPHOR FOR 'THE MIDDLE KINGDOM' REBORN

6. Ibid.
7. Ibid., 276.
8. Ibid.
9. Ibid., 274.
10. Ibid.
11. Ibid., 276.
12. Ibid.
13. Ibid.
14. Kissinger, *On China*, 547.
15. Ibid., xii.
16. Ibid., 546.
17. Fenby, *Tiger Head, Snakes Tails*, 17–8.
18. Ibid., 18.
19. Ibid.
20. Ibid.
21. Beer, *Darwin's Plots*, 81–3.
22. Fenby, *Penguin History of Modern China*, 654.
23. Ibid.
24. *Daily Telegraph*, March 18, 2013, 21.
25. Mangan, "Preface: Geopolitical Games," 2.
26. Gross, *The Oxford Book of Aphorisms*, 116.
27. Mangan and Dong Jinxia (eds), *Beijing 2008: Preparing for Glory*, passim.
28. This point has been made by various commentators including myself. See, for example, Cha, *Beyond the Final Score*, 151.
29. Mangan, "Prologue: 'Middle Kingdom' Resurgent," 5.
30. Ibid., 5–6.
31. Ibid., 8.
32. Ibid., 5–6.
33. Fenby, *Tiger Head, Snakes Tails*, 273.
34. Ibid.
35. See Caffrey (ed.), *The Beijing Olympics: Promoting China*, passim, for an astute appraisal.
36. See especially Mangan et al., "Rivalries: China, Japan and South Korea," and Mangan, Kwon and Kim, "From Honeymoon to Divorce."
37. For a brilliant consideration of metaphor (and analogy), see especially Beer, *Darwin's Plots*, 80–95.
38. Ibid., 88.
39. Ibid., 80.
40. Ibid., 81.
41. Ibid., 83.
42. See Mangan and Dong, "Glittering Guangzhou."
43. See Mangan, "Prologue: 'Middle Kingdom' Resurgent," 2. The quotation is from Xu, *Olympic Dreams*, 267.
44. Mangan, "Preface: Geopolitical Games," 1.
45. Fenby, *Tiger Head, Snakes Tails*, 203.
46. Lovell, "Prologue: Beijing 2008," 13. See also Lovell, *The Politics of Cultural Capital*, passim. It is a penetrating insight into China's 'pathological' obsession with acquiring international cultural 'face'.
47. Gray, *False Dawn*, 66. Grey is quoting Lee Kuan Yew.
48. Darwin, *After Tamerlane*, 14.
49. Ibid., 13.
50. Ibid., 14.
51. Ibid.
52. Ibid.
53. Ibid.
54. Ibid.
55. Lal, *In Praise of Empires*, xxv–vi.
56. Gross, *The Oxford Book of Aphorisms*, 28.
57. Bridges, *The Two Koreas and the Politics of Global Sport*.

58. For an exceptional, and by extension, illuminating discussion of this national preoccupation throughout the history of Europe, see Simms, *Europe: The Struggle for Supremacy*. The analogous extension of this preoccupation to China's long history is highly appropriate.
59. I adopt, adapt and extend an insight of Caffrey outlined briefly in his "Prologue."

References

Beer, Gillian. *Darwin's Plots*. London: Routledge and Kegan Paul, 1983.

Bridges, Brian. *The Two Koreas and the Politics of Global Sport*. Leiden: Global Oriental, 2012.

Caffrey, Kevin, ed. *Beijing Olympics: Promoting China – Soft and Hard Power Politics*. Abingdon: Routledge, 2011.

Caffrey, Kevin. "Prologue: Beijing 2008 – A Production on Many Levels." In *The Beijing Olympics: Promoting China – Soft and Hard Power Politics*, edited by Kevin Caffrey, 1–6. Abingdon: Routledge, 2011.

Cha, Victor D. *Beyond the Final Score: The Politics of Sport in Asia*. New York: Columbia University Press, 2009.

Darwin, John. *After Tamerlane: The Global History of Empire Since 1445*. London: Allen Lane, 2007.

Fenby, Jonathan. *Head, Snake Tails: China Today*. New York: Simon and Schuster, 2012.

Fenby, Jonathan. *Penguin History of Modern China: The Fall and Rise of a Great Power 1850–2008*. London: Allen Lane, 2008.

Gray, John. *False Dawn*. London: Granta Book, 2009.

Gross, John. *The Oxford Book of Aphorisms*. Oxford: Oxford University Press, 1983.

Hamalainen, P. *The Comanche Empire*. London: Yale University Press, 2008.

Kissinger, Henry. *On China*. London: Penguin Books, 2012.

Lal, Deepak. *In Praise of Empires: Globalization and Order*. New York: Palgrave Macmillan, 2004.

Lovell, Julia. *The Opium War*. London: Picador, 2011.

Lovell, Julia. *The Politics of Cultural Capital: China's Quest for a Nobel Prize in Literature*. Honolulu: University of Hawaii Press, 2008.

Lovell, Julia. "Prologue: Beijing 2008 – The Mixed Message of Contemporary Chinese Nationalism." In *Beijing 2008: Preparing for Glory Chinese Challenge in the "Chinese Century"*, edited by J. A. Mangan, and Dong Jinxia, 8–28. Abingdon: Routledge, 2010.

Mangan, J. A. "Preface: Geopolitical Games – Beijing 2008." In *Beijing 2008: Preparing for Glory Chinese Challenge in the "Chinese Century"*, edited by J. A. Mangan, and Dong Jinxia, 1–7. Abingdon: Routledge, 2010.

Mangan, J. A. "Prologue: 'Middle Kingdom' Resurgent! Sports Dominance as Soft Power Politics on the Pacific Rim – Reflections on Rim Realpolitik." In *Post-Beijing 2008: Geopolitics, Sport and the Pacific Rim*, edited by J. A. Mangan, and Fan Hong, 1–26. Abingdon: Routledge, 2011.

Mangan, J. A., and Dong Jinxia, eds. *Beijing 2008: Preparing for Glory – Chinese Challenge in the "Chinese Century"*. Abingdon: Routledge, 2010.

Mangan, J. A., Hyun-Duck Kim, Angelita Cruz, and Gi-Heun Kang. "Rivalries: China, Japan and South Korea – Memory, Modernity, Politics, Geopolitics – and Sport." In *The Asian Games: Modern Metaphor for 'The Middle Kingdom' Reborn – Political Statement, Cultural Assertion, Social Symbol*, edited by J. A. Mangan, Marcus P. Chu, and Jinxia Dong. Abingdon: Routledge, Forthcoming.

Mangan, J. A., Sun-Yong Kwon, and Bang-Chool Kim. "From Honeymoon to Divorce: Fragmenting Relations between China and South Korea in Politics, Economics – and Sport." In *The Asian Games: Modern Metaphor for 'The Middle Kingdom' Reborn – Political Statement, Cultural Assertion, Social Symbol*, edited by J. A. Mangan, Marcus P. Chu, and Jinxia Dong. Abingdon: Routledge, Forthcoming.

Simms, Brenda. *Europe: The Struggle for Supremacy, 1453 to the Present: A History of the Continent Since 1500*. London: Penguin, 2013.

Van Laue, Theodore H. *The World Revolution of Westernization: The Twentieth Century in Global Perspective*. Oxford: Oxford University Press, 1987.

Xu, Guoqi. *Olympic Dream: China and Sport 1895–2008*. Cambridge, MA: Harvard University Press, 2008.

People's Daily: An Evolutionary Narrative on Asia in Its Coverage of the Asian Games

Wenting Xue[b] and Qing Luo[a]

[a]*International Communication Center, Communication University of China, Beijing 100024, P. R. China;* [b]*Beijing Sport University, Beijing 100084, P.R. China*

> Amid the complex international situation and entangled interests, news narration is usually conducted by the government, media and the public together by copying mainstream ideas and concepts. In covering the Asian Games, *People's Daily* takes on a periodical change in its narration about Asia during the history of China's participation in the Games: in the stage of 'alienation and struggle', the narration is focused on politics; in the stage of 'participation and competition', the narration becomes two dimensional, touching on both politics and sport; in the stage of 'hosting the Games and taking the lead', the narration is further diversified and incorporates politics, sport and culture. Such an evolution takes place in a profound international and historical context, reflecting the changes not only in China's sporting events coverage but also in the 'mindset and insight' of Chinese media in covering sporting events and Asia.

Former South African President Mandela ever said that 'Sport has the power to change the world. It has the power to unite in a way that little else does'. In Asia, among interweaving historical grievances and realistic conflicts, as well as intricate internal contradictions and external forces, the Asian Games, founded in 1951, have played such unique roles in 'encouragement' and 'unity', and have become a platform for Asian countries to show their strengths, build up their images and promote mutual exchanges and communication. Following vicissitudes in international politics and the unsteady development of Chinese society, Chinese experience in the Asian Games have basically undergone the three stages of alienation and struggle (1951–1970), participation and competition (1974–1986) and hosting and leading (1990–2010). In this process, Chinese media's coverage of the Asian Games, acting as a 'most typical, widespread and influential narration', has also narrated the story of Asia while recording the history of the Asian Games.[1] What kind of story is it? What features are present in its narration? With *People's Daily*'s coverage of previous Asian Games as the object of study, this paper attempts to reveal typical expressions, Asian stories and narrative features in Chinese media's reportage of the Asian Games, so as to deeply explore the features and functions of Chinese sports coverage, especially international event coverage.

Alienation and Struggle (1951–1970): One-Dimensional Narration Highlighting Political Views

As a result of the Cold War and the deterioration of Sino–Soviet relations, the New China of this period was shifting its diplomatic policies from 'predomination' (of the Socialist Camp) in the initial stage of the New China to 'two-pronged actions' (against American imperialism and the Soviet Union's modern revisionism) in the 1960s, excluding it from the mainstream world order as well as the arenas of the Asian Games. In 1951, the All-China Sports Federation was honoured with an invitation to visit the first Asian Games in New Delhi. In 1954, when the Asian Games Federation invited Taiwan to participate in the second Asian Games, the All-China Sports Federation resolutely cut off all relations with the Asian Games Federation, and since then, it had been isolated from the arenas of the Games for as long as 20 years. In 1962, Indonesia refused to allow Taiwan to participate in the fourth Djakarta Asian Games in order to maintain friendly relationships with the New China, for which it was denounced and sanctioned by the Asian Games Federation and the International Olympic Committee.

In such an international environment of alienation and rejection, with the exception of the Djakarta Asian Games in 1962 and the Bangkok Asian Games in 1966, *People's Daily* basically adopted a 'silent' attitude, defining the position of 'one China' and the disapproval of relevant resolutions of the Asian Games Federation and reducing adverse effects caused by Taiwan's participation in the Asian Games, as shown in Table 1. However, when the situation in the Djakarta Asian Games in 1962 turned out to be favourable to China, *People's Daily* seized the opportune moment to publish news and editorials, supporting the actions of the Indonesian government and condemning the interference of imperialists led by the USA, which completed an Asian narration manipulated by 'American imperialism' with clear demarcation of friends and foes, presenting strong political and ideological views.

Political Narration under Control of 'American Imperialism'

From July of 1962, when Indonesia prevented entry of Taiwanese athletes, to September 5 of that year, the day following the closing ceremony of the Djakarta Asian Games, *People's Daily* published 14 reports, such as 'Under Instigation of the USA, Chiang Kai-shek Clique Steps up Attempts to Sneak into the Asian Games', 'Indonesian Government Announced Denial of Entry of Chiang Kai-shek Clique's "Sports Team"', 'With the Completion of the Fourth Asian Games, Conspiracy of Imperialists and Their Running Dogs Went Bankrupt and India Fled in a Panic under the Drive of Angry Indonesians' and

Table 1. Statistics of the quantity of *People's Daily*'s reports about the Asian Games from 1951 to 1970.

	1951 New Delhi Asian Games	1954 Manila Asian Games	1958 Tokyo Asian Games	1962 Jakarta Asian Games	1966 Bangkok Asian Games	1970 Bangkok Asian Games
Report quantity	0	0	0	8	1	0

Notes: Statistics were only recorded for coverage of the Asian Games during the Games period to facilitate vertical comparison. Full-text search was conducted in the 'Image-text Database of *People's Daily*' with 'Asian Games' as keywords to produce samples. Since the closing ceremony was often covered in the newspaper on the next day, the time for statistics on the coverage quantity started on the day of the opening ceremony and ended on the day following the closing ceremony. The same follows hereinafter.

so on. These reports uncovered Taiwan's conspiracy to participate in the Asian Games, supported the righteous position of Indonesia and vetoed the sanction of the Asian Games Federation and other international sports organisations against Indonesia. In the 14 reports, the use of the word 'imperialism' was very frequent, appearing 71 times, including 53 times in the phrase 'American imperialism'. The report entitled 'Heads of All Chinese Sports Associations Made Speeches to Strongly Blame the USA's Conspiracy by Instigating Chiang Kai-shek Clique to sneak into the Asian Games', included 17 uses of 'imperialism' and referred to 'American imperialism' 16 times. *People's Daily* also quoted the responsible officer of the All-China Sports Federation that

> Now, the bandit gang and American boss of Chiang Kai-shek have not resigned to their failure, as they are using despicable methods ... Under the manipulation of the USA, the International Olympic Committee and other international sports organizations are exerting pressure on Indonesia and other participating countries and regions, in an attempt to coerce delegations from participating countries to dropout of the Games by *derecognizing the fourth Asian Games*.[2]

It is evident that in the eyes of the Chinese government and media, Asia and the Asian Games were manipulated by 'imperialists' led by the USA.

For such manipulation, *People's Daily* severely reprimanded that

> Such coercion and sabotage cannot be allowed in the sports circle of any self-respecting Asian country. Participating countries and international judicial public opinions all come forward to reprove ... Delegations of many participating countries also expressed that they would continue to participate in the fourth Asian Games. Such a firm attitude represents a forceful answer to imperialists and their agents.

People's Daily also expressed its hope that Asia could get rid of the control of imperialism

> Nowadays, Asia is independent and owned by people of all nations ... The age when imperialists had Asian people at their mercy has gone forever. This event will enable people and sports circles in Asian countries to further see through the insidiousness of imperialists, unite on a broader level and fight for the development of sports activities in Asia.[3]

Political Narration with Clear Demarcation of 'Friends' and 'Foes'

As the Taiwan issue related to China's sovereignty, it had been a core issue in the diplomacy of the New China. Based on the attitudes and positions of the Asian countries on Taiwan's representation and participation in the Asian Games Federation, *People's Daily* clearly demarcated 'friends' and 'foes' in its coverage of the Asian Games.

In 1962, apart from Indonesia, which was regarded by China as a 'friend' for its rejection of Taiwan's participation in the Asian Games, Ceylon and Pakistan were also considered by China to be 'friends', since responsible officers of their delegations criticised Indian members for supporting Taiwan's participation in the Asian Games. In response to support from 'friends', *People's Daily* offered affirmation and thanks through its reports and editorials. For example,

> The Indonesian government and people have been widely praised and supported by African and Asian people for safeguarding their country's territorial sovereignty and dignity, maintaining friendly relationships between Indonesia and China, and defending their righteous position for the unity of Africa and Asia. Chinese people would also like to express their heartfelt admiration and thanks to President Sukarno, the Indonesian government and people for their friendly attitude.[4]

At the same time, Japan, the Philippines, India, South Vietnam, South Korea, Israel, Malaysia and Iraq, were taken as 'foes' in addition to 'American imperialists and their running dog Chiang Kai-shek's clique', for they supported Taiwan's participation in the Asian Games. *People's Daily* also sternly criticised them, for example, saying 'American imperialists conspiratorially placed Chiang Kai-shek's clique onto the list of members to be invited to the Games through their Japanese and Filipino lackeys in the Asian Games Federation'.[5] In 1966, *People's Daily* used extremely harsh words for the fifth Bangkok Asian Games, which attracted the participation of 'sports delegations sent by such notorious puppet regimes – South Korea, South Vietnam, Israeli and Malaysian authority delegation under the control of American imperialists' as well as Taiwan delegation

> The fifth 'Asian Games' organized by the so-called Asian Games Federation, manipulated by imperialists and hosted by reactionary authorities of Thailand, was held in Bangkok from December 9 to 20. At the Asian Games, all sorts of ugly behaviors were exposed, such as cheating, brutal fighting, endless cases of deaths and injuries, and messy organization, which turned the Games as a whole into a scene of chaos.[6]

Participation and Competition (1974–1986): Two Dimensional

Narration focusing on both politics and sport from 1974 to 1986, with the mitigated situation of the Cold War, the New China gradually integrated into the international community and entered the Asian Games. On November 16, 1973, the Asian Games Federation confirmed the legitimate rights of the All-China Sports Federation and cancelled the membership of the Taiwan sports organisation. In 1974, China took part in the Asian Games for the first time and ranked third on the gold medal list, catching the eye of Asia and even of the world. In 1978, the Chinese delegation ranked second on the gold medal list, exerting a great impact on Japan's sports dominance in Asia. In 1982, the Chinese delegation ranked first on the list, creating a new era of the Asian Games. In 1986, the Chinese team topped the gold medal list for the second time and kept its leading position in the Asian sports circles. When Chinese sport 'went beyond Asia and went global', *People's Daily* also substantially heightened its attention to the Games and made significant changes to its narration about Asia, as it included both political narration with 'friendship' and 'unity' as key words and focused on sports narration with the 'tripartite competition' among China, Japan and South Korea.

Political Narration Highlighting 'Friendship' and 'Unity'

Different from the Asia with clear labels of 'friends' and 'foes' when China was isolated from the Asian Games, the 'Asia' in the reports of *People's Daily* during this period was marked with 'friendly' and 'united'. As shown in Table 2, *People's Daily* exerted tremendous efforts to promote 'friendship' during the 1974 Teheran Asian Games. Amid 57

Table 2. Statistics of the quantity of *People's Daily*'s reports about the Asian Games from 1974 to 1986 and the frequency of occurrence of 'Friendship'.

Time	1974 Teheran Asian Games	1978 Bangkok Asian Games	1982 New Delhi Asian Games	1986 Seoul Asian Games
Quantity of the Asian Games reports	56	42	68	133
Quantity and propitiation of reports with 'friendship' and 'friendly'	35, 63%	9, 21%	12, 18%	3, 2%
Occurrences of 'friendship' and 'friendly' and average occurrences per report	178, 3.18	10, 0.24	27, 0.40	3, 0.02

reports about the Asian Games, 35 reports contained the words 'friendship' or 'friendly', accounting for over a half of the total reports. In these reports, there were as many as 11 reports with the word 'friendship' in their titles, such as 'The Spirit of Friendship First, Competition Second Deeply Rooted in the Hearts of People', 'Flowers of Friendship Can Be Found Everywhere' and so on. Occurrences of 'friendship' and 'friendly' reached up to 178 with 3.18 times per report. The report 'Friendship Overweighs Success' featured more than 30 occurrences of the said words. At the same time, 'unity' also had a high occurrence frequency, for there were 17 reports with the word 'unity' in their main bodies and six reports with the same word in their titles, such as 'To Further Strengthen Friendship and Unity amid People of All Countries, To Make New Developments in Sports Exchanges with All Countries' and 'A Sports Show with Unity and Friendship'.

'Friendship first, competition second' was the policy for sports endeavours proposed by Premier Zhou Enlai when he led the Chinese delegation to attend the 31st World Table Tennis Championships in 1971, which played positive roles in accelerating the globalisation of Chinese sport and developing a new international political phase. However, with changes in international situations, such a policy triggered doubts and discussions in the 1970s and 1980s, which was then kept away from mainstream discourse. Accordingly, the occurrence frequency of 'friendship' in reports about the Games was also gradually decreased.

Sports Narration Centring on 'Tripartite Competition' among China, Japan and South Korea

If it can be said that China was concerned first and foremost with the verification of its identity in Asia and recognition by other Asian countries when it first came to the Asian Games, then, with the steady rise of its ranking on the gold medal list, China began to pay increasing attention to its status in the Asian sports circles, which was prominently shown in the competition between China and Japan for the number 1 position on the gold medal list in 1982, and the competition between China and South Korea in 1986 for the same purpose. *People's Daily* also shifted the focus of its coverage from 'friendship' to the tripartite competition among China, Japan and South Korea.

In 1982, *People's Daily* published such reports in succession 'By Midway through the Asian Games Season, China's Gold Medals in the Lead', 'By Carrying forward the Fighting Spirit to Earn Honor for the Motherland, Chinese Athletes to Secure China's Number One Position in Gold Medal Count', etc. When the 'gold medal battle' between Chinese and Japanese players turned white-hot in the last lap of the Games, *People's Daily* could not hide its excitement and nervousness in its reportage when waiting for China to outperform Japan in the Games.

> Now, China has overtaken Japan in terms of the total gold medal count and total scores. In the last four days of competition, as long as Chinese players display their normal level of performance and work hard on each event, there is hope that China can outstrip Japan in the aspects of total gold medal count and total scores.[7]

> 'Now, the Chinese team has won one more gold medal than Japan'.[8] 'China's ranking first on the gold medal list at the 9th Asian Games caused great repercussions in Japan'.[9]

During the Seoul Asian Games in 1986, China met powerful challenges from the host country South Korea on its road to stay in the number 1 position for another term. *People's Daily* also published in succession reports such as 'Gold Medal Competition Gets Fierce with the Asian Games Approaching the End, As the Chinese Team Won Five Champions Yesterday and Made the Total Gold Medal Count 85 – 12 More than South Korea', 'As

Gold Medal Competition in the Asian Games Comes to the Last Lap, South Korea's Gold Medal Count Gets Closer to that of China' and 'The 16-Fay Asian Games Will Come to an End Today, and China and South Korea Hold the Same Gold Medal Count', as well as other reports, highlighting the fierceness of the competition and the rise of Chinese competitive sports.

Hosting the Games and Taking the Lead (1990–2010): Three-Dimensional Narration Relating to Politics, Sport and Culture

The 1990 Beijing Asian Games were significant as the first comprehensive international event held by the New China. From the sports perspective, the Beijing Asian Games achieved the transformation from the 'tripartite competition among China, Japan and South Korea' to 'China outshines others, and Japan and South Korea compete for the second place' in the Asian sports circles, which also accumulated useful experience in hosting large events. From the political viewpoint, the success of the Beijing Asian Games gradually led China out of the negative international influence resulting from the political turbulence in 1989 and promoted friendly exchanges between China and other Asian countries. After the Beijing Olympic Games and the Shanghai World Expo, the 2010 Guangzhou Asian Games became another 'symbol' for China's rising international influence. From Beijing to Guangzhou and from 1990 to 2010, the two Asian Games demonstrated the progress of Chinese society and rise of Chinese national strength to Asia and the world (Table 3).

During this period, Chinese media's coverage of the Asian Games also gradually became mature and confident, and paid attention to spread of diversified Asian culture in addition to political narration and sports narration, bringing to the audience a different Asian story.

Political Narration Assisting Official Diplomacy

The Asian Games were not only a sports issue but also a political issue, involving Asian regional relations and even international relations. As a result, reportage of the Asian Games was still politically tainted and undertook the political function of assisting official diplomacy during this period.

The 1990 Beijing Asian Games assumed the diplomatic missions of improving regional atmosphere and strengthening international exchanges. To assist the Asian Games in fulfilling the significant diplomatic missions and implementing the Beijing Asian Games' tenets of 'unity, friendship and progress', *People's Daily* clearly put forward the reporting concept of 'attaching sufficient importance to both competition and friendship' and 'highlighting friendship'.[10] According to statistics, *People's Daily* published 475 reports regarding the Asian Games during the Games period. Among them, there were 91 reports

Table 3. Statistics of quantity of *People's Daily*'s reports about the Asian Games from 1990 to 2010.

	1990 Beijing Asian Games	1994 Hiroshima Asian Games	1998 Bangkok Asian Games	2002 Busan Asian Games	2006 Doha Asian Games	2010 Guangzhou Asian Games
Report quantity	475	127	136	177	132	248

including the words 'friendship' or 'friendly' in their main bodies, accounting for 19% of total reports, and 9 reports including the words 'friendship' or 'friendly' in their titles, such as 'Friendship, Common Pursuit across Borders', 'The Great Wall of Friendship' and so on. In addition to over 30 reports about state leaders meeting with Asian leaders and coming for the Asian Games, *People's Daily* also opened up the special column of 'Interviews with Delegation Leaders', releasing interview records on chiefs of delegations from 39 countries and regions, such as 'Sport as a Symbol for Peaceful Cooperation: Interview of Deputy Leader of the Saudi Delegation', 'A Good Beginning to Go Global: Interview of Acting Leader of Palestinian Delegation', 'Visit, Inspection and Preparation: Interview of Hiroshima Mayor Takeshi Araki' and so on, which was affirmed and welcomed by all delegations for its role in deepening friendships and strengthening communication.

In 1994, centring on the disturbance during the Hiroshima Asian Games,[11] *People's Daily* published in succession over 20 reports, including 'What Do the Taiwan Authorities Pursue "Sport Diplomacy" for?', 'What Should the Japanese Government Do?', 'Responsible Officer of China Olympic Committee (COC) Restates China's Position in Strictly Following the Nagoya Resolution of the IOC', 'Return with Songs of Victories', etc., condemning the Japanese government for allowing Taiwan politicians to attend the opening ceremony of the Games and revealing the international relations and political gaming behind the Games.

It is noteworthy that Asia was not peaceful on the eve of the 2010 Guangzhou Asian Games, as the Games were preceded by Hillary Clinton's speech on the South China Sea issue and joint military manoeuvre of the USA and South Korea, followed by the Chinese hostage-taking incident in the Philippines and Japan's detaining of a Chinese fishing boat. Despite these, China welcomed guests from all countries with a moderate and prudent mindset, as she had grown to be an important international political power and the world's second largest economy. Chinese media as represented by *People's Daily* abided by Guangzhou Asian Games' concept of 'Thrilling Games, Harmonious Asia', and made relatively objective and friendly reports about foreign delegations and athletes, including those from Japan, South Korea and the Philippines. Amid the 247 reports of *People's Daily*, there were 48 occurrences of 'friendship' or 'friendly', such as 'Guangzhou Asian Games harvested not only touching stories about the fighting and pioneering spirit on the sports ground, but also friendships among Asian countries and regions established in harmonious contact and fair competition ...',[12] 'Different from the opening ceremony that focused on Lingnan (the south of the Five Ridges) regional culture, the closing ceremony highlighted Asian elements and praised the exchanges and friendship among athletes from all Asian countries and regions'.[13]

Sports Narration Paying Attention to Development of Asian Sports as a Whole

The hosting of the Asian Games in China and Chinese delegations' outstanding performance in the Games enabled the Chinese government, media and the public to treat medals in a detached manner and broadened the scope of their attention from focusing on Chinese delegations to covering development of Asian sports as a whole and pattern changes in Asian sports.

During the Asian Games in 1990, *People's Daily* clearly put forward the reportage tone of 'highlighting Asia as a whole' and the principle that all countries, big or small, shall be equal, in order to avoid 'despising the poor and currying favor with the rich' and fastening eyes on the several 'major gold winning countries'.[14] The public also reminded the Chinese people and media that 'We shall have the awareness of one Asia while expressing our patriotism',[15] and that 'We shall avoid turning reportage of the Asian Games into that of the National Games'.[16] During the Beijing Asian Games, *People's Daily* properly implemented the idea of 'highlighting Asia as a whole', for it published 97 reports about match performance of athletes from all countries, the situations of watching the Games in different countries and world opinions on the Games, such as 'Winning the Hockey Championship, Pakistanis Dancing with Joy', 'First Gold Medal Winner in Japan', 'Black Lightning in Oman', 'First Burmese Prize Winner Came into Being', 'Winning Silver Medal with a Sword: Brief Introduction to Indonesian "Mother Athlete" Silvia', 'Dyuksang: Eagle of Bhutan' and so on. After that, although *People's Daily* made fewer reports about foreign delegations and athletes, it always paid attention to the development of Asian sports as a whole, as evidenced by the quotes 'Through scattered gold medals and the long gold medal list, we could see the bright prospects with the Asian sports circles going ahead with full steam and the power of Asia shocking the world',[17] and

> The awakening of Asian sports needs not only such Asian sports 'leaders' China, South Korea and Japan, but also the vigorous participation of the 45 members of the Olympic Council of Asia, in order to jointly build the cornerstone for development of Asian sports and create a bright future for Asian sports.[18]

As more countries took part in the Asian Games, *People's Daily* began to use the expressions of East Asia, South Asia, Southeast Asia, West Asia and Central Asia, and paid close attention to trends of the sports patterns in Asian sports circles. In 1990, upon completion of the Games, *People's Daily* published 'East Asia: Showing Strong Sports Strength and Japan Preparing Itself for the Next Games', 'South Asia: Rising from the Bottom', 'West Asia: Presenting Bright Prospects', 'Southeast Asia: Active Participation' and 'Rapid Rise of the Korean Peninsula', making a survey of sports development in various regions. In 1994, *People's Daily* paid attention to the five countries that newly joined Central Asia by successively releasing 'Challenges from Central Asia Rolled in, First Athletes Looked Vigorous and Energetic', 'Central Asia Newly Wakes from Sleep' and other reports, which also anchored its hopes on Central Asia for enhancing Asian sports development. In 2010, *People's Daily* covered the emerging track and field of West Asia and published 'West Asia *Stake* Track and Field and Expects *Counterattack*', acknowledging West Asia's efforts and performance in track and field events.

Cultural Narration Promoting Asian Civilisation

There is no doubt that sport is a kind of culture. Therefore,

> The Asian Games is not only a grand event for sports competition, but also, and more importantly a stage for cultural integration. On this stage, all Asian countries and regions have mutual contact, understand each other's culture and create harmony through cultural exchanges and synergy.[19]

Since 1990, the Chinese government, media and the public have become increasingly aware of the cultural functions of the Asian Games. Luo Jingjun, Head of the Propaganda Department of Guangzhou Asian Games Organizing Committee, even pointed out 'The most prominent feature differentiating the Guangzhou Asian Games from previous ones is that it will also be a cultural event embodying diversified culture in Asia'.[20] For this purpose, the Guangzhou Asian Games Organizing Committee made the opening and closing ceremonies 'based on Chinese culture, integrate Asian culture and highlight Lingnan culture' and creatively used representative symbols of all Asian countries and regions. *People's Daily* also used 'culture' and 'civilisation' many times in its coverage of the Games, such as 'Chinese Chess as the Ambassador of Asian Culture', 'Sport is not only a Sports Show, and also a Stage for Cultural Integration – Many Tourists Get Infatuated with the Cultural Elements in the Asian Games' and so on.

Non-Olympic events in the Asian Games are an embodiment manifesting Asian sports culture and facilitating sports and cultural exchanges in Asia, which are also favoured by Asian people for their absorption of strong connotations of oriental culture as well as national characteristics. For these events, not only does the Chinese government actively promote their entry into the Asian Games, but Chinese media also made massive coverage, in order to present Asia with culture for the audience. In 1990, the Beijing Asian Games increased the martial arts event to the Games and added sepatakraw and kabaddi into the formal events. *People's Daily* published 14 reports about sepatakraw and 12 reports about kabaddi, showing its attention to the non-Olympic events from Southeast Asia and South Asia. The Asian Games was the sports competition with the most newly added non-Olympic events. Chinese media also covered these non-Olympic events. Among them, *People's Daily* released 12 reports containing the words of 'non-Olympic events', such as 'Non-Olympic Events Fight for Their Existence in Asia', 'Non-Olympic Events: Of a Strong Asian Flavor and Closer to People', 'Non-Olympic Events Also Splendid' and so on. In addition, *People's Daily* spoke highly of the cultural meanings of non-Olympic events with the comments that

> The Guangzhou Asian Games, which have both fierce competition in Olympic events and wonderful demonstration of folk sports events from different nations, resemble a majestic and grand book with endless pages organized in a natural and harmonious manner and containing Asia's beauty in diversification and colorfulness. These bring great vitality to the Games and continue Asia's eternal dream of pursuing *peace, friendship and progress.*[21]

People's Daily also introduced 14 non-Olympic events through its reports such as 'Dragon Boat Sails into the Asian Games for the First Time', 'Cricket's First Encounter with the Asian Games', 'Sepatakraw Turns out To Be More Wonderful When Played with More Members', 'Kabaddi with a Strong Resemblance to the Eagle-Grabs-Chicken Game Reminds Audience of Their Childhood' and so on. Some articles even attached tips helping the audience understand the history, culture and viewing etiquettes of the events. For the issue of necessary deletion of non-Olympic events due to shortening of the Asian Games, a journalist of *People's Daily* even proposed the idea of 'holding two Asian Games' and said,

> Modern sports events are dominated by traditional sports events of Western countries, and many countries in Asia have few or no rights of speech in this area. The lower sports level of Asia as a whole is an important cause of being controlled by Western countries in the Asia Games. Since the Asian Games is expanding in size with its development, why not hold two different Asian Games.[22]

Conclusion

News is a kind of narration. Amid complex international situations and entangled realistic interests, news narration is usually conducted by the government, media and the public together by copying mainstream ideas and concepts. In covering the Asian Games, *People's Daily* takes on a periodical change in its narration about Asia over the history of China's participation in the Games: one-dimensional political narration in the 'participation and competition' stage; two-dimensional political and sports narration in the 'participation and competition' stage; three-dimensional political, sports and culture narration in the 'hosting and leading' stage. The periodic and time features presented in the narration about Asia in Chinese media's coverage of the Asian Games stem from changes in the international political setting and of China's relations with other Asian countries, from the development of Chinese society and sports undertakings and from diplomatic needs of the Chinese government.

We must 'understand with compassion' the obvious and continued political narration featured throughout reportage of *People's Daily* about the Games. No one can be divorced from society and, similarly, any period of history cannot be separated from the context of the time. Furthermore, the political roles of sport in building the image of the nation in the international community and uniting the national spirit at home have been obvious to all.

The increase in the narration dimension in *People's Daily*'s coverage of the Games reflects the evolution of the Chinese sport and sports coverage functions, as well as the deepening knowledge of the Games by the Chinese government, media and the public. Also, it embodies changes in the 'mindset and insight' of Chinese media in covering sporting events and Asia. When Wang Yi, Former Chinese Ambassador in Japan, referred to the China Central Television (CCTV) programme 'Insight Japan', he said

> My concern is not having a look at Japan, but showing Chinese media's moderate and objective mindset and insight in covering the world, and that its reform and opening-up has developed to such a stage. That is the impression China shall leave to the world.[23]

Notes on Contributors

Wenting Xue is the Deputy Director of Public Relations Department, Beijing Sport University (BSU); Associated Professor and Master Supervisor in Sport Journalism Department, BSU.

Qing Luo is the Secretary-general of MLeague (International League of Higher Education in Media and Communication); Deputy Director of International Office, Communication University of China (CUC); Associated Professor in International Communication; Visiting Professor nominated by COMUNDUS-Erasmus Mundus, EU, Olympic Studies Center of International Olympic Committee (OSC-IOC) and European Audiovisual Observatory-Council of Europe.

Notes

1. Buyan Fan, "Humble Opinions on News Narration" (*Press Outpost*, 12, 2000, 4).
2. "Head of All-China Sports Federation Reprimanded Imperialists for Scheming to Sabotage the Asian Games and Supported Righteous Position of Indonesia" (*People's Daily*, September 2, 1962).
3. Ibid.
4. "Victory of Asian People in Unity and Friendship" (*People's Daily*, September 6, 1962).
5. "Vainly Attempted to Create 'Two-China' to Destroy Friendship between Chinese and Indonesian People: As the USA Actively Instigated Chiang Kai-shek Clique to Participate in the Asian Games, Indonesian People and Public Opinions Expressed Strong Indignation" (*People's Daily*, July 25, 1962).
6. "The Fifth Asian Games with All Kinds of Ugly Behaviors" (*People's Daily*, December 28, 1966).
7. "Competition Becomes Increasingly Fierce, Chinese People Strives for Greater Victory" (*People's Daily*, November 30, 1982).
8. "13 Gold Medals Came to Winners on the 12th Day of the Asian Games, Chinese Handball Player won Championship" (*People's Daily*, December 1, 1982).
9. "To Carry Forward the Fighting Spirit to Earn Honor for Motherland, Chinese Athletes to Secure China's First Position in Gold Medal Count" (*People's Daily*, December 3, 1982).
10. Asian Games Coverage Team of *People's Daily*, "Review of Coverage of the Asian Games" (*News Front*, 3, 1991, 15).
11. On the eve of the Hiroshima Asian Games, Li Denghui declared that he would attend the opening ceremony of the Games upon invitation of the Olympic Council of Asia, which met with strong opposition and solemn representations of the Chinese government. After the Chairman of the Olympic Council of Asia announced to have revoked the invitation, Xu Lide,

THE ASIAN GAMES: MODERN METAPHOR FOR 'THE MIDDLE KINGDOM' REBORN

'Vice President of the Executive Yuan' assigned by the Taiwan authorities, attended the opening ceremony as a canvasser for 'bidding to hold the 2002 Asian Games' and obtained the entry visa issued by the organising committee of the Hiroshima Asian Games, which gave rise to the China–Japan turbulence.

12. "Thrilling Games, Lifting Hopes: Warm Celebration of Closing of the Guangzhou Asian Games" (*People's Daily*, November 28, 2010).

13. "Play Faster, Higher and Stronger Music and Paint Grand Spectacle of Unity and Friendship to Celebrate Successful Closing of the 16th Asian Games" (*People's Daily*, November 28, 2010).

14. Asian Games Coverage Team of *People's Daily*, "Review of Coverage of the Asian Games" (*News Front*, 3, 1991, 15).

15. "Our Asia" (*People's Daily*, September 25, 1990).

16. "One Sentence Comments" (*People's Daily*, September 25, 1990).

17. "Power of Asia Shocking the World – Reflections upon Closing of the 12th Asian Games" (*People's Daily*, October 17, 1994).

18. "Differences May Be Found in Strength But Not in the Fighting Spirit, and on the Stage of the Asian Games, All Dreams Are Splendid" (*People's Daily*, November 16, 2010).

19. "The Sports Event also Serves a Stage for Cultural Integration – Many Tourists Gets Infatuated with the Cultural Elements in the Asian Games" (*People's Daily*, November 17, 2010).

20. "The Creator Team Uncovers Creativity in the Opening Ceremony of the Asian Game and Creation of the Grand Event" (*People's Daily*, November 13, 2010).

21. "Thrilling Games, Harmonious Asia: Warmly Celebrating Opening of the 16th Asian Games" (*People's Daily*, November 12, 2010).

22. "Why Not Hold Two Asian Games" (*People's Daily*, November 21, 2010).

23. Kai Zhao, "Role of Media in Public Diplomacy: A Perspective Based on the TV News Programme – Insight Japan" (*The Journalist Monthly*, 12, 2009, 26).

The Pursuit of Regional Geopolitical Aspirations: China's Bids for the Asian Games and the Asian Winter Games since the 1980s

Marcus P. Chu

Department of Political Science, Lingnan University, Hong Kong, China

> Any international bid involves a zero-sum competition among two or more national candidates vying for the right to host a particular international event. Chinese cities in total have participated in the Asian Games and Asian Winter Games bids four times since 1980. Beijing's bid for the 1990 Asian Games; Harbin's bid for the 1996 Asian Winter Games; Changchun's bid for the 2007 Asian Winter Games and Guangzhou's bid for the 2010 Asian Games: not one encountered failure. The argument here is that all the bids were used to build up China's hegemonic status in the Asian sports community with wider resonances for the geopolitical hegemonic influence of China. Evidence is drawn from contemporary literature and media reports.

Introduction

The term 'geopolitical hegemony' was coined by Prof. J.A. Mangan, with the aim of drawing a conclusion about the political intentions behind China hosting the 2008 Summer Olympics in Beijing. Throughout the remarkable performance of the opening ceremony and the leading rank taken by the Chinese athletes in the gold medal table, the Games were viewed as an instrument of the government not only to project China as a superpower on the global stage, but also to rebuild it as the middle kingdom in the Asian Pacific Rim. Those political intentions, however, were asserted to be very likely to (1) arouse nationalist, patriotic and/or chauvinistic sentiments among the Chinese, (2) increase the regional fear towards China and (3) challenge the *status quo* of the Rim.[1]

Apart from the 2008 Olympic Games, China also projected its geopolitical hegemony through hosting the Asian Games (AG) and Asian Winter Games (AWG). The AG and the AWG are two of the five international multi-sport events (IMSEs) organised by the Olympic Council of Asia (OCA). While the former has been celebrated 16 times, the latter has been presented 7 times. To date, four Chinese cities, namely Beijing, Harbin, Changchun and Guangzhou, respectively, hosted the 11th AG in 1990, the 3rd AWG in 1996, the 6th AWG in 2007 and the 16th AG in 2010.

As China was widely boycotted by the members of the international community after the Tiananmen massacre of pro-democracy demonstrators in June 1989, the 1990 Beijing AG became a crucial means for the government to boost Chinese patriotic emotion. Therefore, while its preparation and organisation were propagandised as a milestone of the socialist reform through which the Chinese nation had become competent to independently stand up on the regional and world stage, the Chinese delegation's gold medal domination in the 16-day event was interpreted as the removal of the image of the 'sick man of East Asia', which had been a national stigma on China, under the ruling of the Chinese Communist Party (CCP).[2] It should be noted that Beijing's decision to bid for the rights to host 2000 (and later 2008) Summer Olympics was also partly motivated by the success in celebrating the AG.[3]

The 1996 AWG was the first IMSE held in Harbin, a city in north-eastern China close to Russia. The Chinese were proud of this 8-day gathering for three reasons. First, the Chinese delegation placed at the top of the gold medal table. Second, it was up until then the biggest winter-sport event in Asia. Third, Harbin only spent 26 months to prepare the games, which was 34 months shorter than the time taken for the same tasks completed by the other Asian cities for prior games. All the reasons above were correlated with the achievement of China's socialist reform, and China's collectivism led by the then CCP General Secretary Jiang Zemin through which all the Heilongjiang and Harbin residents devoted their greatest efforts to make the games a success.[4] The successful holding of the AWG later even became one of Harbin's motives to bid for the 2010 Winter Olympics.[5] On that occasion, however, Harbin was eliminated by the International Olympic Committee (IOC) in the first round.[6]

Eleven years later, Changchun, also in the north-eastern part of China, became the second Chinese city to hold the AWG. When Harbin prepared the 1996 Games in only 26 months, Changchun prepared for the 2007 Games over almost 5 years.[7] Though the central government used Harbin's speed to praise the collectivism led by the then CCP chief Jiang Zemin, it took Changchun's preparation, through which the city was transformed from an industrial base to a liveable metropolis, to confirm the feasibility of the next CCP General Secretary Hu Jintao's 'Scientific Development Concept' to improve China.[8] While 445 athletes from 17 nations participated in the 1996 AWG, 802 athletes from 26 nations took part in the 2007 AWG. While the Chinese delegation was rewarded with 37 medals, including 15 gold, 7 silver and 15 bronze, in Harbin, China obtained 61 medals, including 19 gold, 19 silver and 23 bronze, in Changchun. While Harbin's Games were described as a successful sports event in Asia, Changchun's Games were praised as the most successful and amazing winter-sport gathering in the OCA's history.[9] Just as holding the 1996 Games motivated Harbin to bid for the 2010 Winter Olympics, so hosting the 2007 Games stimulated Changchun to bid for the 2018 Winter Olympics.[10]

The 2010 Guangzhou AG, in which 9704 athletes from 45 OCA member countries participated, was the biggest sports gathering in Asia so far, and the biggest multi-sport event held in China after the 2008 Beijing Olympics.[11] The following three aspects implied that the 16-day event was being used as another instrument to project China's sports superpower image and boost nationalist and patriotic sentiment among the Chinese. First, since the preparation of the Games, which was under the guidance of the Scientific Development Concept, accelerated Guangzhou's pace of economic growth and social development, it was celebrated as a landmark of the leadership of Hu Jintao and his fellow Party leaders.[12] Second, while the opening ceremony of Guangzhou amazed the OCA officials and international observers, the *People's Daily* editorial pointed out that the games, along with the 2008 Beijing Olympics and the 2010 Shanghai World Expo, had showcased the Chinese style in presenting international mega events.[13] Third, while the Chinese delegation won more medals in Guangzhou than those in any prior AG, China's ambition to become a strong power in sport (*tiyu qiangguo*) was displayed.[14]

This article, however, does not further examine the projection of China's geopolitical hegemony through the actual organisation and execution of the AG and AWG. Rather it aims to study the strategies behind China's bids for the host rights of those games and to unveil the political intentions underpinning those bids. Before analysing the competitions of Beijing, Harbin, Changchun and Guangzhou, respectively, with the other Asian cities, a brief review regarding China's bids for IMSEs since the 1980s will be conducted in the next section.

China's Bids for IMSEs

An international bid refers to a competition among two or more national candidates vying for the right to host a particular international event. For instance, the participants in the 2012 Summer Olympics bid included Havana (Cuba), Istanbul (Turkey), Leipzig (Germany), London (UK), Madrid (Spain), Moscow (Russia), New York City (USA), Paris (France) and Rio de Janeiro (Brazil). It is important to note that since the right to host each IMSE is extremely unlikely to be granted to two or more candidates, the results of international bids are basically zero-sum. A bidder's win hence necessarily means the failure of its competitor/s.

Chinese cities have bid totally for 16 IMSEs since the 1980s (see Table 1). Those events are gatherings in which almost all the countries in the world are permitted to participate, including the Summer and Winter Olympics; the Summer and Winter Youth Olympics; the Summer and Winter Universiade; the World Gymnasiade and the Special Olympics World Summer Games, and celebrations in which states within a specified region may take part, like the AG, the AWG and the East AG. All the bids were overseen by six international sports organisations, including five by the IOC, four by the International University Sports Federation (FISU), four by the OCA, one by the East Asian Games Association (EAGA), one by the International School Sport Federation (ISF) and one by the Special Olympics organisation.

Table 1.   China's bids for IMSEs 1980–2012.

Year of application	Candidate city	Bidding event	International organisation overseen
1984	Beijing	1990 Summer AG	OCA
1988	Shanghai	1993 Summer Universiade[a]	FISU
1991	Beijing	2000 Summer Olympics[a]	IOC
1993	Harbin	1996 Winter AG	OCA
1994	Shanghai	1998 World Gymnasiade	ISF
1998	Beijing	2001 Summer Universiade	FISU
1999	Beijing	2008 Summer Olympics	IOC
2001	Changchun	2007 Winter AG	OCA
2002	Shanghai	2007 Special Olympics World Summer Games	Special Olympics
2002	Harbin	2010 Winter Olympic Games[a]	IOC
2004	Guangzhou	2010 Summer AG	OCA
2004	Harbin	2009 Winter Universiade	FISU
2005	Shenzhen	2011 Summer Universiade	FISU
2007	Tianjin	2013 East AG	EAGA
2008	Harbin	2012 Winter Youth Olympic Games[a]	IOC
2009	Nanjing	2014 Youth Olympic Games	IOC

Source: Author's database.
[a] Refers to China's failed bid.

Of the 16 international bids, China won 12 of them. The win-out rate reached 75%. However, through examining the success rate of the bids overseen by the FISU and the IOC, they were 75% and 40%, respectively. In other words, the former equals the win-out rate of the total bids, whereas the latter was lower than the win-out rate of the total bids. China has not yet encountered failure in the bids overseen by the other international sporting organisations, including the OCA, the EAGA, the ISF and the Special Olympics. Chinese cities totally participated in four OCA bids, whereas they joined one bid only in the EAGA, the ISF and the Special Olympics, respectively. Therefore, China's record in the OCA bids was better than that in the bids overseen by all the other international organisations.

Beijing's Bid for the 1990 AG

Beijing, the capital city of China, was first suggested as a site for staging the 1990 AG by the Chinese Olympic Committee (COC) in 1983. Its application letter was submitted to the OCA in March 1984. In the meantime, Japan's Hiroshima also formally declared its intent to hold the games. A committee was then formed by the OCA, aiming to evaluate which city would be better to be the host. During its 3-day inspection trip in Beijing, the members, including the then OCA President, visited the construction sites of the city's sports facilities that were arranged to celebrate the games and met with the officials from both the national and local levels. In order to increase its odds, Beijing also lobbied the OCA members in 12 countries for support.[15] It eventually obtained the right to host the event in the OCA Assembly on 28 September 1984. The OCA also decided on Hiroshima to stage the 1994 AG on the same occasion.[16] The Chinese later went high profile to publicise Beijing's victory. It, together with the excellent performance of the Chinese athletes in international sports events, was interpreted as the evidence that China's status of an Asian strong power in sport had been confirmed.[17]

Two strategies were the key to persuading the OCA to choose Beijing rather than Hiroshima. First, the bid had obtained the support of the Chinese government. According to the OCA Constitution and Rules, a city rather than the nation is the unit to bid for and later hold the AG or the AWG. Therefore, the national government of a candidate city is not a required unit to be involved in any bid. Nonetheless, the Chinese central government was keen to give support when Beijing was vying with Hiroshima for the right to host the 1990 AG. A letter signed off by the then Chinese Foreign Minister Wu Xueqian was attached to Beijing's application documents, in which the Chinese government's decision to fully support the city to hold the games was highlighted.[18] Later, the then China General Sports Association (CGSA) President Li Menghua promised that Beijing will devote its best efforts to celebrate the event on behalf of the Chinese government in a dinner with the members of the OCA Evaluation Committee.[19] The then Chinese President Li Xiannian also participated in the bid. He, on behalf of the Chinese government and people, appealed to the OCA President and his fellows to support Beijing before the end of the inspection.[20] The appearance of the Chinese officials above implied that the bid was not simply treated as a normal competition with a Japanese candidate. It can be regarded as a diplomatic battle by the Chinese government in which the host right was treated as a part of China's national interest.

Second, holding the 1990 AG was highlighted as a wish of all the Chinese people. This message was respectively expressed by the then Beijing Mayor Chen Xitong and the COC Deputy President Lu Jindong in their meetings with the OCA President.[21] Although the one billion Chinese did not act to support Beijing during the bid, they made a tremendous financial contribution to the games after the hosting rights were given. According to the data disclosed by the *People's Daily*, the Chinese totally donated 600 million yuan (approximately US$ 1.26 hundred millions) to Beijing.[22]

Harbin's Bid for the 1996 AWG

The decision to hold the 1996 AWG in Harbin was initiated by the Heilongjiang provincial government in September 1992.[23] It was approved by the CGSA three months later.[24] When Harbin's application was submitted to the OCA, Seoul of South Korea also joined to bid for the right to host the games. The OCA Evaluation Committee, which was led by the Yasutaka Matsudaira, then President of the Japan Volleyball Association and then Executive President of the International Volleyball Federation, inspected the Chinese candidate in March 1993. Harbin's sports facilities impressed the inspectors.[25] The host right of the 1996 AWG eventually passed to the city on 2 December 1993.

Compared with Beijing's bid for the 1990 AG, Harbin's bid was a low-profile one. It was not stressed as a wish of all the Chinese people, nor did any of the senior national officials, including the then Chinese President Jiang Zemin, the then Foreign Minister Qian Qichen and the then CGSA President Wu Shaozu, take part. The distinctly different treatments of the two projects can be explained by two reasons. First, the status of Beijing and Harbin in China is different. While the former is the capital city of China, the latter is only the capital city of Heilongjiang Province. Second, when Harbin started processing its bidding tasks, Beijing was in the last stages of vying to host the 2000 Olympics. In order to concentrate all China's resources on the Olympic bid, all Harbin's tasks were required by the CGSA to be completed through a low-profile approach.[26]

Although Harbin's experience in the bid for the 1996 AWG was different from that of Beijing in the 1990 AG, it still eliminated its competitor. The victory was determined by the following three factors. First, the city gained strong support from the Heilongjiang Province. In Harbin's application letter, the provincial government and all the Heilongjiang people were stressed as the supporters of the bid.[27] The government also promised to sponsor 30 million yuan (approximately US$ 5.21 million), which was equivalent to one-third of the total budget of celebrating the games, for the city if the host rights were obtained.[28] Heilongjiang Governor Shao Qihui and his colleagues frequently worked alongside the Harbin and COC officials in the following tasks, including entertaining the OCA inspectors and giving advice on the bid publication and the city renovation.[29] Hosting the AWG in Harbin was therefore viewed as a project not resting solely on the city alone. The support of the provincial government and 45 million Heilongjiang people was able to further strengthen the confidence of the OCA regarding the Chinese candidate's competence to celebrate the games in 1996.

Second, the residents of Harbin were organised to participate in the bid. In order to demonstrate that the holding of the 1996 AWG had gained a high popularity in the city, one million local people were organised by the Harbin government to sign their names shortly after the application had been submitted.[30] One thousand and five-hundred residents were chosen to perform a radio calisthenics display when the city was being evaluated.[31] It should be noted that the OCA Constitution and Rule does not stipulate the people of a candidate city, who are needed to take part in a bid.

Third, the strong social network of the Chinese officials in the Asian and international sports community facilitated Harbin to becoming the winner. Before the OCA members decided on the host city, Harbin had successfully gained the support of the OCA President.[32] The then IOC President Juan Samaranch even signed off his name to wish the city good luck. When the OCA Assembly prepared to vote the host city, the Pakistan Olympic Association President Syed Wajid Ali gave a speech in which he suggested Harbin to hold the 1996 AWG and Seoul to host the 1999 AWG. His suggestion obtained the consent of all the attendants, including the President of the South Korean Olympic Committee Kim Un-yong and the members of the South Korean bid delegation.[33] The Chinese candidate thus won the bid without undergoing a vote.

Shortly after Harbin obtained the host rights, the nationalist and patriotic sentiments among the Chinese were aroused. The first piece of evidence was from a celebration meeting held by the Heilongjiang and Harbin governments, in which the political significance of the success was confirmed. It was depicted as a means not only to facilitate the rise of China's status and influence in Asia, but also to accelerate the pace of building up Deng Xiaoping's 'Socialism with Chinese Characteristics' in the province.[34] The second piece of evidence was from Governor Shao Qihui's congratulatory remarks, in which all the Heilongjiang residents were called on to support the preparation of the 1996 AWG as it was deemed to bring honour to the country and the nation.[35]

Changchun's Bid for the 2007 AWG

Changchun, the capital city of Jilin Province, was suggested to host the 2007 AWG by the CGSA after that city had successfully staged the 9th National Winter Games of China in January 2001. Its application and candidature file were, respectively, submitted to the OCA in January and February 2002.[36] Since the Chinese candidate was not the only Asian city formally expressing the intent to host the games, it, together with its competitors, including Almaty (Kazakhstan), Beirut (Lebanon) and Tehran (Iran), needed to be evaluated.[37] Changchun's odds increased after being inspected by the OCA Evaluation Committee. It was partly because of the high praise given by Samih Moudallal, the OCA Deputy President and the chairperson of the Evaluation Committee, regarding the city's sports facilities, and partly due to the withdrawals of Almaty and Tehran.[38] The Chinese candidate eventually was chosen to host the games on 2 October 2002.[39]

Changchun's strategy in the bid for the 2007 AWG was similar to that of Harbin in its bid for the 1996 AWG. First, the bid gained the support of the Jilin provincial government. For instance, Vice Governor Quan Zhezhu, on behalf of Governor Hong Hu and the entire province, introduced Changchun's strengths to hold the event when meeting with the OCA inspectors.[40] He and his colleagues also discussed with the Changchun officials regarding the arrangements for lobbying the OCA members. Second, Changchun people were arranged to take part in the bid. For example, 10,000 local residents and students signed off their names to support the holding of the games when the city was being inspected by the OCA officials.[41] Third, the COC President Yuan Weimin and his colleagues frequently appealed to the OCA members in China and abroad to support the city, including their meetings with the OCA President and the President of the Korean Olympic Committee one day before the vote.[42]

Once the OCA passed the host right to Changchun, the government praised it as a landmark of China's rise, and as a gift to celebrate the opening of the 16th CCP National Congress.[43] In addition, the Chinese official media stressed that the success was another big victory for China's sport diplomacy after Beijing obtained the right to host the 2008 Summer Olympics.[44] The wordings here implied that the Chinese government regarded the bids for all the IMSEs during the 2000s not only as a work to benefit local development, but also as a matter to promote the national interest.

Guangzhou's Bid for the 2010 AG

Guangzhou, the capital city of Guangdong Province in the south of China, raised its intent to host the 2010 AG in 2002 shortly after completing the celebration of the Ninth National Games of China.[45] The intention was then endorsed by the Guangdong government, the CGSA and the State Council in turn.[46] When its bidding documents were submitted to the OCA in March 2004, Amman (Jordan), Kuala Lumpur (Malaysia) and Seoul (South Korea) were also qualified to vie for the hosting right.[47] Guangzhou was informed of the withdrawals of all of its competitors while being inspected by the OCA Deputy President Celso Dayrit and his colleagues in April 2003.[48] Four months later, the Chinese bidder obtained the right to hold the games without undergoing a vote.[49]

Guangzhou adopted all the strategies carried out in China's previous bids for the AG and the AWG, except that the holding of the 2010 AG was not claimed as a wish of all the Chinese people.[50] First, a letter that was signed off by the Chinese Premier Wen Jiabao was attached to Guangzhou's application documents. It referred to Guangzhou's holding of the games having gained the support of the Chinese government.[51] Second, the Guangdong provincial government gave strong support when the bid was taking place, as shown by the fact that Guangdong Governor Huang Huahua participated to entertain the members of the IOC Evaluation Committee, and led the Guangzhou delegation to attend the OCA Assembly in which the host right was given,[52] while Vice Guangdong Governor Xu Deli and his colleagues frequently worked alongside the Guangzhou and COC officials to publicise the city and lobby the OCA members in China and aboard.[53] Third, the Guangzhou residents were arranged to take part in the bid. For instance, in order to motivate the incentive of the public regarding the holding of the games, local residents were invited to design the logo and theme of Guangzhou's bid.[54] Fourth, around 40 OCA members were lobbied in some 20 countries. Guangzhou's intention to host the games obtained most of their support, including that of the OCA President.[55]

In addition to adopting the strategies in China's previous AG and AWG bids, Guangzhou also played the money card to draw the attention of the OCA. When it became clear that the withdrawals of its competitors were due to their lack of funding, Guangzhou Mayor Zhang Guangning promised to spend 220 billion yuan (US$ 26.6 billion) to renovate the city from 2004 to 2010.[56] The amount was similar with Beijing's budget to prepare the Summer Olympics from 2001 to 2008.[57] This tactic successfully strengthened the confidence of the OCA regarding Guangzhou's promise to present the games as the most outstanding sports event in the history of Asia.[58]

The bid once again became an official instrument to propagandise China's rise. For example, Guangzhou Party Secretary Lin Shusen stressed that the high status and good reputation that the Chinese government enjoyed in the international society was the reason for the success.[59] In addition, the ambition of the officials to project China's international profile was motivated when the hosting rights were obtained. For instance, in the State Councillor Chen Zhili's congratulatory telegram, the celebration of the AG was depicted as a channel by which China would be able to further embrace the world.[60] Mayor Zhang Guangning also promised to transform Guangzhou into the most influential metropolis in Southeast Asia in 2010.[61]

Conclusion

Through reviewing the competitions of Beijing, Harbin, Changchun and Guangzhou with the other Asian cities, the extent and nature of China's ambition to be the best place to hold the AG and AWG can be displayed by the following four aspects. First, despite the condition that holding any OCA multi-sport event is required to be the duty of a city, all the Chinese candidates gained the strong support from the national and/or provincial governments. It might well have served to relieve any worries that the OCA had regarding the possibility of a lack of funding to complete the celebrations of those games in China. Second, when tens of thousands of the residents and students were arranged to participate in each bid, it would make the OCA confident regarding the government's capability of organising the Chinese to give support during the preparation and presentation of those events. Third, the Chinese candidates were keen and were certainly active to lobby the members of the OCA and its President. Fourth, the Chinese candidates demonstrated their willingness to spend money for hosting the games. For example, Guangzhou's budget to prepare the 2010 AG was found to be similar to that of Beijing's to prepare the much larger 2008 Olympic Games. The OCA eventually had no reason to pass the host right to its competitors when witnessing the superiority of China. Therefore, apart from the dominance of the Chinese athletes in the medal tables of the AG since the 1990s and the outstanding performances of the Chinese cities in the celebrations of the AG and AWG, the bids themselves have become another means to build up China's hegemonic status in the Asian sports community.

In addition, it can be observed that all the successes of the Chinese candidate cities were asserted to be related to (1) the socialist reform policies conducted by the CCP; (2) the maturity of China in dealing with diplomatic affairs in sport and, most importantly, (3) the rise of China's status in the international society, according to the congratulatory speeches of the officials and the reports of the official media. All the bids hence were confirmed as an instrument of the central government to arouse the patriotic and nationalist sentiments among the Chinese.

If China's bids for any future AG and AWG were to be continually used as a means to build up and express its hegemonic status in Asia and, at the same time, arouse the Chinese patriotic and nationalist sentiments at home, the following scenarios are likely to occur and each of them could affect the harmony of the Asian Pacific region. First, would China's consistent and regular victories gain the adoration of other Asians or boost their jealousy, and would the jealousy deepen the current regional dissatisfaction and hostility towards China?[62] Second, would rising patriotic and nationalist sentiments stimulate the escalation of Chinese chauvinism, and if so, would the Chinese be scornful of, and even belligerent towards, other Asian states? In order to prevent the occurrence of any of the possible scenarios above, the Chinese government is advised to try to treat future Asian sporting bids as simply an international competition rather than a diplomatic battle and to report their success through neutral narration rather than by political propaganda.

Notes on Contributor

Marcus P. Chu teaches Chinese politics and international relations in the Department of Political Science, Lingnan University, Hong Kong. He obtained his PhD from the University of Auckland in May 2012. His thesis reviews the central and local inter-relations in China's bids for international events since the 1980s. He currently works on a project regarding the political preoccupations of East Asian countries at the London 2012 Olympics with Professor J.A. Mangan.

Notes

1. Mangan, "Preface: Geopolitical Games," 751–7; Mangan, "Prologue: Guarantees of Global Goodwill, 1869–83" and Mangan, "Prologue: 'Middle Kingdom' Resurgent," 2333–58.

2. "Zhuhe Di 11 Jie Yayunhui Kaimu (Celebrate the Opening of the 11th AG)" (*People's Daily* (*PD*), September 22, 1990, 1) and "Zhuhe Di 11 Jie Yayunhui Bimu (Celebrate the Closing of 11th AG)" (*PD*, October 8, 1990, 1).

3. "Beijing 2000 Nian Aoyunhui Shenbanwei Chengli (Beijing 2000 Olympics Bid Committee Establish)" (*Beijing Daily* (*BJD*), April 12, 1991, 1) and "Beijing 2008 Nian Aoshenwei Chengli (Beijing 2008 Olympics Bid Committee Establish)" (*BJD*, September 7, 1999, 1 and 2).

4. "Li Tieying Zai Jiejian Zhongguo Huojiang Yundongyuan Shi Gaodu Pingjia Yadonghui (Li Tieying Praises AWG When Meeting With Chinese Medal-Winning Athletes)" (*Harbin Daily* (*HBD*), February 12, 1996, 1) and "Dali Fayang Dongya Jingshen (Strongly Promote the Spirit of Holding AWG)" (*Heilongjiang Daily* (*HLJD*), February 12, 1996, 1 and 2).

5. "Harbin Shenban 2010 Nian Dongaohui (Harbin Bid for 2010 Winter Olympics)" (*HBD*, January 31, 2002, 1).

6. "Harbin Weineng Ruwei (Harbin Failed)" (*China Sports Daily* (*CSD*), August 29, 2002, 1).

7. "Youyuan Xiangqian Cujin Goujian Hexie Yazhou (Step Forward for the Construction of a Harmonious Asia)" (*CSD*, January 28, 2007, 1).

8. The Scientific Development Concept is the official guiding socio-economic ideology of the CCP, since Hu Jintao became the Party chief in 2002. "Shu Bingxue Haoqing Cu Jilin Zhenxing (AWG Will Accelerate Jilin's Development)" (*Jilin Daily* (*JLD*), January 29, 2007, 1).

9. "Disanjie Yadonghui Shengli Bimu (The Third AWG Successfully Close)" (*HBD*, February 12, 1996, 1) and "Diliujie Yadonghui Zai Changchun Bimu (The Sixth AWG Close in Changchun)" (*Changchun Daily* (*CCD*), February 5, 2007, 1).

10. Changchun, however, gave up the right to bid for the Winter Olympics on behalf of China. For details, see "Harbin Changchun Fangqi Shenban 2018 Nian Dongaohui (Both Harbin and Changchun Give Up to Bid for 2018 Winter Olympics)" (*Guangzhou Daily* (*GZD*), October 15, 2009, A15).

11. "Guangzhou Yayun Kepimei Beijing Aoyun (Guangzhou AG is Close With Beijing Olympics)" (*Nanfang Daily* (*NFD*), November 28, 2010, A02).

12. "Yayunhui Yacanyunhui Wei Guangzhou Tisu Shinian (AG Accelerate Guangzhou's Development Pace)" (*GZD*, November 13, 2010, 1 and 2).

13. "Yayun Kaimushi Rang Guangzhou Yiye Chengming (Opening Ceremony Lets Guangzhou be Famous)" (*GZD*, November 14, 2010, 1 and 3) and "Jiqing Shenhui Shenteng Xiwang (AG Raises Hope)" (*PD*, November 28, 2010, 1).

14. "Zuo Tiyu Shizhe Zhan Zhongguo Fengcai (Be Sports Ambassadors and Showcase China's Charm)" (*CSD*, November 12, 2010, 1).

15. Fan, "Communist China and the Asian Games," 83.

16. "Di Shiyijie Yayunhui Zangzai Beijing Juxing (The 11th AG Will be Held in Beijing)" (*BJD*, September 29, 1984, 1).

17. "Weicujin Yazhou Tiyu Yundong Fazhan Zuogongxian (Contribute Asia's Sports Development)" (*PD*, September, 29, 1984, 1).

18. "Woguo Aoweihui Zhengshi Zhihan Yaao Lishihui Zhuxi (COC Submit a Letter to OCA President)" (*BJD*, March 12, 1984, 1).

19. "Yazhou Aolihui Zhuxi Fahede Yixing Daojing Kaocha (OCA President Fahed and his Fellows Will Inspect Beijing)" (*Sports Daily* (*SD*), June 15, 1984, 1).

20. "Li Xiannian Huijian Yazhou Aolihui Zhuxi Fahede (Li Xiannian Meets With OCA President Fahad)" (*SD*, June 18, 1984, 1).

21. "Chen Xitong Huijian Bing Yanqing Fahede Yixing (Chen Meets With Fahed and his Fellows)" (*BJD*, June 16, 1984, 1) and "Fahede Zhuxi Yu Woaoweihui Lingdaoren Huitan (President Fahed Meets With COC Seniors)" (*SD*, June 16, 1994, 1).

22. "Yayunhui jizi Qianyue Yu Liuyiyuan (Around 600 Million Yuan are Raised for AG)" (*PD*, September 11, 1990, 1).

23. "Lishi Fuyu De Qiji (A Historic Chance)" (*HBD*, December 8, 1993, 1).

24. "Guojia Tongyi Woshi Shenban Disanjie Dongji Yayunhui (CGSA Approves Harbin to Bid for AWG)" (*HBD*, December 11, 1993, 1).

25. "Nimen Younengli Juban Dongyahui (Harbin is Capable of Holding AWG)" (*CSD*, March 31, 1993, 1).

26. "Dongyuan Shehui Liliang Zhengqu Shenban Chenggong (Mobilize the Society and Get the Bid Done)" (*HBD*, October 19, 1993, 1).

THE ASIAN GAMES: MODERN METAPHOR FOR 'THE MIDDLE KINGDOM' REBORN

27. "Harbin Shi Juban Disanjie Dongji Yayunhui De Shenqingxin (Harbin's Application Letter for AWG)" (*HBD*, December 3, 1993, 2).
28. "Shao Qihui Juxing Jizhe Zhaodaihui (Shao Holds a Press Conference)" (*HLJD*, December 23, 1992, 1).
29. "Yi Shenban Yayunhui Tuidong Quansheng Gongzuo (To Push Forward All Provincial Tasks by Bid)" (*HLJD*, January 20, 1993, 1) and "Shao Qihui Shenzhang Huijia Bing Yanqing Kaochatuan (Shao Meets With OCA Inspectors)" (*HLJD*, March 31, 1993, 1).
30. "Shenban Dongyayunhui Qianming Huodong Quanmian Zhankai (A Signature Campaign for Supporting AWG Bid Takes Place)" (*HBD*, January 13, 1993, 1).
31. "Woshi Jiangzuzhi Daxing Quanzhong Tiyu Huodong (Harbin Will Organise Sports Activities for the Mass)" (*HBD*, March 25, 1993, 1).
32. "Fahede Qinwang Zhichi Harbin Shenban Dongyahui (Fahed Supports Harbin to Hold AWG)" (*HBD*, December 1, 1993, 1).
33. "Yazhou Xuanzele Harbin (Asia Choose Harbin)" (*CSD*, December 18, 1993, 2).
34. "Shengshi Zhaokai Qingzhu Harbin Shenban Disanjie Dongyahui Chenggong Zuotanhui (Province and City Together Hold a Meeting to Celebrate Harbin's Success)" (*HBD*, December 4, 1993, 1).
35. "Ganxie He Xiwang (Thanks and Hopes)" (*HLJD*, December 3, 1993, 1).
36. "Woshi De Yayuinhui Shenban Zhilu (Changchun's Steps in Bid)" (*CCD*, February 20, 2002, 7).
37. "Changchun Zhengshi Shenban 2007 Nian Diliujie Yazhou Dongji Yundonghui (Changchun Start 2007 AWG Bid)" (*JLD*, February 7, 2002, B4).
38. "Mudalaer Yanzhong De Changchun (Changchun in Moudallal's Eyes)" (*CCD*, March 12, 2002, 1).
39. "Changchun Shenban 2007 Yadonghui Chenggong (Changchun Win 2007 AWG Bid)" (*CSD*, October 4, 2002, 1).
40. "Quan Zhenzhu Huijian Mudalaer Yixing (Quan Zhezhu Meets With Moudallal and his Colleageus)" (*JLD*, March 12, 2002, A2).
41. "Wanren Qianming Zhichi Shenban (Ten Thousand People Sign to Support Bid)" (*CCD*, March 10, 2002, 1).
42. "Hanguo Zhichi Changchun Shenban 2007 Nian Diliujie Yayunhui (South Korea Support Changchun AWG Bid)" (*CSD*, October 2, 2002, 3) and "Yayunhui 1800 Tian (AWG's 1800 Days)" (*East Asia Economy and Trade News*, January 26, 2007, 6).
43. "Guojia Youguan Bumen Shengzhengfu Dianhe Woshi Huo Yadonghui Jubanquan (CGSA and Jilin Government Send Telegrams to Celebrate Changchun's Success)" (*CCD*, October 6, 2002, 1).
44. "Woshi Huode 2007 Nian Yadonghui Jubanquan (Changchun Obtain 2007 AWG Host Right)" (*CCD*, October 6, 2002, 1).
45. "Guangzhou: Shiqinian Menxiang Chengzhen (After Seventeen Years Guangzhou's Dream Come True)" (*PD*, July 2, 2004, 12).
46. "Guangzhou Shenya Chu Benbao Baodao Zao (Guangzhou Daily is the First Media to Report AG Bid)" (*GZD*, July 2, 2004, A12).
47. "Guangzhou Jinri Dijiao Shenya Baogao (Guangzhou Will Submit Candidature File Today)" (*GZD*, March 31, 2004, A1).
48. "Guangzhou Chengweiyi Shenban Chengshi (Guangzhou Become Only City in Bid)" (*NFD*, April 15, 2004, A01).
49. "Yayun Jubanquan Zhangshengzhong Jueding (AG Host Right is Decided in Applause)" (*GZD*, July 2, 2004, A3).
50. It was only claimed as a wish of all the Guangdong people. For details, see "Dongya Diqu Aoweihui Luntan Zai Beijing Juxing (East Asian Olympic Association Forum Take Place in Beijing)" (*NFD*, March 26, 2004, A02).
51. "Chengban Yayunhui Guangzhou Kao Shili (Guangzhou is Competent to Hold AG)" (*GZD*, July 2, 2004, A11).
52. "Huacheng Shengqing Yingjie Yayun Kaoguan (Guangzhou Greet OCA Inspectors)" (*GZD*, April 15, 2004, A1 and A5) and "Guangzhou Shenya Daibiaotuan Fu Duoha (Guangzhou Bid Delegation Flight to Doha)" (*NFD*, June 28, 2004, A01).
53. For details, see my essay "Strict Compliance!: Chinese Conformity and the Guangzhou Bid for the Asian Games' in this volume."

THE ASIAN GAMES: MODERN METAPHOR FOR 'THE MIDDLE KINGDOM' REBORN

54. "Guangzhou Shenya: Qingnin Sheji Biaozhi Kouhao (You are Invited to Design Guangzhou's Bidding Logo and Theme)" (*GZD*, January 24, 2004, A1).
55. "Yaao Zhuxi Zhichi Guangzhou Shenya (OCA President Supports Guangzhou's Bid)" (*GZD*, February 17, 2004, A1).
56. "Guangzhou 2200 Yi Yingyayun Cuchengjian (Guangzhou Will Spend 220 Billion Yuan for AG and Urban Infrastructure)" (*GZD*, June 29, 2004, A1 and A5).
57. Beijing's budget was about 235 billion yuan (US\$ 28.4 billions). See: "Liu Qi Zai Beijing Shenban 2008 Nian Aoyunhui Chenggong Baogaoshang De Jianghua (Liu Qi's Speech Delivered to Celebrate Beijing's Success in 2008 Olympics Bid)" (*CSD*, July 24, 2001, 4).
58. The promise was firstly given by Deputy Guangdong Governor Xu Deli when Guangzhou was being inspected by the OCA officials. See "Guangzhou Wanquan Youshili Juban Yayunhui (Guangzhou is Capable of Holding AG)" (*NFD*, April 16, 2004, A01).
59. "Yayun Jianghui Huanlai Xiandaihua Dadushi (AG Will Make Guangzhou as a Modern Metropolis)" (*GZD*, July 2, 2004, A1).
60. "Chen Zhili Zhidian Zhuhe (Chen Zhili Sends a Congratulatory Telegram)" (*CSD*, July 2, 2004, 1).
61. "Yuan Weimin Huang Huahua Zhang Guangning Changtan Guangzhou Shenya Chenggong (Yuan Weimin, Huang Huahua and Zhang Guangning Talk About Guangzhou's Success)" (*NFD*, July 2, 2004, A02).
62. The dissatisfactory and hostility were caused by China's non-transparent military expansions and its territorial disputes with the neighbours.

References

Fan, Hong. "Communist China and the Asian Games, 1951–1990: The Thirty-Nine Year Struggle to Victory." *Sport in Society* 8, no. 3 (2005): 479–492.

Mangan, J. A. "Preface: Geopolitical Games – Beijing 2008." *The International Journal of the History of Sport* 25, no. 7 (2008): 751–757.

Mangan, J. A. "Prologue: Guarantees of Global Goodwill: Post-Olympic Legacies – Too Many Limping White Elephants." *The International Journal of the History of Sport* 25, no. 14 (2008): 1869–1883.

Mangan, J. A. "Prologue: 'Middle Kingdom' Resurgent! Sports Dominance as Soft Power Politics on the Pacific Rim – Reflections on Rim Realpolitik." *The International Journal of the History of Sport* 27, no. 14-15 (2010): 2333–2358.

Strict Compliance!: Chinese Careful Conformity and the Guangzhou Bid for the Asian Games

Marcus P. Chu

Department of Political Science, Lingnan University, Hong Kong, China

> This article aimed to examine whether the division of labour between the Chinese central and local officials, who came from the China General Sports Administration; the Chinese National Olympic Committee; and the Guangdong and Guangzhou governments, strictly complied with the stipulations of the Olympic Council of Asia in completing Guangzhou's bid for the 2010 Asian Games. The findings confirm Guangzhou as a rule-abiding bidder, and imply China's eagerness to be accepted by the international community and to project itself as a superpower in accordance with its wider political, economic and cultural ambition.

Introduction

China has been on a quest for superpower status on the international stage since the beginning of this century by the following three aspects: (1) Politically, the Chinese government has been keen to ratify international treaties, join international organisations, initiate multilateral cooperation forums, establish regional security and trade mechanisms, and participate in United Nations peace-keeping missions.[1] (2) Economically, the high economic growth rate has ensured that the country no longer can be considered as a second class middle power.[2] Indeed, the massive growth in China's global trade and investment has demonstrated its hunger to gain control on strategic technologies and assets in the West, as well as natural resources from Asia, Africa and Latin America. It has already overtaken Japan and has also been predicted to be the only state able to replace the USA and dominate the world marketplace.[3] (3) Culturally, the Chinese government has become smarter and more mature in exercising soft power worldwide. The ways include setting up Confucius Institutes, giving financial aid to developing countries, sending young talents, like basketball player Yao Ming, abroad, and holding international multi-sport events (IMSEs).[4]

Since Beijing staged the 11th Asian Games (AG) in August 1990, China has in total held 17 IMSEs (see Table 1). All of them are found to showcase China's might and greatness, including the 2010 Guangzhou AG, the biggest Asian regional sports gathering so far. After watching its opening ceremony and visiting its stadiums, Guangzhou's performance in celebrating the AG was claimed to be sufficiently qualified to even meet the requirements of hosting the Summer Olympics.[5] When Chinese athletes dominated the

Table 1.   IMSEs held in China 1990–2012.

Year of holding	Event	Host city
1990	Asian Games	Beijing
1993	East Asian Games	Shanghai
1994	Far East and South Pacific Games for the Disabled	Beijing
1996	Asian Winter Games	Harbin
1996	Special Olympics Asia Pacific Region Games	Shanghai
1998	World Gymnasiade	Shanghai
2001	Summer Universiade	Beijing
2007	Asian Winter Games	Changchun
2007	Special Olympics World Summer Games	Shanghai
2008	Summer Olympic Games	Beijing
2008	Summer Para Games	Beijing
2008	World Mind Sports Games	Beijing
2009	Winter Universiade	Harbin
2010	Asian Games	Guangzhou
2010	Asian Para Games	Guangzhou
2011	Summer Universiade	Shenzhen
2012	Asian Beach Games	Haiyang

Source: Author's database.

medal tables of the Games, China was also marked out to have become a strong power in sport (*tiyu qiangguo*).[6]

This article does not aim to further study how China projected its soft power through the 2010 AG, but rather the intention is to examine whether the division of labour between the Chinese central and local officials strictly complied with the stipulations of the Olympic Council of Asia (OCA) in completing Guangzhou's bid for the right to host the Games. If the Chinese candidate is confirmed as a rule-abiding bidder, the findings may imply China's eagerness to be accepted by, and to display its might and greatness in, the international community. Before reviewing Guangzhou's bid tasks, the reason why strict compliance matters in international bids will be explained in the next section.

Strict Compliance in International Bids

An international bid refers to a zero-sum competition among two or more national candidates vying for the right to host a particular IMSE. All bids have two main characteristics. First, each of them is overseen by the executive body of a particular international organisation. For example, according to the OCA Constitution and Rules, the OCA Executive Board is empowered to determine the bidding procedure, appoint an Evaluation Committee to inspect the bid cities, study the Evaluation Report and shortlist candidates.[7]

Second, the process of bidding for an IMSE is highly regulated. For example, the OCA stipulated that each candidate in an AG bid must complete the following four tasks, including (1) submitting its Letter of Intent (application letter), (2) submitting its Candidature File, (3) entertaining the OCA Evaluation Committee and (4) giving a presentation before the final vote. Apart from the above, each candidate is also allowed to lobby the OCA members and publicise itself at home and abroad after its application is submitted. In addition, what parties need to do to execute an AG bid is stated. They include support from the candidate city and the country's National Olympic Committee (NOC).

Furthermore, a division of labour between the two parties in a bid is also required. The city, as the host unit, needs to play the leading role in the entire bid operation.[8] The NOC must take charge of two duties: (1) giving supervision to the city candidate[9] and (2) putting forward the candidate city to the OCA.[10] In other words, not only does the NOC need to submit the candidate city's Letter of Intent to the OCA, but it assists the local government in completing the bid tasks as well. Hence, each Summer or Winter AG bid is a local-led and central-coordinated project.

It is noted that the executive body of international organisation is empowered to give warnings and even terminate candidacy if any candidate city fails to conform to the bidding stipulations. For instance, the OCA Constitution and Rules Article 45 Item 11 states that

> the OCA Executive Board has the power to disqualify the bidding city, after due warning, if it considers that the, OCA directives and the fundamental principles as enshrined in the OCA Constitution, are not being adhere to in its totality.[11]

Therefore, to win a host right, not only does any candidate need to demonstrate its outstanding capability of staging the IMSE, but it must strictly comply with the stipulations of the international organisation as well.

Guangzhou's Bid for the 2010 AG

From submitting the letter of Intent in late December 2003 to obtaining the host right on July 1, 2004, Guangzhou's bid for the 2010 AG was executed by its Bid Committee in which both Chinese central and local officials participated.[12] The central officials were from the China's General Sports Association (CGSA), one of the 16 organisations directly under the State Council, and its affiliated unit the Chinese Olympic Committee (COC). The local officials were from the Guangdong provincial, and the Guangzhou municipal, governments. They generally worked together in the following six bid tasks, including (1) lobbying the OCA members and executives, (2) publicising Guangzhou in China and abroad, (3) furnishing the bidding documents, (4) entertaining the inspectors, (5) giving the presentation and (6) preparing Guangzhou to hold the AG. Their division of labour in the six tasks will be reviewed one after another in order to understand whether Guangzhou was a rule-abiding candidate in the bid.

Lobbying OCA Members and Executives

In order to gain the support of the OCA members, a number of lobbying activities were carried out on appropriate occasions in China. The local officials were found to play the leading role in all of them. For instance, Deputy Guangdong Governor Xu Deli and Guangzhou Deputy Mayor Li Zhuobin attended the wine party of the 2004 East Asian Olympic Association Forum at Beijing. The occasion enabled the local officials to lobby the representatives of the Olympic Committees of Chinese Taipei, Hong Kong, Japan, Macau, Mongolia and South Korea face-to-face. All the representatives decided to back Guangzhou after Xu discussed Guangzhou's performance in economic development and sports affairs and highlighted that staging the AG was the wish of all the Guangdong people.[13] Xu later met with Lao National Sports Minister and Olympic Committee President Dr Phouthone Seung-Akhom when the Lao sports delegation visited Guangzhou in May 2004. He was informed that the Lao Government and Olympic Committee would support Guangzhou in the 2010 AG bid.[14]

The local officials also led the lobbies abroad. Xu Deli and Li Zhuobin visited 10 countries, including Malaysia, Indonesia, India, the Philippines, Bangladesh, the Maldives, Kuwait, Saudi Arabia, Qatar and Pakistan before the inspection of the OCA Evaluation Committee. In addition to attending the opening ceremonies of the first Afro-Asian Games at Hyderabad where they met with all the NOC presidents of the Asian participants, they also appealed to the NOC representatives of Afghanistan, Bangladesh, Bhutan, India, Malaysia, the Maldives, Nepal, Pakistan and Sri Lanka to support Guangzhou when visiting the 9th South Asian Games at Islamabad.[15]

Apart from the NOC members of the OCA, the local officials also directly lobbied the OCA senior executives, including the OCA President Sheikh Ahmad Al-Fahad Al-Sabah and the OCA Deputy President Celso Dayrit. According to the OCA Constitution and Rules, the President is empowered to appoint the members of the Evaluation Committee for each AG bid, and is allowed to attend the OCA General Assembly meetings at which the host city for each AG is elected.[16] Despite the President not having the right to vote, he can 'establish the regulations for all elections and determined any matter concerning the General Assembly and votes that are not covered in the OCA Constitution and Rules'.[17] Xu Deli and Li Zhuobin met with the President once after the Letter of Intent had been submitted to the OCA. They discussed the progress of Guangzhou's bid and emphasised its ambition to hold the 2010 AG. Reportedly, Ahmad gave his personal support for Guangzhou's intent.[18]

Celso Dayrit was one of the key OCA executive officials in the 2010 AG bid. Although he did not have the right to vote, he was appointed to chair the Evaluation Committee and to draft the report about the hosting capacity of each candidate city. In order to impress Dayrit, Xu Deli and Li Zhuobin specially held a meeting with him in Manila before the inspection trip of the Evaluation Committee. They introduced Guangzhou's social and economic development and performance in organising large-scale multi-sport events. Dayrit was also invited to visit Guangzhou at his convenience.[19]

All the meetings with the OCA members and executive officials in China and abroad were arranged by the CGSA and COC. In order to promote Guangzhou's bid, senior officials of the CGSA and the COC, including Yuan Weimin, Yu Zaiqing, Gu Yaoming, Wei Jizhong and their colleagues, often gave the opening speeches at the meetings. It is important to point out that the central officials never lobbied directly for Guangzhou in their opening speeches, nor did they introduce Guangzhou's social and economic development alongside the local officials. In addition, the wine party held to lobby the East Asian OCA members during the 2004 East Asian Olympic Association Forum was co-sponsored by the COC and the Guangdong government.

Publicising Guangzhou in China and Abroad

The local officials were found to take charge of publicising Guangzhou's bid for the 2010 AG to foreign diplomats and politicians in China and abroad. For instance, Mayor Zhang Guangning particularly emphasised the six advantages of Guangzhou as a host of the event when he met with the then Australian Ambassador to China Alan Thomas in Guangzhou. These were: (1) Guangzhou is a historic city and the local people have a strong sense of international awareness; (2) Guangzhou is one of the Chinese cities with excellent economic and social development; (3) Guangzhou is competent to entertain foreign visitors; (4) Guangzhou has experience in holding large-scale multi-sport events; (5) the local people are enthusiastic about sport and (6) Guangzhou has impressive medical and health care.[20] Deputy Mayor Wang Xiaoling also introduced Guangzhou's bid progress to

Yemeni Prime Minister Abdul Qadir Bajamal when she visited Yemen. The Prime Minister promised on behalf of the Yemen government to support Guangzhou.[21]

The local officials also undertook to publicise Guangzhou to influential figures in the international sports community. For instance, Deputy Governor Xu Deli and Deputy Mayor Li Zhuobin, respectively, met with Sandy Holloway, the President of the Sydney 2000 Olympic Games Organising Committee. The Australian expressed his optimism about Guangzhou's bid and promised he and his Australian colleagues would give assistance if necessary.[22] They later together introduced the bid to Professor Khurshid Anwar Chowdhry, the Chairperson of the International Boxing Association, in Guangzhou. The Pakistani pledged to try his hardest to help Guangzhou's cause.[23]

In addition to promoting Guangzhou to international sporting and political celebrities, the local officials were also in charge of informing Guangzhou residents about the significance of holding the 2010 AG. For instance, at a press conference for the second Session of the 12th Guangzhou People's Congress, Mayor Zhang Guangning stressed that the 2010 AG would not only benefit the development of Guangzhou's tourism and other tertiary industry sectors, but also improve the standards of its urban management and construction.[24] Prior to that, the relationship between the holding of the 2010 AG and Guangzhou's pace of internationalisation was included in Li Zhuobin's speech delivered at the opening ceremony of the 5th Guangzhou Social Sciences Conference.[25]

The central officials assisted in publicising the Chinese candidate on a number of occasions. At the 2004 COC General Meeting, President Yuan Weimin emphasised the significance of holding the 2010 AG for China and required his colleagues to coordinate with the Guangdong and Guangzhou governments in completing bid tasks.[26] In addition, Xu Deli and Li Zhuobin's meeting with Professor Chowdhry was specially arranged by Chang Jianping, Director of the CGSA Boxing and Taekwondo Sports Management Centre, during the 2004 Olympic Games Asian boxing qualifiers in Guangzhou.[27]

Furnishing the Bidding Documents

Each candidate for the 2010 AG was required to submit two documents to the OCA: a Letter of Intent and a Candidature File. The Letter of Intent informs the OCA that the city has decided to bid for the AG. In order to comply with the requirements of the OCA outlined the beginning of Section 5.3, Guangzhou's Letter of Intent was drafted, and handed to the OCA, by the COC officials.[28]

The Candidature File must be submitted after the city had been approved as one of the candidates. It must contain concrete information about the following 24 subjects: (1) the nation and its international relations, (2) candidature city, (3) immigration, (4) climate, (5) environment, (6) security, (7) finance, (8) heath and medicinal facilities, (9) accommodation, (10) reception and hospitality, (11) transportation, (12) schedule, (13) spots, (14) art exhibition, (15) the OCA General Assembly session, (16) ceremony, (17) media, (18) communication, (19) the internet, (20) marketing, (21) schedule, (22) law, (23) experience of organising multi-sport events and (24) ticket sales.[29] The Candidature File was delivered to Kuwait City by the central and local officials, but the person who handed it to the OCA President was Deputy Governor Xu Deli.[30]

It should be noted that once the preliminary draft of the Candidature File was completed by the officials and professionals of Guangzhou,[31] it was passed to Wei Jizhong and his colleagues in the CGSA and COC. Their main role was to suggest revisions to the local officials based on their experience in dealing with international sporting organisations, and to proofread the English.[32] The final version of the Candidature File, hence, was completed with the assistance of the central officials.

Entertaining the Inspectors

After submitting the Candidature File, all the candidature cities in the 2010 AG bid were inspected by the OCA Evaluation Committee. The Evaluation Committee was composed of six OCA executive officials. Its main duty was to evaluate whether the candidature cities were competent to fulfil their intention of holding the AG over the course of a two-day inspection and then write a report. Their report is the most important reference for the OCA members during the vote.[33] Before inspecting Guangzhou, the Guangzhou government officials formed the Guangzhou AG Bid City Work Committee. Under the leadership of Mayor Zhang Guangning, its duty was to prepare Guangzhou for inspection in accordance with the instructions of the Bid Committee.[34]

In order to motivate Guangzhou officials and residents to complete the preparations for the entertaining of the Evaluation Committee, the City Work Committee organised two activities. The first was a mobilisation meeting in which around 200 middle-level officials from the Guangzhou district governments attended. In addition to introducing the significance of holding the 2010 AG for Guangzhou, Deputy Mayors Shen Bonian and Li Zhuobin instructed the officials to devote their best efforts to presenting a civilised and harmonious Guangzhou during the inspection of the OCA Evaluation Committee.[35] Later, the City Work Committee organised a long-distance running competition, which was aimed more at citizens. Around 12,000 Guangzhou residents, including the senior officials of the provincial and city Party committees and governments and the Guangdong-trained Olympic medallists, participated in it. Besides running, all the participants were invited to sign off their names on a 100 metre long 'I Support Guangzhou to Hold the 2010 AG' banner. The banner was later displayed in front of the OCA inspectors.[36]

Besides preparing Guangzhou, the city officials were also in charge of entertaining the OCA Evaluation Committee, together with the provincial officials. When the OCA Deputy President Celso Dayrit and his colleagues arrived at Guangzhou International Airport on April 14, 2004, the welcome ceremony was chaired by Mayor Zhang Guangning and his deputy Li Zhuobin.[37] They also said farewell to the inspectors from there as well.[38] Governor Huang Huahua and Mayor Zhang each held dinners with the inspectors on behalf of the Guangdong and Guangzhou governments after the Evaluation Committee had finished their day's work.[39] Deputy Governor Xu Deli and Zhang held a press conference after accompanying the OCA executives on the inspection. In response to the Evaluation Committee's praise regarding Guangzhou's performance, Xu promised on behalf of the Bid Committee that Guangzhou would stage the 2010 AG as the most outstanding event in the history of the OCA.[40]

In addition, the OCA Evaluation Committee was given a group presentation during the inspection. The presentation was to inform the inspectors about the superiorities of Guangzhou for hosting the 2010 AG. After Mayor Zhang Guangning delivered a welcome speech, Guangzhou's urban planning, sports history and tradition, immigration and transportation, reception, medical and health, security, media and telecommunications, and marketing were, respectively, introduced by eight people. Four of them were senior officials of the Guangdong and Guangzhou governments. The others were professors and experts from Guangzhou.[41] It is noted that the presenters were exclusively selected by the City Work Group. All the inspectors were impressed with their performance and presentation content.[42]

The central officials supervised Guangzhou's preparations. Before the official inspection of the OCA Evaluation Committee, officials of the CGSA and COC came down three times to examine Guangzhou. The first examination was led by President Yuan Weimin and his deputy Yu Zaiqing. They focused on the local transport facilities, including the airport, exhibition centre and underground rail, and then passed on their suggestions to Governor Huang Huahua.[43] The COC Deputy President Tu Mingde and the CGSA Aquatic Sports Department Headperson Zhang Qing chaired the second examination. This was to double-check on the venues Yuan and Yu had inspected in the first examination. Tu and Zhang were also arranged to watch a presentation rehearsal together with Deputy Mayor Li Zhuobin. The central officials commented on the presentation content and the presenters' performance.[44] Wei Jizhong directed the last examination, making a final check of all the places the inspectors would visit.[45]

The central officials also assisted the local officials in entertaining the inspectors. For instance, the CCSA President Yuan Weimin and his deputy Yang Shu'an invited all the Evaluation Committee members to have lunch at the Mingquanju Hotel in Guangzhou on the second day of the inspection. In addition to introducing Guangzhou's advantages, Yuan also promised the inspectors that the CGSA and COC would give their all-out support to Guangzhou to hold the event.[46]

Giving the Presentation

Each candidate city was required to give a presentation to all the OCA members before the final vote. The presentation must cover two parts: (1) the city's promise to comply with the OCA regulations and (2) its detailed arrangements for holding the 2010 AG. The presentation was given by both central and local officials, and the local officials were in charge of making the promise and explaining the detailed arrangements. After Guangdong Governor Huang Huahua assured the audience that the Guangdong government would ensure that the 2010 AG would be the most outstanding event in the history of the OCA, Mayor Zhang Guangning promised that Guangzhou would strictly comply with the OCA Rules and Constitution and provide excellent conditions for all the participants.[47] In the second part, Guangzhou's venue arrangements for the 2010 AG were explained by two local officials, the Guangdong Government External Affairs Deputy Officer Qian Hongjie and the Guangzhou Government Deputy Secretary Gu Shiyang.[48]

The opening remarks were delivered by the CGSA and COC President Yuan Weimin. It had only one key sentence: that on behalf of the COC he supported Guangzhou's bid to hold the 2010 AG. There was no other senior official of the CGSA or the COC appointed to assist the local officials in giving the promise and explaining the arrangement. Nor were any Chinese athletes who had previously won gold medals in the AG assigned to deliver speeches.[49]

Preparing Guangzhou to Hold the AG

In order to achieve the goal of staging the most outstanding AG in the history of the OCA, Mayor Zhang Guangning announced that the Guangzhou government had decided to spend 220 billion yuan (US\$ 26.6 billions) on the renovation of the city. Of this sum, 9 billion yuan (US\$ 1.09 billions) would be spent on the construction of the sports facilities, with the rest assigned to the expansion of the highways, airport, underground railway, train stations, wharfs, facilities for civil education and sewage works. Guangzhou would have a 240 km underground railway network connecting the entire region's cities and townships. The Mayor would lead his colleagues in securing finance for the event in China and abroad. However, Zhang did not mention that the national government would invest in the AG, nor participate in financing Guangzhou's preparations.[50]

To assist the local officials to prepare for the AG, the CGSA organised a seminar at Guangzhou after the Letter of Intent had been submitted. Members of the Beijing 2008 Olympics and Changchun 2007 Asian Winter Games Organising Committees and representatives of the CGSA Liaison Office and the COC were invited to participate in it. Under the auspices of CGSA Deputy President Yu Zaiqing, the visitors not only shared their experiences in collaborating with the central officials in their bids, but also introduced their budgets for the Olympics and the Asian Winter Games. Deputy Governor Xu Deli, Deputy Guangdong Government Secretary Cheng Liangzhou and Guangzhou Deputy Mayor Li Zhuobin participated in the discussions. However, the CGSA and the COC did not participate in the budgeting for the 2010 AG with the Guangzhou government afterwards.[51]

Conclusion

Through reviewing all the six tasks above, it is plain to see Guangzhou's bid is a local-led but central-coordinated project. In other words, the division of labour between the central and local officials in the entire bidding journey was consistent with the stipulations of the OCA. The Chinese candidate, therefore, can be confirmed as a rule-abiding bidder.

It is noted that the findings of this article are different from those of some previous academic works, which concluded that the Chinese officials were reluctant to conform to international rules and regulations when dealing with global or regional affairs.[52] International sporting bids, hence, can be viewed as a means for the Chinese government to alter the negative impression of the international community on China's poor records in complying with international laws, and to demonstrate China's competence to be a responsible international actor. They imply that China has no longer an intention to ostracise itself from world affairs. It has been eager to engage, and to be fully accepted by, the international society.

In addition, to strictly comply with the stipulations of international organisations such as the OCA also reflected China's determination to win all the bids that it undertakes. It is because the government tended to correlate all the bidding victories with the socialist reform conducted by the Chinese Communist Party, the maturity of China in dealing with diplomatic affairs in sport, and, most importantly, the rise of China's status in the international society. Hence, apart from actually hosting IMSEs, bidding for them has been another official means to project the national might and greatness by which China's superpower status in the world stage can be achieved.

Notes on Contributor

Marcus P. Chu teaches Chinese politics and international relations in Department of Political Science, Lingnan University, Hong Kong. He obtained his PhD from the University of Auckland in May 2012. His thesis reviews the central and local inter-relations in China's bids for international events since the 1980s. He currently works on a project regarding the political preoccupations of East Asian countries at the London 2012 Olympics with Professor J.A. Mangan.

Notes

1. Chan, *China's Compliance in Global Affairs*; Economy, "The Impact of International Regimes," 230–53; Gill and Medeiros, "Foreign and Domestic Influences," 66–94; Johnston,

THE ASIAN GAMES: MODERN METAPHOR FOR 'THE MIDDLE KINGDOM' REBORN

Social State; Kent, *Beyond Compliance*; Lanteigne, *China and International Institutions* and Zhao and Ortolano, "The Chinese Government's Role," 708–25.

2. The term 'second class middle power' was coined by Gerald Segal to describe a country which has a lack of weight in aspects of the international trade and investment, and has a small and comparatively less significant market. For details, see Segal, "Does China Matter," 25.

3. Michael Elliot, "China Takes on the World." (*TIME*, January 11, 2007). Available at http://www.time.com/time/printout/0,8816,1576831,00.html. Accessed October 24, 2010; Ted. C. Fishman, "The Chinese Century" (*New York Times*, July 4, 2004). Available at http://www.nytimes.com/2004/07/04/magazine/the-chinese-century.html. Accessed October 24, 2010; Hale, "China's Growing Appetites," 137–47 and Hughes, "A Trade War with China," 94.

4. Gill and Huang, "Sources and Limits of Chinese Soft Power," 17–36; Larmer, "The Centre of the World," 66–74; Kurlantzick, *Charm Offensive*; Joseph Nye, "The Olympics and Chinese Soft Power" (*The Huffington Post*, August 24, 2008). Available at http://www.huffingtonpost.com/joseph-nye/the-olympics-and-chinese_b_120909.html. Accessed October 8, 2009; Paradise, "China and International Harmony," 647–69 and Ding and Saunders, "Talking up China," 3–33.

5. "Guangzhou Yijubei Juban Aoyunhui De Nengli (Guangzhou is Competent to Hold Olympics)" (*China Sports Daily (CSD)*, November 16, 2010, 1).

6. "Zuo Tiyu Shizhe Zhan Zhongguo Fengcai (Be Sports Ambassadors and Showcase China's Charm)" (*CSD*, November 12, 2010, 1).

7. Article 42 paragraph 3 and Article 45 paragraphs 3 and 4, *OCA Constitution and Rules*, 69, 72 and 73.

8. Article 45 paragraph 5, *OCA Constitution and Rules*, 73.

9. Article 45 paragraph 10, *OCA Constitution and Rules*, 73.

10. Ibid.

11. Ibid.

12. The members of the 2010 Guangzhou AG Bid Committee include (1) President(s): *Yuan Weimin* (CGSA President and COC President) and *Huang Huahua* (Guangdong Governor); (2) Executive President(s): *Yu Zaiqing* (CGSA Deputy President and COC Deputy President), *Xu Deli* (Guangdong Deputy Governor) and *Zhang Guangning* (Guangzhou Mayor); (3) Deputy President(s): *Xiao Tian* (CGSA President Assistant and Athletic Officer and COC Deputy President), *Gu Yaoming* (CGSA Liaison Officer and COC Secretary), *Cheng Liangzhou* (Deputy Secretary, Guangdong Government), *Li Zhuobin* (Guangzhou Deputy Mayor) and *Yang Naijun* (Guangdong General Sports Administration President); (4) Secretary(s): *Gu Yaoming*, *Yang Naijun* and (5) Deputy Executive Secretary(s): *Chen Yaoguang* (Secretary, Guangzhou Government) and *Liu Jiangnan* (Guangzhou General Sports Administration President). For details see: "Guangzhou 2010 Nian Shenyawei Zucheng Renyuan He Jigou (Guangzhou 2012 AG Bid Committee Members and Units)" (*Guangzhou Daily (GZD)*, April 9, 2004, A1).

13. "Dongya Diqu Aoweihui Luntan Zai Beijing Juxing (East Asian Olympic Association Forum Take Place at Beijing)" (*Nanfang Daily (NFD)*, March 26, 2004, A02).

14. "Xu Deli Huijian Laowo Tiyu Daibiaotuan (Xu Deli Meets With Lao Delegation)" (*NFD*, May 29, 2004, 03).

15. "Yaao Zhuxi Zhichi Guangzhou Shenya (OCA President Supports Guangzhou's Bid)" (*GZD*, February 17, 2004, A1); "Guangzhou Shenyatuan Fangfei (Guangzhou Delegation Visit the Philippines)" *GZD*, March 8, 2004, A5 and "Sui Shenyatuan Guanmo Nanya Yundonghui (Guangzhou Delegation Visit South Asian Games)" (*NFD*, March 30, 2004, A02).

16. Article 18 paragraph 2 and article 45 paragraph 3, *OCA Constitution and Rules*, 27, 28 and 72.

17. Article 18 paragraph 2 and bye-law to article 18 paragraph 3, *OCA Constitution and Rules*, 27, 28 and 30.

18. "Yaao Zhuxi Zhichi Guangzhou Shenya (OCA President Supports Guangzhou's Bid)" (*GZD*, February 17, 2004, A1).

19. "Guangzhou Shenyatuan Fangfei (Guangzhou Delegation Visit the Philippines)" (*GZD*, March 8, 2004, A5).

20. "Guangzhou Shenya You Liuda Youshi (Guangzhou has Six Advantages in Bid)" (*GZD*, February 18, 2004, A1 and A5).

21. "Yemen Zhichi Guangzhou Shenya (Yemen Support Guangzhou's Bid)" (*NFD*, June 3, 2004, A12).

22. "Guangzhou Shenya Youshi Wuyu Lunbi (Guangzhou's Advantages in Bid are Unmatched)" (*NFD*, February 25, 2004, A03).

THE ASIAN GAMES: MODERN METAPHOR FOR 'THE MIDDLE KINGDOM' REBORN

23. "Guoji Quanlian Zhuxi Biaoshi Jiangjinli Tigong Zhichi (IABA President Promises to Give Support)" (*NFD*, March 21, 2004, 01).
24. "Zhang Guangning Zhaokai Jizhe Zhaodaihui (Zhang Guangning Holds a Press Conference)" (*GZD*, March 26, 2004, A2).
25. "Women Shengjuan Zaiwo (We Sure Win)" (*NFD*, February 25, 2004, A03).
26. "Zhongguo Aoweihui Quanli Zhichi Guangzhou Shenya (COC Fully Support Guangzhou's Bid)" (*NFD*, February 28, 2004, 08).
27. "Guoji Quanlian Zhuxi Biaoshi Jiangjinli Tigong Zhichi (IABA President Promises to Give Support)" (*NFD*, March 21, 2004, 01).
28. "Zhongguo Aoweihui Yizhengshi Dijiao Shenbanshu (COC Confirm to have Submitted Application Letter)" (*China Sports Daily*, December 23, 2003, 2).
29. "Guangzhou Shenya Baogao Shenmi Chulong (Guangzhou's Candidature File Comes Out)" (*NFD*, March 26, 2004, A02).
30. "Guangzhou Zuori Dijiao Shenya Baogaoshu (Guangzhou's Candidature File was Submitted Yesterday)" (*GZD*, April 1, 2004, A1).
31. "Shenban Baogao (The Candidature File)" (*GZD*, March 25, 2004, A28).
32. "Shenya Baogao Yingyuban Chutai Neimu (Inside Story About Drafting the English-Version Candidature File)" (*GZD*, March 30, 2004, A28) and "Guangzhou Shenya Baogao Kaoti Jiedu (Review Guangzhou's Candidature File)" (*GZD*, April 1, 2004, A28).
33. Article 45 paragraph 3 and 4, *OCA Constitution and Rules*, 72 and 73.
34. The Members of the Guangzhou AG Bid City Work Committee include (1) Director: *Zhang Guangning* (Guangzhou Mayor); (2) Executive Director: *Li Zhuobin* (Guangzhou Deputy Mayor); (3) Deputy Director(s): *Chen Yaoguang* (Secretary, Guangzhou Government), *Chang Min* (Deputy Secretary, Guangzhou Government), *Gu Shiyang* (Deputy Secretary, Guangzhou Government) and *Liu Jiangnan* (Guangzhou General Sports Administration President); (4) Secretary: *Chen Yaoguang* and (5) Deputy Secretary(s): *Gu Shiyang* and *Liu Jiangnan*. For details see "Shenya Chengshi Gongzuo Weiyuanhui Chengli (AG Bid City Work Committee Establish)" (*GZD*, March 30, 2004, 1).
35. "Guangzhou Shenya Zuo Shizhan Yanlian (Guangzhou Made a Rehearsal Yesterday)" (*GZD*, April 10, 2004, A1).
36. "Wanren Changpao Wei Guangzhou Shenya Jiayou (Ten Thousand People Participate in a Long Distance Running Competition)" (*GZD*, April 11, 2004, A1).
37. "Huacheng Shengqing Yingjie Yayun Kaoguan (Guangzhou is Passionate to Greet OCA Inspectors)" (*GZD*, April 15, 2004, A1 and A5).
38. "Shenya Pinggutuan Manyi Lisui (OCA Evaluation Committee Left Guangzhou with Satisfaction)" (*GZD*, April 17, 2004, A1).
39. "Huacheng Shengqing Yingjie Yayun Kaoguan (Guangzhou is Passionate to Greet OCA Inspectors)" (*GZD*, April 15, 2004, A1 and A5) and "Shenya Nengfou Chenggong Haikan 7 Yue 1 Ri (Whether Guangzhou Holding AG will be Determined on July 1)" (*GZD*, April 16, 2004, A1 and A5).
40. "Guangzhou Wanquan Youshili Juban Yayunhui (Guangzhou is Capable of Holding AG)" (*NFD*, April 16, 2004, A01) and "Guangzhou Yao Zhengban Yijie Zuichuse Yayunhui (Guangzhou Intend to Hold the Most Outstanding AG)" (*NFD*, April 16, 2004, A03).
41. Guangzhou's presenters for briefing the OCA Evaluation Committee include (1) Urban planning section: *Li Yongning* (Professor, Guangzhou Academy of Social Sciences); (2) Sports history and tradition section: *Liu Jiangnan* (President, Guangzhou General Sports Administration); (3) Immigration and transportation section: *Qian Hongjie* (Deputy Officer, Guangdong Government External Affairs Office); (4) Reception section: *Zhou Haiying* (Liaison officer, Guangzhou AG Bid Committee); (5) Health and medical facilities section: *Xiao Haipeng* (Professor, Sun Yat-Sen University); (6) Security section: *Zhang Zhengui* (Deputy Head, Guangzhou Dongshan District Police Station); (7) Media and communication section: *Yin Jie* (Deputy Head, Guangzhou Television Station News Department) and (8) Finance and marketing section: *Sun Lei* (Deputy President, Guangzhou Economic Development Bureau). For details see "Guangzhou Shenban 2010 Nian Yayunhui Chenshu Baogaohui Zuo Juxing (Presentation Meeting of Guangzhou 2010 AG Bid Took Place Yesterday)" (*GZD*, April 16, 2004, A2).
42. Ibid.

43. "Siyue Shisiri Guangzhou Shenya Yingkao (Guangzhou will be Inspected on April 14)" (*GZD*, April 9, 2004, A1 and A8).
44. "Shenya Chenshu Caipai Yingde Maitangcai (The Presentation Rehearsal is Cheered)" (*GZD*, April 11, 2004, A1) and "Kaoguan Keganshou Guangjiaohui Shengkuang (Inspectors Feel Ganton Fairs' Grand Occasion)" (*GZD*, April 11, 2004, A2).
45. "Guangzhou Shenyawei Zuo Zuihou Yici Jiancha Gekaochadian (Guangzhou AG Bid Committee did an Inspection Yesterday)" (*GZD*, April 14, 2004, A1).
46. "Shenya Nengfou Chenggong Haikan 7 Yue 1 Ri (Whether Guangzhou Holding AG will Determine on July 1)" (*GZD*, April 16, 2004, A1 and A5).
47. "Guangzhou Shenya Daibiaotuan Daibiao Zhichi (Guangzhou Delegation Representatives' Speech)" (*GZD*, July 1, 2004, A2).
48. "Chenshu Neirong Xuandeng (Presentation's Selected Content)" (*GZD*, July 2, 2004, A3).
49. "Guangzhou Shenya Daibiaotuan Daibiao Zhichi (Guangzhou Delegation Representatives' Speech)" (*GZD*, July 1, 2004, A2).
50. "Guangzhou 2200 Yi Yingyayun Cuchengjian (Guangzhou will Spend 220 Billion Yuan for AG and Urban Infrastructure)" (*GZD*, June 29, 2004, A1 and A5).
51. "Shenban Dishiliujie Yayunhui Yantaohui Zuozai Guangzhou Juxing (A Seminar About AG Bid Took Place in Guangzhou Yesterday)" (*GZD*, December 23, 2003, A26).
52. Foot, "Chinese Power," 1–19; Feinerman, "Chinese Participation in the International Legal Order," 186–210; Kent, *China, the United Nations and Human Rights* and Potter, "China and the International Legal System," 699–715.

References

Chan, Gerald. *China's Compliance in Global Affairs: Trade, Arms Control, Environmental Protection, Human Rights*. Singapore: World Scientific, 2006.

Ding, Sheng, and Robert A. Saunders. "Talking up China: An Analysis on China's Rising Cultural Power and Global Promotion of the Chinese Language." *East Asia: An International Quarterly* 23, no. 2 (2006): 3–33.

Economy, Elizabeth. "The Impact of International Regimes on Chinese Foreign Policy-Making: Broadening Perspective and Policies … But Only to a Point." In *The Making of Chinese Foreign and Security Policy in the Era of Reform, 1978–2000*, edited by David M. Lampton, 230–253. Stanford, C.A: Stanford University Press, 2001.

Feinerman, James V. "Chinese Participation in the International Legal Order: Rogue Elephant or Team Player?" *The China Quarterly* 141 (1995): 186–210.

Foot, Rosemary. "Chinese Power and the Idea of a Responsible State." *The China Journal* 45 (2001): 1–19.

Gill, Bates, and Evans S. Medeiros. "Foreign and Domestic Influences on China's Arms Control and Non-Proliferation Policies." *The China Quarterly* 161 (2000): 66–94.

Gill, Bates, and Yanzhong Huang. "Sources and Limits of Chinese Soft Power." *Survival* 48, no. 2 (2006): 17–36.

Hale, David. "China's Growing Appetites: Demand for Industrial Raw Materials Impacts Trade, Foreign Policy." *National Interest* 76 (2004): 137–147.

Hughes, Neil C. "A Trade War with China?" *Foreign Affairs* 84, no. 4 (2005): 94–106.

Johnston, Alastair Iain. *Social State: China in International Institutions 1980–2000*. Princeton, NJ: Princeton University Press, 2008.

Kent, Ann E. *Beyond Compliance: China, International Organizations, and Global Security*. Stanford, CA: Stanford University Press, 2007.

Kent, Ann E. *China, the United Nations and Human Rights, the Limited of Compliance*. Philadelphia, PA: Penn State Press, 1999.

Kurlantzick, Joshua. *Charm Offensive: How China's Soft Power Is Transforming the World*. New Haven, CT: Yale University Press, 2007.

Lanteigne, Marc. *China and International Institutions Alternative Paths to Global Power*. London: Routledge, 2005.

Larmer, Brook. "The Centre of the World." *Foreign Policy* 150 (2005): 66–74.

Olympic Committee of Asia. *OCA Constitution and Rules*. Accessed May 24, 2012. http://www.ocasia.org/OCA/Download/Default/1/OCA/4/1OCA400150.pdf

Paradise, James F. "China and International Harmony, The Role of Confucius Institutes in Bolstering Beijing's Soft Power." *Asian Survey* 49, no. 4 (2009): 647–669.

Potter, Pitman B. "China and the International Legal System: Challenges of Participation." *The China Quarterly* 191 (2007): 699–715.

Segal, Gerald. "Does China Matter?" *Foreign Affairs* 78, no. 5 (1999): 24–36.

Zhao, Jimin, and Leonard Ortolano. "The Chinese Government's Role in Implementing Multilateral Environmental Agreement: The Case of the Montréal Protocol." *The China Quarterly* 175 (2003): 708–725.

'Glittering Guangzhou': The 2010 Asian Games – Local Rivalries, National Motives, Geopolitical Gestures

J.A. Mangan[a], Jinxia Dong[b] and Di Lu[b]

[a]*University of Strathclyde, Glasgow, UK;* [b]*Department of Physical Education, Peking University, Beijing, P.R. China*

> The Guangzhou Asian Games of 2010 was the deliberate outcome of an intense regional rivalry, a careful national balancing act and a geopolitical marketing momentum embedded in a provincial and civil reconstruction that mirrored a wider national reconstruction: Guangdong and Guangzhou – 'the city', the Games City and Chinese performances were statements about the controlled advance of the 'Middle Kingdom' to a regained hegemonic status in the western Pacific. This is a verbal and visual depiction of the cosmopolitanism and confidence of the New China: word and picture meshed to demonstrate vividly the modern ascendancy of the 'Middle Kingdom'.

Precisely because we live in a culture dominated by evolutionary ideas it is difficult for us to recognize their imaginative power in our daily readings of the world. We need to do so.[1]

Contrary to the old western view of China as stagnant or unchanging, as almost without history, the story of how China came to be the huge country we know today is full of drama. In each period Chinese have made use of what they inherited, but also have come up with new ideas and practices as they struggled …, to impose their will or contend with opponents, to survive and thrive.[2]

In every epoch Chinese have made use of the resources they inherited-material, intellectual, and institutional-to set goals, respond to new challenges, to protect themselves, and advance their interests.[3]

Introduction: Investment, Infrastructure, Performance

Only two years after the 2008 Beijing Olympic Games, once again China thrust itself onto the world stage via a mega-sports event. In yet another dramatic manifestation of 'China Ascendant', Guangzhou, the capital city of Guangdong in the south of China, hosted the 2010 Asian Games. The Games left its mark on the history of the event with the greatest number of records, the largest number of events, the largest sponsorship income and the greatest number of participants. Furthermore, the Guangzhou Asian Games caught international attention with its spectacular ceremonies, the state-of-art stadiums and not least the crushing dominance of the Chinese athletes (Table 1).

Table 1. The 2010 Guangzhou Asian Games medal table.

Rank	Nation/region	Gold	Silver	Bronze	Total
1	China	199	119	98	416
2	South Korea	76	65	91	232
3	Japan	48	74	94	216
4	Iran	20	14	25	59
5	Kazakhstan	18	23	38	79
6	India	14	17	33	64
7	Chinese Taipei	13	16	38	67
8	Uzbekistan	11	22	23	56
9	Thailand	11	9	32	52
10	Malaysia	9	18	14	41

Source: *Sina*, 'Asian Games medal table', available at *http://match.2008.sina.com.cn/asia2010/totalmedal.php* (accessed August 10, 2012).

What motivated China to host the Asian Games in the immediate aftermath of the Beijing Games? Why did Guangzhou make a huge investment in the Games? How did other regions react to the Games investment, infrastructure and performance, and what role did the national government play in ensuring success?

The motives of China, Guangdong and Guangzhou and the responses of other regions will be considered more in an effort to answer these questions through an analysis of investment in facilities, construction and medal dominance. This will involve discussion of the varied ambitions of politicians – national, regional and civic, the coverage by the media and responses of the public, the different interests of central, regional and local government, the intense competition between the regions and leading cities and the complicated relations and ambitions of these forces.

The Asian Games and Regional Rivalries

Given the huge cost and tremendous effort associated with organising the event, especially after Beijing had already hosted a spectacular Olympic Games, why did Guangzhou want to host the Asian Games? To answer this question, it is necessary to look at the recent social and economic development of Guangdong and its status relative to other provinces in China (Figure 1).

Guangdong, located in southern China, is currently the largest populated province in the country with over 100 million permanent residents. Since the economic reforms of 1979, Guangdong has been the engine for the nation's phenomenal economic propulsion.[4] Three of the four Specialised Economic Zones, initially established in 1979, are situated in the province.[5] The province is currently the biggest GDP contributor on the Chinese mainland, accounting for 11.2% of the country's total GDP in 2011.[6] Its *per capita* GDP increased from 370 Yuan (US\$ 220) in 1978 to 15,365 Yuan (US\$ 1856) in 2002 when Guangzhou bid for the Games.[7]

Intense territorial competition exists in China, a vast country with 32 provinces, municipalities and autonomous regions and with a population of over 1.3 billion. In this century, in consequence other regions represented by the Bohai-Rim Economic Circle in the north and the Yangtze River Delta in the east have experienced strong economic growth and posed intense challenges to Guangdong. By 2011, Beijing, Shanghai and Tianjin were classified as 'superior urban societies', and Guangdong was classified only as an 'intermediate urban society' (Figure 2).[8]

THE ASIAN GAMES: MODERN METAPHOR FOR 'THE MIDDLE KINGDOM' REBORN

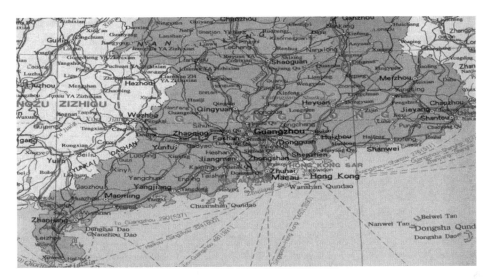

Figure 1. Map of Guangdong Province. *Source*: *China Maps*, 'China Map of Guangdong Province', available at http://www.chinamaps.org/china/provincemaps/guangdong.html (accessed January 18, 2013).

Competition, as noted earlier, is the outcome of the economic reforms of the late 1970s. Reforms characterised by regional decentralisation guaranteed local administrations more freedom and provided them with incentives to compete by linking regional government officials' career paths with regional economic performance. Regions,

Figure 2. Map of Chinese Provinces. *Source*: *China Highlights*, 'Map of China Provinces', available at http://www.chinahighlights.com/map/china-provincial-map (accessed November 20, 2012).

provinces and cities over recent decades have striven to amass the greatest resources, bargaining for the most favourable policy concessions and seeking to generate the highest growth rates. How to maintain Guangdong's leading position in a fast changing country is an issue facing the decision-makers of the province. When Beijing won the right to host the 2008 Olympic Games, hosting a mega-sports event such as the Olympics was believed to stimulate national and regional social and economic development through 'games-related expenditure, job creation, provision of new sports facilities and infrastructure, urban revival, enhanced international profile, increased tourism and more inward investment'.[9]

A City Transformed

Beijing's successful Olympic bid in 2001 inspired Guangdong. In late 2002, Guangdong Provincial Government and Guangzhou City Government officials jointly expressed their wish to host the 2010 Asian Games. To stage the Games was a chance for Guangzhou to upgrade its infrastructure, quicken the pace of economic development and then showcase to Asia and the world a new, vigorous image of an open, modernised and advanced metropolis. In addition, the hope was that the Asian Games would pave the way for Guangdong to play a greater part in national affairs and provide a broad bridge to Asia (Figure 3).

In 2004, with both central and provincial governmental support, Guangzhou, the capital city of Guangdong Province, won the Asian Games bid by a large margin. Guangzhou on the Pearl River Delta is the second Chinese city to host the Asian Games (the first was held in Beijing in 1990). With the 'opening up' in late 1970s,[10] the city had seized its opportunity and achieved economic lift-off. However, just as Guangdong has faced challenges from other provinces, Guangzhou has challenges from other cities in the past 10 years and has been overtaken by Hong Kong, Shanghai and Beijing. In 2011, these three cities went ahead of Guangzhou on the index of city scientific development.[11]

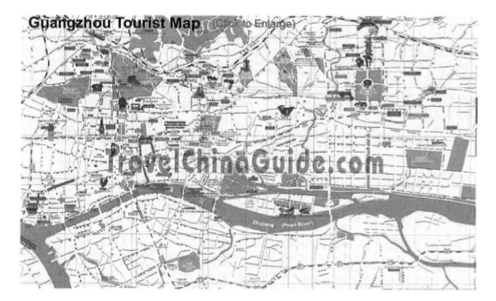

Figure 3. Map of Guangzhou in Guangdong Province. *Source*: *Travel China Guide*, 'Guangzhou Maps', available at http://www.travelchinaguide.com/map/guangzhou/ (accessed January 26, 2013).

Guangzhou has also been challenged by Tianjin, another municipal city in the Bohai-Rim. Consequently, Guangzhou has had to shift from an exclusively economic emphasis to broader social and cultural emphases involving socio-political institutions, value systems and quality life improvements. Hosting the Asian Games, the second largest global multi-sport event after the Olympic Games, provided Guangzhou with a golden opportunity to promote not only its economic but also its social and cultural development.

Immediately after Guangzhou won the bid, a vast investment and construction programme was put in place. A total of 17.48 billion Yuan (US$ 2.67 billion) was invested in the game-related projects, of which 6.05 billion Yuan (US$ 0.92 billion) went to the operating funds of Guangzhou Asian Games Organizing Committee, 7.25 billion Yuan (US$ 1.11 billion) to the construction of venues, 3.51 billion Yuan (US$ 0.54 billion) to transportation, volunteers and urban landscaping, and 0.67 billion Yuan (US$ 0.10 billion) to the operating funds of Guangzhou Para Asian Games Organizing Committee.[12] The small budget for the Games itself had a sound reason. Guangdong's prosperous economy had paved the way for its sports development. 'Guangdong was in the forefront of virtually every major sport reform. It pioneered commercial clubs, individual sponsorship and athlete transfer'.[13] The province had built impressive facilities and held big national and international competitions in the 1980s and 1990s. Before it applied to host the Asian Games, it had staged the National Games twice – (1987 and 2001) and the First Women's World Soccer Championships (1991). Thus, Guangdong had most of the venues and facilities required for the Asian Games when it bid to host the event. To refurbish 58 venues and build 12 new venues needed only 6.3 billion Yuan (almost US$ 1 billion), the smallest budget of the Asian Games (Figures 4–7).

These images reveal a national, regional and city mindset: energetic, ambitious and confident. They are visual demonstration of achievement and ambition. They fuse political policy, commercial acumen and civic satisfaction with a single strand of shining success. They are mirrored by the city Asian Games images.

The Guangzhou Asian Games Venues

The Guangzhou Asian Games had six venues including the Guangzhou Asian Games City, the Guangdong Olympic Sports Centre and the Guangzhou University City Sports Centre.

Figure 4. Glittering Guangzhou: a panoramic view of Guangzhou. *Source*: *Beauty Places*, 'Guangzhou', available at http://beauty-places.com/guangzhou/ (accessed November 20, 2012).

Figure 5. Glittering Guangzhou: central business districts. *Source*: *Beauty Places*, 'Guangzhou', available at http://beauty-places.com/guangzhou/ (accessed November 20, 2012).

The Guangzhou Asian Games City comprising seven components and covering 120 hectares was located in Panyu district. This Games City breaks the grounds for the future development of the Guangzhou New City that will have 1 million residents. The creation of sports facilities and venues was an integral part of the development. Each district was planned to have at least one competition venue for the Asian Games.[14] Thus, a balanced development of Guangzhou was purposefully planned (Figures 8–11).

A Provincial and City Project

The Beijing Olympic Games was considered a national political project and obtained the nation's support. The Guangzhou Asian Games was regarded as the Games of Guangdong Province and received support mainly from the Guangdong Provincial Government and the Guangzhou City Government. This was reflected in the composition of the Games budget: 180 million Yuan (US$ 27.47 million) from the central government, 4.25 billion Yuan (US$ 0.65 billion) from the Guangdong Provincial Government, 9.5 billion Yuan

Figure 6. Glittering Guangzhou: Pearl River at night. *Source*: *Travel Blog*, 'Guangzhou TV Tower at Night', available at http://www.travelblog.org/Photos/5712731 (accessed January 19, 2013).

THE ASIAN GAMES: MODERN METAPHOR FOR 'THE MIDDLE KINGDOM' REBORN

Figure 7. Glittering Guangzhou: Pearl River night tour. *Source*: *China Absolute Tours*, 'Night Tour on the Pearl River', available at http://www.absolutechinatours.com/Guangzhou-attractions/Pearl-River-Night-Tour-88.html (accessed January 19, 2013).

(US$ 1.45 billion) from Guangzhou government and 2.89 billion Yuan (US$ 0.44 billion) from the marketing and the donation of the Asian Games Organizing Committee.[15]

Has this massive capital investment achieved its ends: the creation and projection of an advanced modern metropolis? The transportation system in Guangzhou has been significantly upgraded, with some 76 Asian Games bus lanes and six newly opened subway lanes now in service with extended service times. In addition, a new bus rapid transit (BRT) that seamlessly connects passengers to both the metro system and the city's new bike-share network was built to reduce carbon monoxide emissions and traffic congestion. Opened in February 2010, 9 months before the Games, the BRT system carries 800,000 passengers per day. Furthermore, more high-speed bullet trains were opened to the public. In addition, the new Guangzhou Baiyun International Airport was upgraded to meet the need of the massive increase in the volume of passengers with 12 new aviation routs opened to Asian countries. The eye-catching Asian Games Village, the state-of-art airport terminal and modern subway lines, among other things, dramatically and purposefully changed the appearance of Guangzhou, as the Olympic Games changed

Figure 8. Huangpu Centre Gymnasium. *Source*: *Joy*, 'Huangpu Central Gymnasium', available at http://sports.joy.cn/2010-09-15/100883640.html (accessed November 20, 2012).

THE ASIAN GAMES: MODERN METAPHOR FOR 'THE MIDDLE KINGDOM' REBORN

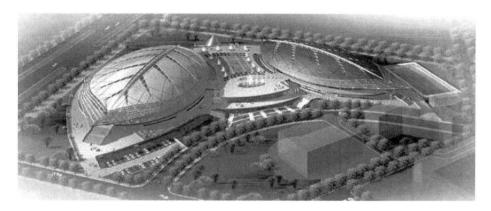

Figure 9. Guangzhou University Town Sports Centre. *Source*: *Sina*, 'Asian Games Venues: University Town Central Stadium', available at http://yayun2010.sina.com.cn/venue/ (accessed November 26, 2012).

Figure 10. Huadu Stadium. *Source*: *Sina*, 'Elegant Demeanor of Asian Games Venues: Huadu Stadium', available at http://slide.gd.sina.com.cn/news/slide_17_2890_13031.html (accessed January 19, 2013).

Figure 11. Asian Games Town Gymnasium. *Source*: *Chinese Radio*, 'A Glimpse of the Asian Games Town Gymnasium', available at http://gb.cri.cn/1321/2010/11/18/157s3060378.htm (accessed November 20, 2012).

Beijing and the World Expo changed Shanghai. 'The Asian Games would create a new Guangzhou', claimed Wang Qinliang, the mayor of Guangzhou.[16] He was correct.

Not only was a 'new Guangzhou' created, but with increased job opportunities, migrants flooded into the fast economically expanding province. The number of migrants in Guangdong increased from 81,830 in 1978 to 145,490 in 2006 though it did decrease slightly to 110,560 in 2008 due to the increasing impact of the global financial crisis, and Guangzhou was one of the major cities in China that attracted thousands of migrant workers.[17]

The vast infrastructural construction and the building of sports venues and facilities not only created a significant number of employment opportunities but also facilitated developments in commerce, construction, real estate, transportation, sport, finance, insurance, education, media and advertising. Guangdong's GDP reached 2.59 trillion Yuan (US\$ 330 billion) in 2006 but increased to 5.3 trillion Yuan (US\$ 840 billion) in 2011.[18] It has been estimated that the Games could increase Guangzhou's annual GDP growth by 5%.[19]

In addition, improving the environment was a major aim associated with the Games captured in the mantra: 'Welcome to the Asian Games for the creation of good life'. A low-carbon development environmental model was introduced, and making the city fit for living became a primary objective associated with the Asian Games. Advanced technology, remarkable energy-reducing achievements and rapid low-carbon industry expansion have made, in fact, a low-carbon economy possible.[20]

Just as Beijing did, Guangzhou took a series of environmental measures including adjusting the industrial economic structure, controlling industrial pollution, suspending or closing seriously contaminating plants, removing the most 'purulent' plants from within the four ring-road systems, intensifying industrial pollution source management, publicising clean manufacture and recycling to turn the skies bluer, making the water cleaner and ensuring a smoother flow of the traffic.[21]

Improved natural environment brought about changes of standards, which were instrumental in the pursuit of a new lifestyle. The Games to a degree, without question, has helped the Chinese to become more conscious of the need to balance economic development and environmental protection. In a decade before Guangzhou hosted the National Games in 2001, it was decided that the year of 2010 should witness significant changes in Guangzhou's environment. It was also in 2010, according to the Guangdong Provincial Government plan, that Guangdong would realise modernisation. Therefore, staging the Asian Games in 2010 had a special significance. It would have a marked impact on the development of Guangzhou, Guangdong and the Pearl Delta Area.[22] Making use of the chance to host the Asian Games, as it has been estimated, accelerated the construction of Guangzhou by at least 5 years. The economic impact of the Asian Games is expected to reach 800 billion Yuan (US\$ 120.80 billion) in a short span of time.[23]

Guangzhou's preparation for the Asian Games partially coincided with global financial crisis that had a negative impact on Guangdong's export-based manufacturing industry. To stimulate the Chinese economy, the Chinese government adopted a more relaxed financial policy and encouraged local government to increase investment for infrastructural construction. Taking advantage of this policy, Guangzhou stepped up its effort to invest in city infrastructure. For example, the project of Guangzhou Tower that integrated TV transmitter, tourism industry, hi-tech exhibitions, cultural entertainments, meteorological research and a command and control centre needed 2.7 billion Yuan (US\$ 407.69 million). The government lent the TV Tower company 40 million Yuan (US\$ 6.04 million) as start-up capital and the rest was acquired through business financing.[24]

Finally, encouraged by the success of the Beijing Olympics in 2008 and concerned about the possible post-Olympic fatigue, to sustain the enthusiasm of Chinese people and maintain the Beijing Olympic legacy were challenges to the Chinese Government. The Guangzhou Games was one possible solution.

To ensure the success of the Games, many experts responsible for the success of the Beijing Olympic Games were sent to Guangzhou to help organise the Asian Games. Everything was modelled on the Beijing Games: security, transportation, media and communication, competition management, volunteers' training and marketing. Taking the volunteer programme as an example, more than 1.5 million volunteers were deployed to assist in the operation of the Games. During the Games, volunteers were provided with transportation and meal allowances, as well as uniforms.

Political and Geopolitical Ambitions

Sport has been used as a bright metaphorical mirror in China.[25] After Beijing's successful bid for the Olympics in 2001, the Chinese Government gave a green signal to Guangdong's application to host the 2010 Asian Games. Hosting another international event in the south of China would not only once again stimulate national pride in the whole country but also promote the balanced development of different regions and cities.

In China, Beijing, Shanghai, Shenzhen and Guangzhou are the four most important developed first-tier cities. Beijing, as China's political, economic and cultural centre, has staged a spectacular and exceptional Olympic Games and raised its international profile to a new level. Shanghai, a world-famous international metropolis, has also successfully hosted the World Expo in a display of its modern image to the whole world. Shenzhen and Guangzhou are two cities located in Guangdong. To promote the balanced development of major cities, the central government gave its support to Guangzhou to host the 16th Asian Games and to Shenzhen, the fastest developed city in the country since 1980, to host the 2011 World University Games. The host city has to take responsibility, however, for organising and running the Games. Nevertheless, the support of the central government is crucial.

As already made clear, hosting the Asian Games was intended to enlarge Guangdong's national and international profile. To showcase to the world the profound, unique and impressive Lingnan culture through the Games was thus one ambition. The word 'Lingnan' comes from the eastern Zhou Dynasty (770BC−221BC) and generally refers to Guangdong, Guangxi and the region of north Vietnam. Guangzhou is the centre of Cantonese culture along the Pearl River. The Cantonese dialect, Cantonese Opera, Lingnan calligraphy, Cantonese cuisine, art, architecture and miniascape as well as music and handicrafts are all reflection of this culture. However, Lingnan culture, compared with other traditional Chinese culture, is not widely known. To increase an awareness of Lingnan culture was a priority. Staging the Asian Games offered opportunities for an appreciation of the uniqueness of Lingnan culture and was undoubtedly an imperative for the local government. In preparing the Games, it took various measures to infuse Lingnan culture elements into the Games. For the first time in history, the Opening Ceremony in Guangzhou was moved from the traditional indoor location in the main stadium to an external location, Haixinsha Island along the Pearl River, in an attempt to promote the ceremony's water-themed features. Water has been crucial to Guangzhou's existence and prosperity. Facing the sea, Guangzhou has more than 1300 rivers in the city and 121 rivers flow through the 'downtown' area. The mighty Pearl River which flows through the city is regarded as the river of motherhood and maternal symbol of the city.

China, itself, was similarly showcased by the Games. From 2008 to 2010, China hosted three mega-events, the Beijing Olympic Games, the Shanghai World Expo and the Guangzhou Asian Games. All caught world attention. All pronounced China's rise: undoubtedly one of the greatest global dramas of the twenty-first century. China's rise to superpower status is underpinned by the fact that China has become the world's second largest economy in 2010 – fittingly the year of the Guangzhou Asian Games. More significantly, perhaps China's contribution to world economic growth increased to 20% between 2002 and 2011.[26] China's extraordinary economic explosion and soft power diplomacy in recent years are transforming East Asia, and future decades will see even greater increases in Chinese influence in both soft and hard power.

Regional Harmony and Disharmony: Romance and Realism

Though not as globally popular as the Olympic Games, the Asian Games demonstrated China's substantial wealth and its impressive economic power, while promoting with opulent ostentation the shining new image of the nation and thus reinforcing the pride and cohesion of the Chinese with a display of dazzling modernity: staging the Asian Games had a message and a meaning beyond mere sport. In addition, the successful holding of the Games offers China opportunities to build all-around and multilevel cooperation with other Asian countries, to enhance mutual understanding and confidence, to consolidate and improve relationships with its peripheral countries and regions. This ambition is clearly illustrated in the Games' vision: 'Thrilling Games, Harmonious Asia'. This is a bold even audacious ambition. The concept of the Harmonious Society was wedged into the pronouncements of President Hu Jintao and has resonated in his speeches for several years and has become a cornerstone of the 'theory of Scientific Development' and is drawn, of course, from Chinese history and culture.[27] It is a modern version of the imperial legitimation of the Mandate of Heaven.[28] It was employed, therefore, as an appropriate pronouncement for the Guangzhou Asian Games.

Historical Realism and Regional Disharmony

To be sanguine is laudable. However, to be realistic is sensible. The history of East Asia and especially the history of Sino-Japanese relations argue for the latter. It must be recognised that the holding of the recent Asian Games in China with a display of ostentatious affluence, efficiency, confidence and success at all levels carries the clear danger of interpretation by other nations in the region, not least Japan, of the Games as a naked display – political and geopolitical – of soft power assertion eventually to be allied to 'hard power' domination. The holding of the recent Asian Games in China, hard on the heels of the impressive Beijing Olympics, brings with it – rather than an appreciation of a national government preoccupation with balancing the internal opportunities of provinces and cities – the possible conviction among the nations of the region that it is manifestly a statement of regional hegemonic aspiration and a conviction that the 'Middle Kingdom' is again reverting to a once 'natural' and central location as the controlling force in East Asian inter-relationships. And in fact, in the wake of the savage twentieth-century confrontation of appalling ruthlessness between Japan and China, it can be argued that China will be even more committed to this control than in centuries past. Thus, the recent Asian Games has the potential for promoting harmony and provoking disharmony in East Asia.

It has been written by one Western commentator that

> ... the greatest concern about China as a global power is its deeply rooted superiority complex. How that will structure and influence Chinese behavior and its attitudes towards the rest of the world remains to be seen, but it is clear that something so entrenched will not dissolve or disappear. If the calling card of the West has often been aggression and conquest, China's will be its overweening sense of superiority and the hierarchical mentality this has engendered.[29]

Is this assertion widely supported throughout East Asia? Sport is invariably linked to politics. Indeed, even at times, a surrogate source of conflict: famously described as war without weapons! The crushing of the Asian nations by the 'Middle Kingdom' renascent could be realistically interpreted not as an act of cooperation but of confrontation. The future will test the value of the Guangzhou Asian Games as a measure of harmonious reconciliation in the region. The dominance of the Chinese athletes and the display of conspicuous materialistic consumption – technologically, architecturally and promotionally – could have an impact which in the future will be far from harmonious in consequence. Time will tell. Is the recent confrontation between China and Japan over the Diaoyu or Senkaku Islands more of a harbinger of East Asian future relations than a triumphant Chinese Asian Games? With regard to soft power politics to what extent is this assertion true:

> As a matter of course, hegemonic powers seek to project their values and institutions on to subordinate nations and the latter, in response, will, depending on circumstances, adapt or genuflect towards their ways; if they don't hegemonic powers generally seek to impose those values and arrangements on them, even in extremis by force.[30]

It has been recorded that a leading Chinese political figure has recently stated of the clash between China and Japan over the islands:

> China is equivalent of smaller powers ... But ... Japan is different. There is history between us. Japan regards itself as a regional, and sometimes, a world power ... *You cannot poke us* [emphasis added]. You cannot make a mistake.[31]

Did China poke Asia in Guangzhou in 2010?

Conclusion: Local Rivalries, National Motives, Geopolitical Gestures

In summary, the Asian Games was used by the regional government as a political project to upgrade its infrastructure, promote economic development, build a new image and thus to win an improved status in a huge competitive populated country. For the central government, it was a chance to promote the balanced development of major cities including Beijing, Shanghai, Shenzhen and Guangzhou – and a testing ground for the national athletes who would compete in the Olympic Games in 2012. Without question, the 2010 Asian Games, through the successful organisation of the event and the remarkable athletic performances, helped advance the international image, esteem and dignity of China as a nation, Guangdong as a province and Guangzhou as a city. But will there be a long-term price to pay?

Understandably, politicians, public and media looked at the Games from different angles. Central government officials put a special emphasis to the total number of Gold medals won by Chinese athletes; provincial government officials focused on the successful organisation of the Games and the image of Guangdong; Guangzhou was concerned with bettering its city rivals and demonstrating modern facilities, good services, efficient practice, openness to the media and local athletes' performances. Many residents, on one hand, supported the Games by participating or serving as volunteers, whereas on the other hand, some complained about the inconveniences caused by the Games. Praise for the Games was reported by most of the media, but there was questioning of the Games by the

Figure 12. The Guangzhou city at night. *Source*: *Beauty Places*, 'Guangzhou', available at http://beauty-places.com/guangzhou/ (accessed November 20, 2012).

parts of the media with a major concern being the appropriateness of the huge spending involved in the hosting of the Games. This involvement of both the cities and the media in a spirit of openness was perhaps a previously unconsidered positive development.

Beyond all doubt, the 2010 Asian Games provided a platform for Guangzhou to leap to prominence as an international modern city in the face of intense competition from the major cities of Tianjin, Shanghai and Beijing that were ranked as the top three in terms of per capital GDP in 2011. Guangzhou endeavoured to raise the 'index of citizens' happiness' and strengthen their sense of civic pride.[32] More than this, however, Guangzhou was a project backed by the national government as a shining symbol of a Chinese twenty-first century city – efficient, dynamic, indeed 'glittering' and of a new China: China Renascent.

This is dramatically expressed through the medium of powerful visual imagery (Figures 12 and 13).

The ambition of all concerned was to explode into the consciousness of the world, not least the Asian world, and to send an unequivocal message that Guangzhou was a totemic

Figure 13. The Games City. *Source*: *Sina*, 'Elegant Demeanor of Asian Games Venues: Guangdong Olympic Center', available at http://slide.gd.sina.com.cn/news/slide_17_2890_12846.html#p=2 (accessed January 19, 2013).

statement – both of present partial realisation and of future complete realisation: 'the Middle Kingdom' if not now then soon was to be reborn.

This essay is a verbal and visual depiction of the cosmopolitanism and confidence of the New China: word and picture meshed to demonstrate vividly the modern ascendancy of the 'Middle Kingdom'.

For as Ikinberry suggests, China 'emerges not from within but outside the established post-World War II international order, it is a drama that will end with the grand ascendance of China and the onset of an Asian-centered world order',[33] whereas Jacques goes further maintaining that

> The Western world is over; the new world, at least for the next century, will not be Chinese in the way that the previous one was Western. We are entering an era of competing modernity, albeit one in which China will increasingly be in the ascendant and eventually dominant?[34]

Was the Guangzhou Asian Games a harbinger of such things to come?

Notes on Contributors

J.A. Mangan, Emeritus Professor, University of Strathclyde, FRHS, FRAI, FRSA, D. Litt. is Founding Editor of *The International Journal of the History of Sport* and the series *Sport in the Global Society* and author of the globally acclaimed *Athleticism in the Victorian and Edwardian Public School, The Games Ethic and Imperialism* and *'Manufactured' Masculinity: Making Imperial Manliness, Morality and Militarism* and author or editor of some 50 publications on politics, culture, and sport.

Jinxia Dong, Ph.D. from University of Strathclyde (UK) in 2001 and a visiting scholar in Yale University, USA in 2009, is a professor of Peking University. She has published books and articles in both English and Chinese, including the world acclaimed *Women, Sport and Society in Modern China* and *The Olympic Culture: An Introduction.*

Di Lu obtained her bachelor's degree from Sun Yat-sen University, majoring in English. She is now a graduate student in Peking University for a master degree program in sports sociology. Her research interest is sport and gender. She was an intern for the Guangzhou Asian Games.

Notes

1. Beer, *Darwin's Plots*, 2.
2. Ebrey, *Illustrated History of China*, 7.
3. Ibid.
4. Chen, "Guangdong Reform and Opening-up," 9.
5. Ibid., 10.
6. *National Bureau of Statistics of China*, "Bulletin of the National Economic and Social Development in 2011," http://www.stats.gov.cn/tjgb/ndtjgb/qgndtjgb/t20120222_402786440. htm and *Statistics Bureau of Guangdong Province*, "Major Statistical Indicators of Guangdong Province from January to December in 2011," http://www.gdstats.gov.cn/tjsj/zh/gmjjzyzb/201203/t20120308_89666.html both (accessed January 26, 2013).
7. *Guangdong Statistical Yearbook 2012*, Section 3.
8. "City Blue Book" (*Baidu*, August 10, 2012), http://wenku.baidu.com/view/b80539cd050876 32311212b0.html.
9. Li, "Analysis of the Promoting Effects," 132–3.
10. Guangzhou, the capital city of Guangdong Province, has three specialised economic zones initially established in 1979 and has been the engine for the nation's phenomenal economic thrust forward.
11. "The Blue Book of the Competitiveness of Chinese Cities in 2011 Published, Hong Kong, Shanghai and Beijing Ranked the Top Three" (*China News*, November 20, 2012), http://www.chinanews.com/cj/2011/05-06/3021523.shtml.

12. *People's Government of Guangdong Province*, "The Audit of Financial Revenues and Venue Construction of 2010 Guangzhou Asian Games and Para Asian Games," http://www.gd.gov.cn/govpub/gsgg/201111/t20111125_152664.htm (accessed November 20, 2012).
13. Dong, *Women, Sport and Society*, 118.
14. "Zhang Guangning Details the Asian Games Cost" (*Nanfang Daily*, November 20, 2012), http://news.southern.com/d/2010-10/25/content_16978804.htm.
15. *People's Government of Guangdong Province*, "The Audit of Financial Revenues and Venue Construction of 2010 Guangzhou Asian Games and Para Asian Games," http://www.gd.gov.cn/govpub/gsgg/201111/t20111125_152664.htm (accessed November 20, 2012).
16. "The Mayor of Guangzhou: The Asian Games Will Leave Three Legacies and its Impact Will Match the Olympics and the World Expo" (*Sohu*, November 20, 2012), http://sports.sohu.com/20101013/n275606930.shtml.
17. *Guangdong Provincial Statistics Bureau*, "Guangdong Statistics Yearbook 2011," http://www.gdstats.gov.cn/tjnj/2011/table/4/c4-04.htm (accessed November 20, 2012).
18. *Statistics Bureau of Guangdong Province*, "Major Statistical Indicators of Guangdong Province from January to December in 2006," http://www.gdstats.gov.cn/tjsj/zh/gmjjzyzb/200701/t20070124_45459.html (accessed November 20, 2012).
19. "Guangzhou: The Status of National Central City is Laid Down and the Asian Games Generate the 5% of GDP Growth" (*China Economy*, November 20, 2012), http://www.ce.cn/cysc/newmain/pplm/qyjj/201011/17/t20101117_20544944.shtml.
20. "Asian Games Changes Guangzhou" (*China Daily*, November 23, 2010), http://www.chinadaily.com.cn/opinion/2010-11/23/content_11596951.htm (accessed November 20, 2012).
21. "Make the City A Green Card" (*Sun Yat-sin Library*, November 20, 2012), http://eelib.zslib.com.cn/ShowArticle.asp?ID=5238.
22. Chen, "Impact of the 2010," 28.
23. Ma and Zuo, "Study of the Economic Impact," 46.
24. "The New TV Tower is Officially Named as Guangzhou Tower" (*Oeeee*, September 29, 2010), http://www.oeeee.com/a/20100929/935165.html (accessed November 15, 2012).
25. Mangan, "Prologue," vii.
26. "China's GDP per Capita Reached US\$5,432 in 2011" (*Digitimes*, August 17, 2012), http://www.digitimes.com.tw/tw/dt/n/shwnws.asp?CnlID=&id = 0000298564_53G6BIG451D3TH5OIZ4LG (accessed August 30, 2012).
27. Burman, *China: The Stealth Empire*, 247.
28. Ibid., 248.
29. Jacques, *When China Rules*, 32.
30. Ibid., 8.
31. "Military Conflict looms between China and Japan" (*The Telegraph*, February 1, 2012), http://www.telegraph.co.uk/news/worldnews/asia/china/9571032/Military-conflict-looms-between-China-and-Japan.html (accessed August 10, 2012).
32. "Citizens Welcome Asian Games, and the Index of Happiness Is Estimated to Rise after Games" (*China Daily*, September 16, 2010), http://www.chinadaily.com.cn/dfpd/2010gzyyh/2010-09/26/content_11348116.htm (accessed August 10, 2012).
33. Ikenberry, "The Rise of China," 58.
34. Jacques, *When China Rules*, 433.

References

Beer, Gillian. *Darwin's Plots: Evolutionary Narrative in Darwin, George Eliot and Nineteen-Century Fiction*. London: Routledge & Kegan Paul, 1983.

Burman, Edward. *China: The Stealth Empire*. Barrie: The History Press, 2008.

Chen, Jiangling. "Guangdong Reform and Opening-up and the Upsurge of Chinese Specialist Socialism (Guangdong Gaige Kaifang Yu Zhongguo Tese Shehui Zhuyi Moshi Jueqi)." *Lingnan Journal*, no. 1 (2009): 9–12.

Chen, Jianhua. "Impact of the 2010 Asian Games on Guangzhou City Plan (2010 Nian Yayunhui Dui Guangzhou Chengshi Guihua De Yingxiang)." *Planner*, no. 12 (2004): 28.

Dong, Jinxia. *Women, Sport and Society in Modern China: Holding up More than Half the Sky*. London: Frank Cass, 2003.

Ebrey, Patricia Buckley. *The Cambridge Illustrated History of China*. Cambridge: Cambridge University Press, 1999.

Guangdong Statistical Yearbook 2012. Beijing: China Statistic Press, 2012.

Ikenberry, John G. "The Rise of China and the Future of the West: Can the Liberal System Survive?" *Foreign Affairs*, no. 1 (2008). Accessed November 26, 2012. http://www.foreignaffairs.com/articles/63042/g-john-ikenberry/the-rise-of-china-and-the-future-of-the-west

Jacques, Martin. *When China Rules the World: The End of the Western World and the Birth of a New Global Order*. London: Penguin, 2012.

Li, Fenzhen. "Juban Daxing Tiyu Saishi Dui Quyu Chengshi Jingji De Tuidong Xiaoying Sikao (Analysis of the Promoting Effects on Regional Economy by Hosting Large-Scale Sports Events)." *Commercial Times*, no. 14 (2011): 132–133.

Mangan, J. A. "Prologue." In *Sport in Europe: Politics, Class, Gender*, edited by J. A. Mangan, i–vii. London: Frank Cass, 1999.

Ma, Feixiong, and Liancun Zuo. "Guangzhou 2010 Yayunhui Jingji Xiaoyi Tantao (Study of the Economic Impact of the 2010 Asian Games in Guangzhou)." *Statistics and Consultancy*, no. 5 (2006): 46.

Chinese Desires? Olympism and Dominance, Guangzhou and Missed Opportunity, Major Leagues and Isolation on the Pacific Rim

John D. Kelly

Department of Anthropology, The University of Chicago, Chicago, IL, USA

Understanding the situation of China's self-promotion via Olympism requires us to connect two patterns. China is successful at Guangzhou and in Beijing Games at sponsoring and competing in Olympic-style sports festivals, but also surrounded by highly popular professional team sport leagues in baseball, rugby and cricket from Japan to India. China is successful in the promotion of its new capitalist economy but is critically short of energy sources and its aggressive diplomacy in pursuit of energy by land and sea has led to confrontations from Japan to Burma and even to the US 'pivot' to Asia. Review of theories of situation demonstrates that while a Debord-style spectacle theory might seem to explain the sporting spectacles and a realism in the tradition of Clausewitz might seem suited to the military situation, in fact approaches to situation combining realist and constructivist elements are stronger; a Deleuzian emphasis on will to power needs to be supplemented by Weberian attention to ends and ideas. Neither pattern explains the other; they connect. China makes history and its internal debates over state and middle class values can be tracked observing promotion of professional team sport in urban China and the scale of state sponsorship of Olympic-style games.

Introduction

Guangzhou, the 2010 Asian Games, was the best of times for China – or was it? China set all time marks for winning medals and for hosting events and participants at their fourth Asian Games. Careful management of unprecedented spectacle consolidated China's standing as unmatchable host as well as dominant competitor in Olympic-style events. But these games made space for professional team sports that are either excluded or banished from the Olympic movement, and this ambition made the situation more complicated.

The 2008 Olympic Gold medal-winning South Korean baseball team showed up and was very pleased to win Gold in open quest of military service exemptions. But the soon-to-be world-champion Indian cricket team declared that it had other obligations and did not attend. Weak cricket sides from Sri Lanka and Pakistan left the Gold medal to Bangladesh and the Silver to Afghanistan. In baseball, Japan (two-time World Baseball Classic (WBC) champion and dominant nation in the Asia Series) sent an inferior team and did not finish first or second. Attendance at baseball events, even those including China in the medal round, was miniscule. And play was not competitive until the final rounds; only 4 games out of 12 among the 8 teams in pool play avoided early termination under a 'mercy rule'. Finally, the Guangzhou Asian Games, as with the Olympic Games, had no full-sided rugby football competition and the rugby sevens involved only lowly ranking sides: Japan winning Gold in the men's competition and Kazakhstan in the women's.

The bigger picture bifurcates. While China elevates Olympism to new levels of public investment in spectacle, transnational venues for team sport club competitions effloresce elsewhere. The postcolonial global south inspires much of the best rugby in the world, now consolidated in the 'Super Rugby' premier league made up of teams from cities and urban neighbourhoods in New Zealand, Australia and South Africa, an ironic inversion of the British Empire. As Horton shows, Australia is attracted to the Asian sporting world.[1] But it also needs consolidated opportunities for major team sports and their massive fandom.

Meanwhile, cricket in the fan-friendly Twenty20 format centres increasingly in India, with its own Premier League and postcolonial story. The baseball played in Korea and Japan may be the equal of any in the world, Japanese eyes fixed squarely on competing with the Americans, with Korean eyes on the Japanese. Cricket has its own transnational champion's tournament connecting India, South Africa and Australia as hosts. And Major League Baseball (MLB) hosts a preseason 'World Baseball Classic', albeit against increasing Japanese resistance. While MLB thwarts a truly global postseason champions' tournament or premier league, nonetheless an 'Asia Series' has emerged connecting the championship clubs, now, of professional leagues in five nation-states, including China's. So, China dominates in Olympic sport and proudly displays its national pride within the rituals of Olympic internationalism. And it is hemmed in by increasingly international leagues of professional clubs in team sports: cricket to its southwest, rugby to its south and baseball to its north and east.

Our task is to situate this pattern in public sport, to track the relationship of events and structures, and not only for the sporting world. These Asian Games make global references and connect to global aspirations. In myriad aspects of their constitution, these games reflect and are affected by global politics. But what is really interesting is that they, also, have their effects: how and when sports make history. To understand China's efforts in the Guangzhou Games, their success and its limits, to pursue what China wants and how far it succeeds, we need to know how sports make history, and not just as they please. For this we need a strong approach to 'situations', and in situations the ability to connect meanings and powers not only within their own domains but beyond them. The situation of the Asian Games is not merely given to China, the way the rules of a sport are regulated for the teams by referees. This situation is constituted by China as well as for China. China sought out the games and invented much of the pageantry aspiring to the standing of ritual. Thus, the irony of our volume title, Asian Games in metaphor and reality. We study the political, social and cultural games in the Asian Games. But how do we frame the study, not of a people (a city, an ethnicity, a nation) nor an institution (a state, a corporation, a club) nor a system (e.g. cultural, social, linguistic or material) nor an event (a feast, a coronation, a war) nor even a thing (assembled, coherent, knowable) but rather a situation, which can heterogeneously involve all these but be fully defined or controlled by none?

There are two major approaches to the study of situations, but we can live wholly with neither. Guy Debord and his Situationists, aesthetic revolutionary post-Marxists, sought to overcome existential ennui and resolve the search for a method by adding deliberate embrace of the meaning-making power of spectacle to a revolutionary dialectical theory. To Debord the society and social movement as strong as they were could, and did, via spectacle, reinvent itself and its world.[2] Spectacle overcomes in the dialectical sense all prior restraints, as if China could constitute a hegemonic position by announcing one and winning the most. Debord's extreme constructivism (born to save the hope of revolution, remember, not to describe things as they regularly are) is the antithesis of the most developed approach to the definition of situations, that of the military following especially Clausewitz: the Clausewitzian premise of realism, finding situations in reality beyond all mere human conventions and definitions.[3] In its most extreme forms, preferred by the mechanically minded among realists, causalities are wholly material and events fully a function of contexts, as if China has no real choices but responds reflexively to the fatalities of its environment, needs, exigencies and resources. As if the swimmers, divers and gymnasts, but not rugby players or cricket players, grew on Chinese trees. Of course, even the trees in capitalist societies produce commodities by nature and also by culture, and are themselves products of deliberate cultivation towards goals both desired and possible. The study of actual situations requires more than extremes of realism or constructivism.

We might turn to Gilles Deleuze for a vocabulary, an approach finding things, sense and value connected to underlying flows and connections of force; 'the sense of something is its relation to the force which takes possession of it, the value of something is the hierarchy of forces which are expressed in it as a complex phenomenon'.[4] Or, if we dislike the Deleuzean and Foucauldian tendency to describe everything in flamboyant metaphors of force and war, especially because we plan to discuss the relationship of actual games to actual military force and war, then we can return to Max Weber. Where Deleuze sees forces behind meanings and values of things, to Weber ideal and material interests were the engines of history, but, Weber added in his famous metaphor, ideas like switchmen sometimes set the tracks.[5] Deleuze is right to focus on the constitution of complex phenomena he calls things, but Whorf was right to point out that 'thing' is a term of 'cosmic scope of reference' in standard average European grammar, that it is in that grammar, not in reality, that events are a kind of thing and not vice versa. Situations have an 'eventamentality' that does not readily reduce to a collection of things, even connected things in a single manifold; situations always also have a temporal texture and a connection of sites and, most frequently, wills that makes even concepts of underlying forces into a reification of events in train including ideas pursued and wills in dialogue.

Readers of this volume will get from all its chapters a sense of the Guangzhou Asian Games as an event. History in Asia is now being made in complex fields connecting ritual, capitalist culture and state self-assertions surrounding China's new ventures. To see, measure and contemplate China's effort to set new tracks, a good place to look is these sporting spectacles, not merely models of the forces behind them but models for what they seek to organise and direct. In global baseball, the US-based corporate consortium called MLB has gone a long way towards establishing its hegemony without dominance on the field.[6] Meanwhile, China is dominant and yet isolated, missing its opportunity to convert Olympic dominance into sporting hegemony. China in the Guangzhou Asian Games renewed the public proof of its Olympian dominance both in the Gold medal count and in the rituals of contest, but was still unable to sustain pre-eminence and control in public culture. In this light, the most important ongoing contest in global capitalist culture continues to be that between Olympism and its centralising spectacle, and professional team sports with their valorisation of the private in the public sphere.[7] And its most important venues continue to be Asian.

China's Energy and Its Hunt for Energy,
'Superficial Friendship' and 'America's Pacific Century'

So, What Does China Want? We will start with two very different answers from political scientists who teach in mainland China, then consider answers from Deleuzean first principles, before hearing what the Games tell us about themselves: that China wants to sustain the venues, in which China can win.

The last few years, David Zweig shows, a crisis is building in predictable consequence of an asymmetric and unstable energy situation.[8] Energy shortfall drives China to extreme and unwisely aggressive action, from Burma diplomacy to South China Sea bombast. Demand growing sharply, supplies insufficient and delivery routes plagued by piracy and 'warlordist' taxations, China moves to secure its own energy future by way of dam projects and closer control of the roads in Highland Burma, anti-piracy measures and extreme claims of heritage ownership of every island group and thereby all of the South China Sea. Sea-borne confrontations proliferate, rhetoric escalates, the Americans are drawn in and, Zweig finds, intellectuals in China are unnerved as, 'for the first time in decades, Chinese foreign-policy researchers see most of China's external problems emanating from its own behavior'.[9]

In the same years, then, of Beijing and Guangzhou triumphs, with rituals and contests declaring victory, arrival and greatness past, present and future, China has desperately sought oil, natural gas and other energy sources, and its intellectuals watch militarised South Seas policy with dismay. Zweig also tracks the newly aggressive counter-posture of the USA.[10] The US Secretary of State Hillary Clinton (at the high-water moment for the concept of 'pivot') published 'America's Pacific Century'.[11] This manifesto (1) redirected (pivoted) the US military away from expensive counterinsurgency fiascos in Iraq and Afghanistan, relabelling their failures not bombastic and bloody folly but poor prioritising in light of need for smart deployments in the more strategically significant periphery of China, and (2) answered rhetoric anticipating the decline of Pax Americana after the failures of ill-deployed US military, and the emergence of the new twenty-first century as China's century, with a (second) pivot, redefining the twentieth century not, as Luce had it, as 'America's Century', but instead as 'America's Atlantic Century'. 'We will need to accelerate efforts to pivot to new global realities,' Clinton had concluded in her October 2011 paper. 'This kind of pivot is not easy.' As Tsinghua University political scientists Yan Xuetong and Qi Haixia have recently detailed,[12] accelerate they did. By January 2012, US President Obama had issued under his own signature a new strategic defense guidance titled 'Sustaining U.S. Global Leadership: Priorities for 21st Century Defense', including both the news that the US army would no longer 'be sized to' conduct large-scale counterinsurgency operations[13] and that 'we will of necessity rebalance towards the Asia-Pacific region'.[14] And the USA did more than talk: in between these two papers, in November 2011, for the first time in its history it permanently stationed US troops in Australia.

As Zweig details, this new, US forward presence in Australia was a remarkable response to Australia's first significant show of independence of military mind towards the Americans.[15] Despite their record as the only independent nation-state in the world to join every US war coalition in the years of Pax Americana, including in Korea, Vietnam, Afghanistan and Iraq, the Australians withdrew from 'Malabar' naval war games planned for summer 2011 in the Indian Ocean and elsewhere. China had objected vehemently when, in 2007, the USA had expanded its bilateral US–India 'Malabar' war games to include Australia, Singapore and Japan as well as India. Thereafter, the USA and India reverted to bilateral, Bay of Bengal exercises, but in 2011 the USA again advocated multinational games, this time off the coast of Okinawa, and in February 2012 the largest ever, back in the Indian Ocean.

In light of China's uncompromising claims to own the South China sea, and on the other hand the US 'pivot' towards China and these encircling war games, Yan and Qi are not surprised by academic opinion predicting a new Cold War, or worse, between the USA and

China. They argue forcefully, however, for continuation instead of the current diplomatic posture of 'superficial friendship'.[16] Ironically for us, the two Chinese political scientists resort to sporting metaphor to conclude that US–Chinese relations are not on the verge of Cold War. The Cold War had enlisted client states in ramifying division and seemingly endless military confrontation; the new strategic quest for support and emulation builds international interrelations in economy, science and technology while competing for moral high ground: 'If we compare competition between the United States and the Soviet Union to a boxing match, we might compare that between China and the United States to a game of football. The former was characterized predominantly by violence, and whereas the latter will involve occasional conflicts, violence is not the primary means.'[17]

Yan and Qi's claim moves events from a Cold War fought metaphorically in an Olympic sport towards a new era and a team sport. But there are several obvious problems. First, Yan and Qi envision victory in enlistment of allies, which mixes metaphors since it implies growing the team larger, not winning the game in contest. Second, much as Foucault and Deleuze undermine our ability to conceptualise actual war, struggle and violence using force, strategy and deployment metaphors for all social relations, just so, we cannot study games in reality if we make politics, always, a game. Our ability to measure the significance of actual boxing, and Olympic rivalries generally, between the Soviets and Americans and the actual new premier leagues in Asian professional team sports are here swept into the undertow as pieces at best emblematic for 'comprehensive national power' in a 'strategic competition' between nations presumed, in typical political science realism, to be inevitable. If we do not make teams and games, their rituals and violence into metaphors for alleged inevitabilities of security, how shall we situate our Asian Games? Once we have separated the real games from the real guns, should our task be rendering one of the patterns of isolation for an active, triumphalist and waxing powerful China, hemmed in from Japan around to India, into the function, if not the metaphor, of the other? Should the situation of China triumphant in Olympic-style sporting championships, but hemmed in by burgeoning professional team leagues and champions, become a mere function or cultural expression of a security situation, the increasingly organised seaborne military encirclement? As an approach to situation, such an assertion of cultural dialectics is actually radically simplifying. Much too simplifying. It is a species of the theory of will to power that Deleuze criticises as Hegelian:

> What the wills in Hegel want is to have their power *recognized*, to *represent* their power. According to Nietzsche we have here a wholly slave's conception, it is the image that the man of *ressentiment* has of power. '*The slave only conceives power as the object of a recognition, the content of a representation, the stake in a competition, and therefore makes it depend, at the end of a fight, on a simple attribution of established values.*'[18]

In its extreme, this Deleuzian critique of cultural dialectics finds slave thinking even in diplomatic demands for the recognition of state prerogatives and attribution of established values. It would block any interpretation of Chinese Olympism as a quest for recognition in established terms. Alas, what Deleuze prefers instead is a distillation of Nietzsche into a vintage of Debord: an assertion of new values as the essence of will for-itself, a state like any other self not so much playing established games as pursuing new art for art's sake.

We could retreat to some other kind of reassuring, totalising cultural dialectic, perhaps a Gramscian variant reifying not desire of the master for recognition but that of the slave for resistance as an end in itself. We could figure the sporting events, the Guangzhou Games in particular, as commentary on the politics and economics of Pax Americana. But such an approach is problematic in two ways: first, as Sahlins has argued, such reifications of resistance are a species of functionalism with all its limitations, a power functionalism.

Second, more importantly, they make very little sense of the events themselves.[19] While there is an unmistakable element of insistence and ideological fragility in much of China's triumphalist ritual and discourse, almost as evident in Guangzhou and Beijing Olympic pageantry as it is in South China Sea diplomacy, the major articulation within Chinese Olympic triumphalism is triumph, the joy of victory in international competition. Whether or not games as a metaphor help us to understand the major moves of China's military and Chinese diplomacy (or even, whether assertion of inevitable political-economic, military or diplomatic games in reality gives us an actual political science), we can be certain *because we know about the Guangzhou Asian Games* that China likes to win as a nation in international competitions.

'One World, One Dream', slogan of the 2008 Beijing Games, was not only a bromide to please the IOC and a reversal, hidden to much of the visiting world, of a classic Chinese aphorism, 'one bed, two dreams'[20] on the 'more critical, less condescending' Japan-based response, including Farrer's own, to Beijing's 2008 competitive spectacle. It was also crystallisation of continuing desire among large and varied portions of the decision-makers who collectively act as China's state: not merely to play the games that they have to play, because they have to, nor to find themselves in the future, transcending and dialectically cancelling their past, a new work of ritual and art, but to connect past, present and future, and China to the rest of the world, by playing the games China wants to play. China, clearly, wants one world with one dream, a dream of competing with China, as China. It does all it can, not to survive a world of strategic competition among nation-states but to sustain one.

Zweig is entirely right that energy crisis poses China fundamental risks and obstacles.[21] But as Ruth Benedict pointed out in the 1930s, in *her* much more plausible critique of Nietzsche, it is neither the Apollonian nor Dionysian and certainly not their synthesis in the spirit of tragedy that Deleuze attempts to revive, that informs the love of games in contemporary capitalist culture.[22] Benedict borrowing also from Spengler called it Faustian, the structuring of self as finding value in struggle, meaning in obstacles and nemesis challenged and overcome.[23] Valorising this Faustian attitude is a critical part of *Pax Americana* and the neo-liberal American export of game theory, and its Chinese reiteration is no mere dialectical fulfilment or function of global capitalist exigencies, but a grounded, dynamic and dialogical response. Taking little part, despite its market making, in global Hayek–Friedman critique of regulation, China wants what it wants, states and their nations as global players. Thus the effort, as I have said largely unsuccessful, in Guangzhou is to enlist the major Asian and global team sports into pinnacle competition within the national, statist and Olympic competitive format.

To better understand, then, what China does not want, we need an excursus into a very different capitalist, sporting dreamworld. Baseball, as I have pointed out elsewhere, is not accidentally the first professional team sport, the first to organise private clubs into a professional league and also the last to organise, and to date, still, to organise half-heartedly, a high-level transnational championship between teams representing nations. Baseball had a real 'World Series' either first, or not yet, depending on how you look at it. So let us take a brief excursus, away from Guangzhou and into 'the country of baseball'. How easily and flatly how can flags and baseball mix?

Flags and the Sacred in the Country of Baseball

The problem with flags and baseball is not that either is an object with a developed sense of ritual proprieties, but that both are, not that one builds an environment of fundamental meanings, and demarcates them with ritual over-determination, but that both do. Both make surprising, situated claims to precedence at their sites, turning their sites into particular, even sacred places. Flags should not touch the ground, so should they touch baseball fields or players' faces or bodies, fans' noisemakers or clothing? What happens when baseball drapes itself with the flag? The question of the sacred is raised specifically in an online chat mostly among Asian-Americans, concerning patriotic incidents in the World Baseball Classics of 2006 and 2009.

MLB and its Players Association are the owners and organisers of the World Baseball Classic, a tournament for the best baseball playing nations. They attempt to frame their games in ritual, but only somewhat successfully. Their games begin with ceremonies, increasingly elaborate as the tournament proceeds, involving players and others, emblems, inflated globes, marching bands, a symphonic orchestra, and above all national anthems (and nation-like anthems) and flags. None of these ritual efforts have ever generated particularly excited public participation or discussion. Something else has, however: the Korean team's use of the Korean flag. After a key defeat of Japan in 2006, and again after defeating Japan in 2009, the Korean team dug into the dirt of the pitcher's mound and planted their flag in their post-game celebration. What does it mean? While several web discussions of the events are more active, my interest here is an objection to them raised by an interlocutor on Yahoo.com. On the website Yahoo! Answers, 'what was the flag thing about?' is still an 'undecided question'. Part of proposed answer number six particularly interests me: 'The whole point of that is that it is so insensitive and disrespectful to plant your country's flag on a (sacred) playing field of baseball.'[24]

In this view, what is sacred in the country of baseball is not the nation or its flag. A crucifix or a Buddha image might not have fared any better; consider what happens to 'John 3:16' signs held up in television range. Many have connected transcendent concepts to the green grass of the field in the ballpark: But more sacred than the nation, at least in its place? A contending principle of the sacred is in play. More than flags are tightly controlled inside the country of baseball. MLB more than other professional league has resisted allowing commercial emblems and slogans to visually dominate its venues, despite enormous counter pressure to seek advertising revenue from various kinds of emblems and billboards, and despite technologies making electronic product placement easier and more graceful. The grandeur of the playing field has a kind of timelessness (though not placelessness; every home park strives in fact for unique and self-emblematic features). It promises relaxation and green fields pleasure, justifying Donald Hall's localisation 'in the country of baseball',[25] including its resonating double sense of country (nation-state and rural scene). 'I don't care if I ever get back' goes the lyric of the famous song, 'Take Me Out to the Ball Game'[26] sung collectively by baseball fans during the seventh-inning stretch at many baseball 'parks'.

When national teams play, flags in the stands can express fervent affiliation and joy. Victory laps by teams led by a flag, or surrounding a giant flag, are commonplace in international sport, readily adopted at the WBC. The pitcher's mound was another matter. Most observers celebrated the exuberance when Korean players planted a flag after their upset of in 2006 (in a tournament eventually won by the Japanese). But as the gesture was expanded and routinised in 2009, a new squeamishness emerged.[27] Much commentary resembled that in the Yahoo chat room, wondering if somehow something had gone too far, flags and patriotism intruding somewhere different and differently sacred.

As MacAloon has shown, the Olympic movement integrated sports with national symbolism long before most other forms of international ritual were routinised.[28] The Olympic movement was strong enough and careful enough in its protocols for flags and national emblems, and defensive enough of its own international symbolism, that it even refused UN efforts to adopt Olympic emblems, especially the five rings, as the symbol for the UN when it was formed. The country of baseball, especially in its MLB-sponsored form known as 'Organised Baseball', has shown less interest until recently in integrating its logos, uniforms and rituals with national 'sacreds'. Of course, there is one ritual connecting baseball and the nation, the people-freezing, dutiful playing of the 'national anthem' at the outset of baseball games, after 9/11 extended many places to include also the song 'God Bless America' in the seventh-inning stretch – Dialectical synthesis? It often feels like paying a toll at the border of the more joyous country, with an exit marked by more carnivalesque music immediately following, often pop music in the first inning, and 'Take Me Out to the Ballgame' in the seventh.

From 'One World, One Dream' to 'I Don't Care if I Ever Get Back': The Guangzhou Games in the Dialogics of Global Capitalist Sport

Baseball: last to embrace a global championship of national teams, first to allow professionals and first to centre on leagues of professional teams representing cities. The Olympics: first to embrace nations and last to allow professionals: Nothing for cities except 'hosting'. Though the Olympic movement has abandoned its moral resistance to pay for athletes, it is worth reflecting on what made them the last to give in.

The glories of amateurism as a vehicle to gentlemanly virtues (in practice, a marker of gentlemanly leisure) had a much longer run in the British imperial sporting world than they did in the American. While twentieth-century MLB in the urban USA began to show what careful merchandising could do to increase the pleasures of the professional game and its parks,[29] British ambivalence and Whiggish triumphalism led, among other things, to limits on commercial development of cricket, cacophony in soccer and the split of rugby between union and league. Rugby provides the clearest depiction of an additional dimension: anticolonial significances. In rugby the global south rules. And it has always marked its hegemony by its own flamboyant and faux-autochthonous magic: the legendary All-Black haka, New Zealand rugby team appropriation and development of the traditional Maori challenge chant. New Zealand's travelling rugby teams have been performing hakas for more than a century. Pregame ritual hakas were established decades before any European or American sporting events opened with national anthems.[30]

Rugby was almost as dominated by the amateurist muscular Christian ideal as was Olympism and cricket. The split between League and Union in rugby in the United Kingdom, and the prestige of amateurist Union, led the virtual world championship to emerge in the Home Nations tournaments, which became the Five Nations, in reality in 1947 when rugby union resumed following World War Two.[31] With the entry of Italy in 2000 it, logically, became the Six Nations Championship. From the early 1900s rugby teams both union and league had toured and beaten the sides in Great Britain and France, but it was only with the establishment of the Rugby World Cup in 1987 that a true world championship was played; the inaugural was won by the New Zealand All Blacks, the second in 1991 by Australia and the third in 1995 by South Africa. It became impossible to deny that the founders of the 'game' were being beaten by the 'colonies'. Rugby union football formally became a professional sport in 1995 and with a form unique in sporting history: New Zealand, South Africa and Australia built their first fully professional teams as national teams, and it became impossible to ignore their quality in staging any world championship.[32] In 1996, the Tri-Nations tournament between the three great southern powers emerged to counterbalance the then Five Nations tournament in Europe. In 2012, Argentina joined to form 'The Rugby Championship' which now directly opposes the

European Six Nations competition.[33] In 1993, an inter-state/province (theoretically) amateur competition, the Super 10, was formed by the rugby unions of the three southern hemisphere powers and this has grown into the Super 15 championship and is the professional base for the national sides of Australia, New Zealand and South Africa.[34] With Argentina now playing in the Championship, there is talk of adding teams from Argentina, Samoa or Fiji, though this is difficult to figure financially.[35]

Thus, professional team sports emerged nationally in rugby, in this powerful settler colonist challenge to European domination. The haka made an uncanny claim to a different kind of substance, memory and masculinity. And professional play stabilised in a league of capital city and provincial clubs, much as Japanese baseball moved from a national team, for competition with US professional all-stars in the 1930s, into a permanent professional league by moving to urban and corporate sponsorship. Challenges to European and American hegemony in sports, East–West and North–South, have always involved both states and their missions and publics and their pleasures. But where are both, now, not only for China but also in China?

The question of the meaning of sports for fans, their uncanny centrality in urban public life, has vexed serious analysis because it is powerful but not serious. Sports scholars have proved much more insightful analyzing ethical dimensions of sport, starting with the extraordinary development of 'muscular Christianity' as an imperial ethic,[36] than they have with the vaudeville roots of 'Take Me Out to the Ballgame' and the uncanny importance of sport in urban leisure. In another, companion essay I will more fully pursue this urbanisation of desire.[37] Here, to conclude our reflections on the situation of the Guangzhou Games, I want to reflect on the implications of this complexity as we figure the dialogue really involved in these Asian Games.

My comparison with security diplomacy constitutes the key dialogue between state actors; Hillary Clinton is also talking to China by talking to her constituents about China. The Guangzhou Games attempted to 'talk to' cricket, rugby and baseball, but were marginally successful at best, principally because the Koreans really wanted their military exemption. The club championship formats still draw greater excitement. Meanwhile, the MLB league model has gone global as 'premier leagues' emerge first in European soccer and now in many major team sports. In the same motion they have gone Asian with alacrity and success. Observing this species of globalisation we need not forget the differences, also, between the sports, their histories and their postcolonial and other politics.[38] As we notice the differences between the sports and their centres, our sense of a simple, two-sided figure erodes, which is a good thing. Even better is to reconsider complexity of agency within China, state and society, commercial and public. In the end, the negotiations that will determine the significance of the Guangzhou Games and the routinisation of Chinese Olympism will happen in China, between various agencies constituting its state and those that actually constitute urban public life. What, after all, does urban China want? Efforts to expand professional team sport leagues not only surround them but also fitfully emerge in partnerships between Chinese and expatriate team sport entrepreneurs. Globally pre-eminent professional sports leagues, including IRB Rugby Sevens, NBA basketball and MLB baseball, have made significant efforts to set down roots, various ways, in urban China. While ownership structures remain a significant stumbling block, the prospects for articulation with, and resistance of, centralised state sporting spectacle remain. Amid glimmerings that China does want the kind of consumer middle class that makes premier leagues what they are, China's major sporting investments to date seem intent on elaborating and reviving Olympic-style imperium. Tracking Asian Games, more broadly, thus provides us with a unique point of entry into the changing structure of capital investment, the movements of middle class culture and even the fate of empires old and new. Some very interesting decisions are being made as China constitutes and consolidates its sporting institutions.

Notes on Contributor

John D. Kelly, Professor in Anthropology and the College at the University of Chicago, does research in Fiji and in India and highland Asia, on topics including ritual in history, knowledge and power, semiotic and military technologies, colonialism and capitalism, decolonisation and diasporas. Recent books include *Represented Communities: Fiji and World Decolonisation*, co-written with Martha Kaplan, *Anthropology and Global Counterinsurgency* (co-editor) and *The American Game: Capitalism, Decolonisation, World Domination and Baseball*. He publishes frequently in *IJHS* on global baseball.

Notes

1. Horton, "Guangzhou: The Asian Games and the Chinese 'Gold-Fest'."
2. Debord, *The Society of the Spectacle*.
3. von Clausewitz, *On War*.
4. Deleuze, *Nietzsche and Philosophy*, 8.
5. Weber, *From Max Weber*, 280.
6. Kelly, *The American Game*, 25.
7. Kelly, "One World, Real World, Memory and Dream," 2608–41.
8. Zweig and Bi, "China's Hunt for Global Energy," 25–38; David Zweig, "Spooked By China's Hawks? So Are the Chinese" (*Wall Street Journal*, November 11, 2010). Accessed January 7, 2013. http://online.wsj.com/article/SB10001424052748703848204575607752838513836.html and Zweig "Resource Diplomacy under Hegemony."
9. David Zweig, "Spooked By China's Hawks? So Are the Chinese" (*Wall Street Journal*, November 11, 2010). Accessed January 7, 2013. http://online.wsj.com/article/SB10001424052748703848204575607752838513836.html
10. Ibid. and Zweig, "Resource Diplomacy under Hegemony."
11. Hilary Clinton, "America's Pacific century" (*Foreign Policy*, November 2011). Accessed August 31, 2012. http://www.foreignpolicy.com/articles/2011/10/11/americas_pacific_century.
12. Yan and Qi, "Football Game Rather Than Boxing Match," 105–27.
13. *Sustaining U.S. Global Leadership*, 12.
14. Ibid., 8.
15. David Zweig, "Spooked By China's Hawks? So Are the Chinese" (*Wall Street Journal*, November 11, 2010). Accessed January 7, 2013. http://online.wsj.com/article/SB10001424052748703848204575607752838513836.html and Zweig, "Resource Diplomacy under Hegemony."
16. Yan and Qi, "Football Game Rather Than Boxing Match," 105–27.
17. Ibid., 127.
18. Deleuze, *Nietzsche and Philosophy*, 10.
19. Sahlins, *Waiting for Foucault, Still*, 12.
20. Kelly, "One World, Real World, Memory and Dream" and James Farrer, "One Bed, Different Dreams: The Beijing Olympics as seen in Tokyo" (*Policy Innovations*, August 28, 2008). Accessed August 31, 2012. http://www.policyinnovations.org/ideas/commentary/data/000079/:pf_printable.
21. Zweig and Bi, "China's Hunt for Global Energy," 25–38.
22. Benedict, *Patterns of Culture*.
23. Ibid.
24. "WBC 2006 Japan VS Korea," *Yahoo*. Accessed January 6, 2013. http://answers.yahoo.com/question/index?qid=20090318155153AAP9oWt.
25. Hall, *Dock Ellis in the Country of Baseball*.
26. *Baseball Almanac*, "Take Me out to the Ball Game." Accessed January 13, 2013. http://www.baseball-almanac.com/poetry/po_stmo.shtml.

27. It did not help that in 2009, one of the Korean players added a second, smaller Korean flag next to the first that his team planted on the mound, and told the media that it was for Dokdo, an island disputed between South Korea and Japan (who call it Takeshima). Korean and Japanese dispute over the island continues, further stressing East Asian maritime policies. See Martin Fackler, "Dispute Over Islands Reflect Japanese Fear of China's Rise" (*New York Times*, August 21, 2012). Accessed January 8, 2013. http://www.nytimes.com/2012/08/22/world/asia/dispute-over-islands-reflect-japanese-fear-of-chinas-rise.html?pagewanted=all&_r = 0.
28. MacAloon, *This Great Symbol*.
29. White, *Creating the National Pastime*.
30. The US national anthem was borrowed from the US military for the World Series in wartime 1918, before it was officially the US national anthem. One wonders if its role in baseball had something to do with the song's official future. And yet baseball crowds clearly prefer 'Take Me Out to the Ballgame,' the song that took over the seventh-inning stretch; duty before pleasure. The rugby haka; from its nineteenth century origins to their contemporary vicissitudes, connect much more closely to the actual games. See Luke Cyphers and Ethan Trex, "The Song Remains the Same" (*ESPN the Magazine*, September 8 2011). Accessed January 8, 2013. http://espn.go.com/espn/story/_/id/6957582/the-history-national-anthem-sports-espn-magazine.
31. Zakus and Horton, "A Professional Game for Gentlemen," 148–53.
32. Ibid., 142–98.
33. *SANZAR*, "About the Rugby Championship." Accessed February 10, 2013. http://www.sanzarrugby.com/therugbychampionship/about-trc/.
34. *SuperRugby*, "Super XV Rugby – Introduction." Accessed February 10, 2013. http://www.rugbyfootballhistory.com/superrugby.html.
35. *SuperXV*, "Super Rugby Expansion likely to Exclude Islands," January 27, 2013. Accessed February 10, 2013. http://www.superxv.com/news/super15_rugby_news.asp?id=37507
36. Mangan, *The Games Ethic and Imperialism*.
37. Kelly, "The Urbanization of Desire and Professional Team Sports."
38. Kelly, *The American Game* and Kelly, "Reason and Magic in the Country of Baseball," 2491–505.

References

Benedict, Ruth. *Patterns of Culture*. New York, NY: New American Library, 1934.
Debord, Guy. *The Society of the Spectacle*. Detroit, MI: Black & Red, 1970.
Deleuze, Gilles. *Nietzsche and Philosophy*. New York, NY: Columbia University Press, 2006.
Hall, Donald. *Dock Ellis in the Country of Baseball*. New York, NY: Simon and Schuster, 2010.
Horton, Peter. "Guangzhou: The Asian Games and the Chinese 'Gold-Fest' – Geopolitical Issues for Australia." *The International Journal of the History of Sport* (2013).
Kelly, John D. *The American Game: Capitalism, Decolonization, World Domination and Baseball*. Chicago, IL: Prickly Paradigm Press, 2006.
Kelly, John D. "One World, Real World, Memory and Dream: Shadows of the Past and Images of the Future in Contemporary Asian Sports Internationalisms." *The International Journal of the History of Sport* 27, no. 14–15 (2010): 2608–41.
Kelly, John D. "Reason and Magic in the Country of Baseball." *The International Journal of the History of Sport* 28, no. 17 (2011): 2491–505.
Kelly, John D. "The Urbanization of Desire and Professional Team Sports: Races, Nations, and Public Private Participation." Paper presented at IJHS/Yale University Workshop, September 14–15 2012.
MacAloon, John J. *This Great Symbol: Pierre de Coubertin and the Origins of the Modern Olympic Games*. Chicago, IL: University of Chicago Press, 1981.
Mangan, J. A. *The Games Ethic and Imperialism*. London: Frank Cass, 1986.
Sahlins, Marshall. *Waiting for Foucault, Still*. Chicago, IL: Prickly Pear Pamphlets, 1999.
Sustaining U.S. Global Leadership: Priorities for 21st Century Defense. Washington, DC: Department of Defense, 2012. Accessed August 31, 2012. http://www.defense.gov/news/defense_strategic_guidance.pdf
von Clausewitz, Carl. *On War*. Princeton, NJ: Princeton University Press, 1976.
Weber, Max. *From Max Weber*. New York, NY: Oxford University Press, 1946.

White, G. Edward. *Creating the National Pastime: Baseball Transforms Itself 1903–1953*. Princeton: Princeton University Press, 1996.

Whorf, Benjamin Lee. *Language, Thought and Reality*. Cambridge, MA: MIT Press, 1964.

Yan, Xuetong, and Haixia Qi. "Football Game rather than Boxing Match: China – US Intensifying Rivalry Does Not Amount to Cold War." *The China Journal of International Politics* 5 (2012): 105–27.

Zakus, Dwight, and Peter Horton. "A Professional Game for Gentlemen: Rugby Union's Transformation." In *The Games are Not the Same: The Political Economy of Football in Australia*, edited by Bob Stewart, 142–98. Melbourne: Melbourne University Press, 2007.

Zweig, David, and Jianbai Bi. "China's Hunt for Global Energy." *Foreign Affairs* 84, no. 5 (2005): 25–38.

Zweig, David. "Resource Diplomacy under Hegemony: The Sources of Sino-American Competition in the Twenty-First Century?." Lecture given at Vassar College, November 18, 2011.

Guangzhou 2010: Eastern Orwellian Echoes – Yang Shu-chun and a Taiwanese Patriotic Media Offensive

Chen-Li Liu[a], Ping-Chao Lee[b] and J.A. Mangan[c]

[a]Department of Sports Information and Communication, Aletheia University, New Taipei, Taiwan; [b]Department of Physical Education, National Taichung University of Education, Taichung, Taiwan; [c]Strathclyde University, Glasgow, Scotland, UK

> Taiwanese 'sports stars' have been receiving national media attention for over a decade. In particular, the so-called Honour of Taiwan has been especially celebrated: for the media they have epitomised the nation's strength, symbolised its self-belief and represented its self-assertion. This essay explores the Taiwanese media reaction to an incident at the Guangzhou Games involving the Taiwanese athlete 'super-star' Yang Shu-chun, which reveals another aspect of this media attention and exposes national jealously, distrust and dislike – sport seemingly a surrogate for political point-scoring.

Guangzhou: Contradiction!

Soft Power Misplaced

> A country may obtain the outcomes it wants in world politics because other countries want to follow it, admiring its values, emulating its example, aspiring to its level of prosperity...[1]

Democratic Implementation and Taiwan Media Expansion

Because Taiwan, formally known as the Republic of China (ROC), could not take a seat in the United Nations (UN), it was replaced by the People's Republic of China (PRC) in 1971. Most sovereign states switched their diplomatic recognition to the PRC, recognising it as the sole legitimate representative of the whole of China. Taiwan's expulsion from the UN led to an increasingly limited field of international relations. With the loss of Taiwan's UN seat, disrupting its previous relationship with the United States, and with the new president of the International Olympic Committee (IOC), Juan Antonio Samaranch, favouring China, the IOC decided to welcome the PRC back into its organisation in 1971. China's entry was, however, based on the proviso that the PRC would respect the Olympic rules and that Taiwan would not be expelled from the games.[2] Taiwan's Olympic committee was ultimately forced to change its name to the 'Chinese Taipei Olympic Committee' (CTOC) and to adopt a new flag and emblem in April 1981.[3] After compromises by both China and Taiwan and some delicate diplomacy involving major sporting nations within the IOC, the bitter dispute was eventually settled in 1979 when the

'Olympic Formula'[4] was devised to handle the 'Two Chinas' issue'.[5] To a considerable extent, the 1980s was a turning point in Taiwan's sports development. Taiwan was permitted to participate in international games hosted by non-governmental organisations under the 'One Country, Two Systems' formula proposed by Deng Xiaoping in 1982, which sought to mitigate poor relations with Taiwan and to 'create favourable conditions for reunification'.[6] However,

> one element of the world community from which Taiwan is certainly not formally excluded is international sport. The country's relationship with the Olympics, and with international sport more generally, has for many years been in circumstances chosen by others, specifically the IOC and the PRC, rather than by the people of Taiwan themselves.[7]

With martial law rescinded in 1987,[8] Taiwan has experienced significant change in politics, the economy and the media. Taiwan's regime transformed from an authoritarian single-party system to a democratic multi-party system. The economy began to grow rapidly, and Taiwan became one of the four dragon economies of Asia.[9] Furthermore, after the lifting of a newspaper ban in 1988 and the creation of an open policy on cable television in 1993, not only did the number of media outlets dramatically increase, but media practitioners were afforded far greater reporting freedom. Furthermore, since the Hong Kong-based tabloids *Next Magazine* and *Apple Daily* entered Taiwan in 2001 and 2003, respectively,[10] most of Taiwan's media has been engulfed into a tabloid whirlpool. Journalists, or paparazzi, have pursued celebrities, including major sports stars, for a long time. Over the past decade, many distinguished Taiwanese athletes, such as the pitcher Wang Chien-ming in the U.S. Major League Baseball[11], the tennis player Lu Yen-hsun[12] and the 'golf queen' Tseng Ya-ni,[13] have been acclaimed by the media as well as on the Internet. The media's role in broadcasting sporting events has led the Taiwanese to become ever more enthusiastically involved in the performance of its national delegations in international sport.

After its 'unpleasant experiences' in the 2008 Beijing Olympic Games (including the issue of the Olympic Torch relay passing through Taiwan, the marching order of Chinese Taipei in the opening ceremony and a much poorer performance than in the 2004 Athens Olympic Games), Taiwan's successful hosting of the 8th World Games and the 21st Summer Deaflympics in Kaohsiung and Taipei in 2009 made its citizens proud. Inspired by the positive circumstances surrounding these 'sporting successes', the Taiwanese anticipated improved performances by their athletes in the Guangzhou Games. The Taiwanese media routinely featured news of the Games in the lead-up to the event, although the story was not seriously covered in depth until four days before the Games' opening. This delay was due to metropolitan and municipal elections held on November 27, 2010, as well as the revelations of a financial scandal involving former President Chen Shui-bian's family members, particularly his wife, several Chen-appointed officials, and his business associates. All were charged with corruption.[14] This political scandal occupied most newspaper space. Coverage of the Guangzhou Games took a back seat.

Newspapers coverage of the Games began in earnest on November 8, 2010. The first crucial focus was on the *order* in which the flags were to enter the arena. Originally, the *Chinese Taipei* flag, representing the ROC/Taiwan, was to be alongside Hong Kong and Macau. This gave rise to Taiwan resentment and a protest by the CTOC, who argued that such an arrangement would be an insult to Taiwan's international status. After negotiations, the Guangzhou Games Committee (GAGC) stated that the marching order was an unfortunate mistake. The Taiwanese delegation was eventually listed in alphabetical order under 'T', based on the 'Olympic Formula', for entry to the sports arena at the opening of the Games on November 12, 2010. The second focus was on the expectation, fuelled by the Sports Affairs Council (SAC), that the performances of Taiwanese athletes would surpass their performance at the Doha Asian Games in 2006, at which Taiwanese athletes won more than nine gold medals.[15] The third focus was the expectation of the Taiwanese people that their athletes would break through the barrier of the disappointing results in recent Games that had taken place in China, such as the 1990 Beijing Asian Games and the 2008 Beijing Olympics.

The Taiwanese media provided clear schedules of events on television and in newspapers to encourage people to follow the results of the Games and to support the Taiwanese athletes. Ultimately, Taiwan won a total of 67 medals, which included 13 gold, 16 silver and 38 bronze medals; these results met the anticipation of the Games.[16] Regrettably, however, a renowned Taiwanese taekwondo athlete, Yang Shu-chun, was disqualified for cheating in the women's 49-kilogram category.[17] This resulted in an enormous controversy driven by the media. The provoked public vented its anger on South Korea and China.[18] After exploring the unfolding events of the incident, this essay analyses the Taiwanese media's fuelling of Taiwanese fury.

Guangzhou 2010: The Yang Shu-chun Incident

From the perspective of the Taiwanese nation and media the Games passed without incident prior to November 16, 2010. However an outrageous incident (as interpreted by the Taiwanese media and public) occurred the following day. When the Taiwanese Yang Shu-chun was competing in the first-round bout in the 49-kilogram category of the women's taekwondo competition, dominating the match with a 9–0 lead over her Vietnamese opponent, she was suddenly halted for an exceptional reaction from her sensor socks. This was discovered by a South Korean engineer from the electronic equipment manufacturer, who was asked to carry out a check by the technical committee, comprising a Korean-Filipino, Hong Sung Chon, and a Chinese, Zhao Lei.[19] They subsequently ruled that there had been a rule violation in Yang's use of the electronic sensor socks and that Yang would be disqualified for cheating. The unexpected setback astonished Yang She saw this as unacceptable. She defended herself, and although the head coach, Liu Ching-wen, also attempted to file a complaint, it proved fruitless. Yang broke down in tears and was unwilling to leave the arena with her coach Liu Cong-da, protesting the unfair ruling. Later, the World Taekwondo Federation's (WTF) Secretary-General Yang Jin Suk and Zhao Lei upheld the original judgment at an official meeting dealing with the 'banned' sensor socks Yang wore. They also implied that Yang had cheated and was dishonest.[20] The Chinese Taipei team responded by arguing that they had never received any notice from the WTF or the socks' manufacturer about banned electronic socks. Taiwanese journalists demanded clarification, but the official Chinese interpreter provided an incorrect translation of the request, which provoked a shouting match between Taiwanese and Chinese journalists. All the Taiwanese journalists then withdrew in protest from the press conference.

In accordance with the rules, each taekwondo athlete was to carry out pre-match equipment checks of his or her electronic protection with inspectors. When Yang was checked, the inspector asked her to change to a new pair of sensor socks, as the reaction of one of the sensor patches was not *adequate*. Therefore, Yang changed into a new pair with a sensor patch on each heel and passed the check. She was then led to the match arena by a guide. The chief referee asked the two competitors to test their footwear again and then demanded that Yang remove the two sensor patches stuck on her heels *before* the start of

Figure 1. Yang weeping and sitting down in protest after disqualification ruling. *Source*: authorised by an anonymous Taiwanese journalist.

the match. She complied.[21] In other words, during the match, she wore the socks without the patches on her heels. A member of the security staff, Liu Wan-li, who had been accompanying Yang, witnessed the whole process. Nevertheless, the WTF and the Asian Taekwondo Union (ATU) categorically insisted that Yang had taken off the sensor patches on her heels *during* the match.[22] However, in reality, all the photographs and video footage from the various Taiwanese mainstream newspapers and television channels accurately represented the circumstances and demonstrated the false ruling.[23]

On November 18, 2010, a startling headline, 'Shocking Act of Deception by Chinese Taipei' (see Figure 2), was displayed on the official website of the ATU, which accused Yang and the Taiwanese coaches of cheating, and announced the intention to ban them from the competition, and to investigate the Chinese Taipei Taekwondo Association (CTTA).[24]

The harsh statement not only invoked intense outrage on the part of the Taiwanese public and the media, but also motivated a hacker to invade the website and leave the message 'Shame on You' with photographs and videos to demonstrate that Yang did not deceive the officials. The ATU deleted the news report immediately.[25] In response to Taiwanese indignation, the WTF Secretary-General Yang Jin Suk held a second press conference and noted that no matter whether the permitted sensor socks were old or new models, Yang had stuck the two sensor patches in the wrong place, which had not been officially authorised by the WTF. Yang responded that if the socks had not been authorised, then how had she been able to pass two checks? Moreover, she had stuck the sensor patches behind the heels on the basis of official instructions. The Taiwanese public could not accept this distorted evidence and even many foreign journalists questioned Yang Jin Suk's contradictory explanation. The websites of *CNN, The Telegraph, BBC News* (ASIA-PACIFIC) and *ESPN STAR.com* reported Yang's event at that time. The *CNN news* presenter commented, 'It's a strange story' and 'That is most peculiar indeed'.

To avoid fanning the flames further, Yang Jin Suk conducted a third press conference on November 19, 2010 and said that the WTF would look into the incident after the Games. He

Figure 2. *Source*: Shot from Wikipedia (the news has been deleted on the ATU official website).

ultimately admitted that Yang Shu-chun had taken the sensor patches from her heels *before* the match started. He still presumed, however, that Yang was requested to take off the patches during the pre-match check and stealthily stuck them back on her heels when she entered the match arena based on video evidence that was provided by two witnesses. The Taiwanese team called for a confrontation with the witnesses and wanted to watch and analyse the video, but the Secretary-General of the WTF refused. Having amassed a substantial amount of evidence, the Chinese Taipei delegation and the Taiwan Sports Minister Tai Hsia-ling officially filed a complaint with the Olympic Council of Asia (OCA) and responded to the WTF's claims at a foreign press conference. The OCA official Haider Farman indicated that Yang Shu-chun was an honest athlete and that she would only have violated the regulation due to ignorance. The judgment seemed to be very harsh. Farman further argued, after watching the video, that the interpretation of the WTF did not match the evidence displayed in the video.[26] A Taiwanese manager from the 'LaJust' agency,[27] Tsai Chih-kai, showed an illustration of a complete set of electronic protection equipment and highlighted all the legal equipment certificated by the WTF. The electronic socks had been permitted until 2012 according to the International Taekwondo Regulations manual.

Finally, three representatives of the technical committee from Iran, Thailand and Lebanon were appointed by the chairman of the ATU, Lee Ta Chun, to investigate the case. The Secretary-General of the CTOC, Chen Kuo-yi, the Director-General of the CTTA, Chen Jian-ping, and Yang Shu-chun were asked to attend an inquiry on November 20, 2010. After the meeting, the three inquirers apologised for the overly zealous news coverage on the ATU's website but not for the disqualification.

Taiwanese Media Responses: Fury and Suspicion

The Yang incident provoked furious reaction in Taiwan. After the occurrence on November 17, 2010, the Taiwanese media – covered by the media worldwide incidentally – reported not only a stunned public but also considerable pressure on the Taiwanese team members directly involved in the event. This seemed to fit perfectly the profile of a struggle against a type of hegemony that usually embraces the cycle of conflict, communication and negotiation.[28] The official negotiators, however, seemed to the Taiwanese to be duplicitous! The Taiwanese media went to war. It played a critical part in the confrontation, but reporting content and style differed in each medium. Indeed, there was a wide use of symbols (semiotic language) – political, hegemonic and commercial. The following Taiwanese responses to the Yang incident present significantly different meanings.

A Struggle against Regional Hegemony

Gramsci argues that, 'the supremacy of a social group or class manifests itself in two different ways: "domination", or coercion, and "intellectual and moral leadership". The latter constitutes hegemony'.[29] He further notes that 'hegemony is the predominance obtained by *consent* rather than force of one class or group over other classes'.[30] The core of Gramsci's cultural hegemony lies in the ruling class engaging in the process of ideological struggle to consolidate its hegemony.[31] Thus, although South Korean and Chinese officials did not pursue their hegemonic ambition with force, they certainly urged others to accept their official authority and leadership in a struggle to consolidate their control in the ostensibly bizarre instance of the Yang Shu-chun Incident.

When news of Yang's disqualification broke in Taiwan, there was both anger and incredulity coupled with national suspicion born of long simmering resentment. Most Taiwanese felt instinctively that the incident had stemmed from a *conspiracy* involving the Chinese and Korean referees. For some time, the dominant position of Korean Taekwondo and the threat of the Chinese regime have profoundly troubled the Taiwanese.

Gramsci suggests that mass communications play a significant role in hegemonic struggle. The media embodies ideological interests.[32] Thus, it is not difficult to imagine the following headlines: 'Despicable Act! Chinese and Korean Referees collaborate to Kick Yang Shu-chun Out!', 'Korean Secretary-General of the WTF, Bull Shit!', and 'Korean Liar! Changeable Diction in 3 Days', with vivid cartoons (one shows Yang crying, another shows Yang kicking the WTF Secretary-General Yang Jin Suk and one, in particular, represents the Secretary-General as Pinocchio, indicating that he was a liar); all of these headlines appeared in the tabloid *Apple Daily* on November 18–20, 2010 respectively (see Figures 3, 4 and 5).

Further, in Taiwan those who supported the opposition party (the Democratic Progressive Party, or DPP) and were strongly opposed to China suggested that the controversial incident was a Chinese machination, as Yang had been a serious challenge to the Chinese taekwondo gold medal hope, Wu Jing-yu. It was rumoured that, to allow Wu Jing-yu to win the gold medal, Zhao would secretly sabotage Yang's chances of a win. Eventually, Wu did win the gold! On November 20, 2010, one headline in the pro-DPP newspaper *Liberty Times* read: 'Legislator: Chinese Technical Commissioner Protects Pupil with Disguised Trick'. An article in the same newspaper on November 21, 2010 stated that if Wu had not won the gold, Zhao's future as the Chinese Technical Commissioner would have been jeopardised. Zhao thus appeared to be the principal offender, with the Korean official as willing accomplice.[33] The generally pro-Nationalist Party newspapers *United Daily* and the *China Times* both remained fairly balanced in their coverage and refrained from using emotional or overblown rhetoric to slur the South Korean or Chinese referees but they took Yang's side.

As Althusser argues, the media has relative autonomy when permitted, exercising conscious choices and actions. Althusser is applicable here, given the present

THE ASIAN GAMES: MODERN METAPHOR FOR 'THE MIDDLE KINGDOM' REBORN

Figure 3. *Source*: 'Despicable Act! Chinese and Korean Referees Collaborate to Kick Yang Shu-chun out!', *Apple Daily*, November 18, 2010.

circumstances of the Taiwanese media.[34] Gitlin indicates that the media is part of a capital enterprise and does not usually challenge the essential advantage of the ruling system.[35] Hall considers the media to be an instrument of ideological reproduction, with its power to alter public opinion usually making it a dominant social force in ideological struggle.[36] He argues that media messages are primarily semiotic. Thus, it could be argued that the

Figure 4. *Source*: 'Korean Secretary-General of WTF, Bull Shit', *Apple Daily*, November 19, 2010.

Figure 5. *Source*: 'Korean Liar! Changeable Direction in 3 Days', *Apple Daily*, November 20, 2010.

Taiwanese media coverage, in general, of the Yang Shu-chun Incident was not a close coverage of the issue, but in reality rather a semiotic sign system, intended to deliver a specific message of national harassment and patriotic response as exemplified in this Taiwanese newspaper headline (see Figure 6).

Figure 6. *Source*: 'Korean Liar Spoofs! Taiwanese Do Yang Justice', *Apple Daily*, November 21, 2010.

Guangzhou and Internal Taiwanese Politics

Initially, the event involving Yang was purely a sports controversy. Nevertheless, it became a political wrestling match between the two main Taiwanese parties, the Kuomintang (KMT) and the DPP, and ultimately, was used to serve their own political interests. Immediately after the incident, the Deputy Minister of the SAC, Chen Hsian-zong, argued, at a press conference of KMT deputies in the Legislative Yuan [Taiwan's Parliament], that despite the protest of the Chinese Taipei team, the frustrating result had to be 'swallowed' or accepted.[37] Chen thought, since the ruling had been made, athletes should respect it but that SAC could ask for the ATU to re-investigate later. Because the incident had occurred at the international level, some DPP candidates for municipal mayoralties felt that Chen's position was questionable because, as a Taiwanese government official, they believed Chen should have defended his own athletes and refrained from commenting passively on the incident. Most people, including Yang's parents, indicated that they could not 'swallow' the insult. On November 20, 2010, the *Liberty Times* reported that the KMT candidate for mayor of Taipei City, Hao Long-bin, would be leading a march to support Yang's plight on November 21, 2010. The DPP candidates and some of the general public criticised the fact that the march was originally organised against anti-corruption, then for judiciary reformation, then as a Carnival and, finally, in support of Yang. The DPP, and others, believed that the KMT was using a cynical elective tactic by exploiting Yang; in other words, the main purpose of the march was to gain an electoral advantage. In contrast, the other three major papers (the *United Daily News*, the *China Times* and the *Apple Daily*) did not criticise the government. Instead, they highlighted the public's anger and the claims of the government officials. For instance, the headline 'The Fury of the Ruling Party and Opposition: This Is an International Joke!' appeared on the second page of the *Apple Daily* on November 18, 2010. The *United Daily News* ran the headline 'President Ma Supports Yang and Calls for Justice from the ATU' on page four two days later. As for the *China Times*, it published 'Sports Minister Tai Hsia-ling Strongly Protests against the ATU Trick' on the same day. What this illustrates is a sports controversy of national prominence reduced to an internal political push and shove for political advantage and sordid political advantage.

An Additional Influential Element: Internet Communities

Internet communities also exerted a substantial influence. The four main national newspapers all covered the consensus opinions of the public based on its Internet communities. When the news of Yang's disqualification was released, the fury of Taiwanese spread rapidly across *BBS*, *Facebook*, *Plurk* and *Twitter*. According to newspaper coverage on November 19, 2010, over 300,000 people signed their names through *Facebook* in support of Yang and urged that the government strongly protested against the immoral message of the ATU and pressured the WTF to apologise. Some even suggested refusing to watch South Korean dramas and boycotting South Korean products. Any English news of the Yang issue was also produced to make the international community aware of the truth. Others uploaded video frames of Yang's match on *YouTube*, which attracted over one million viewers. To an extent, all these reactions achieved a startling effect.

Dahlgren suggests that the Internet can play a function in the public sphere and provides the communicative space with a new interactive mode. This space is, however, a type of 'private publicity', not 'agora publicity'; Dahlgren terms this space an 'alternative public sphere'.[38] However, many argue that the Internet cannot become an ideal public sphere due to its fast turnover rate and propensity for simplification. More specifically, the Internet can lack serious, politically detailed and complicated arguments, and thus, reduces the quality of democratic rational debate. Hurwitz maintains that the Internet can be easily utilised by an interest group to sway public opinions. In other words, although the Internet offers a capacity to disseminate information, it is not an ideal platform for public exchange.[39] In the book *Republic.com 2.0*, Sunstein indicates that Internet communities will normally form groups pushing common and dominant views.[40] Alternative views get marginalised and democratic diversity is not adequately represented. Nevertheless, this Internet solidarity is a powerful modern influence.

Taiwanese Hostility Towards South Korea

Taiwanese hostility to China needs no explanation. The two nations essentially remain in sharp political confrontation: a democracy state head-to-head with a despotic state – which claims it. However, why did the Taiwanese strongly protest against South Korea? There are three main reasons. First, taekwondo originated in Korea and has been promoted by Koreans abroad. Not surprisingly, the major positions of the ATU and the WTF are filled by South Korean nationals. South Korea is the main source for referees at international taekwondo matches and is thus in a position to manipulate competitions, making many countries question their fairness. In previous years, taekwondo controversies involving Taiwanese or other foreign competitors confronted by South Korean referees or recorders have occurred.[41] In the 2009 Hong Kong East Asian Games, for example, a Korean male taekwondo athlete made an improper hit against the Taiwanese competitor Tseng Jing-hsiang's neck. Tseng had to be taken to hospital for treatment. However, the South Korean arbitration committee felt that it was a legal hit and gave victory to the South Korean. A similar dispute happened in the 2002 Busan Asian Games, South Korea. Chu Mu-yen, a Taiwan outstanding male taekwondo athlete, dominated a South Korean rival. Nonetheless, the South Korean referee ruled unexpectedly that the Korean athlete was the victor. This, and other similar disputes, had already influenced the Taiwanese perception of the Korean hierarchy.

Second, Taiwan and South Korea have a similar historical background in terms of both politics and the economy. Both were Japanese colonies and were two of the four small economic dragons in the 1970s and 1980s. South Korea has viewed Taiwan as a competitive rival and at times has been 'unfriendly' to Taiwan in diplomacy, commerce and sport. Thus, the relationship between Taiwan and South Korea has always been tense. This explains why the Taiwanese become so emotional about South Korea whenever these controversies occur.[42]

Third, South Korean cultural products have been 'invading' Taiwan since the late twentieth century with a profound influence on Taiwanese lives and bringing economic benefits to South Korea. Due to the Yang incident, the public refused to watch South Korean dramas or sport, or eat Korean food. Some technology and computer stores refused to sell Korean products. The business of Korean travel agencies was reduced by almost half. Many in show business declared their support for Yang and their anger towards South Korea. Some called for a collective boycott of Korean artists. The most-publicised protest came when someone threw eggs at the gate of a Korean school in Taipei on November 20, 2010. The next day, a headline in the *Apple Daily* read: 'Korean School Washed with Eggs, Parents Are Uneasy' (see Figure 7). In addition, most television channels covered the Incident.

Figure 7. *Source*: 'Korean School Washed with Eggs, Parents are Uneasy', *Apple Daily*, November 21, 2010.

The Minister of Foreign Affairs released a message calling on Taiwanese protesters to calm down and act rationally, as this controversy did not relate to the South Korean government or the Korean people; it was simply a problem related to the referees. In general, the Taiwanese public condemned any violent protest.[43] This wider public reaction arguably did not receive sufficient affection – for two good reasons: it was not newsworthy and it was not in accord with the patriotic purposes of the media!

In a liberal democracy, theoretically, individuals have the freedom to freely express their ideas and opinions. However, given the current commercialisation of the media, political debate in the public sphere is gradually collapsing. As Habermas argues, 'the public sphere became a field for business advertising, with the transformation of the public sphere into a medium of advertising met halfway by the commercialisation of the press'.[44] In accounts of Taiwanese anger towards South Korea, the media amplified reaction with sensationalist coverage to increase sales, thereby stimulating the public to direct a fierce hostility towards South Korea. Habermas also advocates the concept of 'communicative rationality'. Any effective communicative action must satisfy four efficient claims: the comprehensibility claim, the truth claim, the rightness claim and the truthfulness claim. In the process of communication, both sides must acknowledge these efficient claims to achieve mutual understanding.[45] However, for the Taiwanese public, it seems to be difficult to reach an 'ideal communication situation'. In short, it is difficult to practise communicative rationality with a media that indulges in distorted communication. Nevertheless, the Taiwanese media was undoubtedly tapping into a flow of national resentment towards both China *and* South Korea. It channelled and increased the flow effectively combining patriotism with effective commercialisation.

Conclusion: The Ideal and the Real

In an ideal political world, sport, arguably, should promote political animosity although being an exciting friendly competition. This seldom happens: sport is often an extension of antipathetic political, historical and economic attitudes born of the past and the present and shaping the future.

At the Guangzhou Games a classic case-study was created. It set the Taiwanese against the Chinese and the South Koreans. The Yang Shu-chun Incident is the clearest evidence of the propensity for future East Asian nations – with the West almost off their backs imperially – to project their animosity more effectively towards each other.

Modern sport offers the opportunity to revitalise old as well as reflect modern grudges. As sport becomes more and more significant as a manifestation, demonstration and declaration of national pride, national capacity and national superiority, the East Asian nations will become more acerbic towards each other in regional and international sports events. And doubtless the media will lead the charge as nations clash in efforts to display the supremacy of their political, economic and cultural systems.

Post-Script: A Penchant for Controversy

The 2010 Guangzhou Games ended: Yang's capacity for provoking controversy continued. Yang's three-month ban from competition did not take effect until the conclusion of the games due to the final ruling of the WTF in 2011. Then she went on to capture the silver medal at the 2011 World Taekwondo Championships in Gyeongju, South Korea, in May. On July 2011, Yang finished third in a world qualifying competition to secure a place at the 2012 London Olympics. She was one of the first Taiwanese taekwondo athletes to qualify for the Olympics.[46]

The Taiwanese hoped for victories from their athletes, particularly from the 'Honour of Taiwan', at the 2012 London Olympics. Unfortunately, Yang was knocked out by a Thai opponent in the second round in London, which shocked and disappointed the Taiwanese. It gave rise to yet another controversy: Why has she done so badly? Another celebrated case-study resulted, but this time provoking internal national confusion and irritation.[47]

Coubertin was well and truly dated. It was not the 'the taking part' that mattered but the successful taking part! For a long time, of course this had been the reality. This reality will become more and more significant in East Asia. In the decades ahead much will be expected of the nations by public and media with the coming East Asian Epoch.

Notes on Contributors

Chen-Li Liu is an Assistant Professor in the Department of Sports Information and Communication, Aletheia University. Her research interest includes the issues on tabloidisation, media ethics and broadcasting.

Ping-Chao Lee is Professor of the Department of Physical Education at National Taichung University of Education in Taiwan. He has published papers in leading sport journals such as *European Sport Management Quarterly*. His current research interests include sport politics and the field of the governance of professional baseball in Asia.

J.A. Mangan, Emeritus Professor, University of Strathclyde, FRHS, FRAI, FRSA, RSL, D.Litt. is Founding Editor of *The International Journal of the History of Sport* and the series *Sport in the Global Society* and author of the globally acclaimed *Athleticism in the Victorian and Edwardian Public School, The Games Ethic and Imperialism* and *'Manufactured' Masculinity: Making Imperial Manliness, Morality and Militarism* and author or editor of some 50 publications on politics, culture, and sport.

Notes

1. Joseph Nye, quoted in Ferguson, *Colossus*, 19.
2. Hill, *Olympic Politics*, 161–3.

THE ASIAN GAMES: MODERN METAPHOR FOR 'THE MIDDLE KINGDOM' REBORN

3. Liu and Tsai, "President of International Olympic Committee."
4. Liu, "Study of Signing of Lausanne Agreement."
5. Chan, "From 'Olympic Formula' to Beijing Games."
6. Yu and Mangan, "Dancing Around the Elephant," 831–2.
7. Bairner and Hwang, "Representing Taiwan," 2.
8. When the Nationalist Party (KMT) was defeated by the Chinese Communist Party (CCP) and retreated to Taiwan in 1949, the KMT's leader Chiang Kai-shek declared *Martial Law* to confront an unstable domestic situation, rooted in the native Taiwanese population's continuing resentment of the February 28, 1947 incident and its aftermath, and the tense international situation then followed the onset of the Cold War.
9. In the 1970s and 1980s, the economy of Taiwan, Korea, Singapore and Hong Kong had dramatically risen, hence they were called the Asian four dragons.
10. The owner of the Hong Kong *Next Media* is Mr Li Chi-ying. He invested a substantial sum in launching Taiwanese versions of *Next Magazine* and *Apple Daily*.
11. Wang Chien-ming had been an ace pitcher for the New York Yankees in 2006 and 2007, winning 19 games in both years in the American League.
12. Lu Yen-hsun is a Taiwanese best tennis player and has a long-term title of number one in Asia. He created astonishing play at Wimbledon in 2010 and became the first Taiwanese player to advance to the quarter-finals of a Grand Slam.
13. Tseng Ya-ni was the youngest female golfer, at 23, to win the four major LPGA championships and currently ranks number one in the Women's World Golf Rankings.
14. Gold, "Taiwan in 2009."
15. Taiwan won nine gold medals in the 2006 Doha Asian Games, so the Sports Affairs Council expected that its athletes were able to surpass the results.
16. *Liberty Times*, November 28, 2010; *China Times*, November 28, 2010; *Apple Daily*, November 28, 2010.
17. The brilliant female Taiwanese taekwondo athlete, Yang Shu-chun, has been one of the best 49-kilogram level taekwondo athletes in the world in recent years. Many top-notch talents regarded her as an admirable opponent. With Taiwanese anticipation, she was most likely the person to win the first gold medal in the taekwondo match.
18. Because Taiwanese athletes had been treated unjustly by South Korea and China in various sports events, the Taiwanese vented their anger on these nations.
19. *United Daily News*, November 18, 2010; *China Times*, November 18, 2010; *Liberty Times*, November 18, 2010; *Apple Daily*, November 18, 2010.
20. Ibid.
21. *Apple Daily*, November 19, 2010; *China Times*, November 19, 2010; *Liberty Times*, November 18, 2010; *United Daily News*, November 19, 2010.
22. *Liberty Times*, December 18, 2010.
23. *China Times*, November 18, 2010; *United Daily News*, November 19, 2010; *Apple Daily*, November 18, 2010; *Liberty Times*, November 18, 2010; "Dirty Taekwondo 2010", *eProMotor Blog*, November 19, 2010. http://backtrue.pixnet.net/blog/post/27647825 (accessed June 21, 2011).
24. *Apple Daily*, November 19, 2010; *United Daily News*, November 20, 2010; *Liberty Times*, November 20, 2010; *China Times*, November 21, 2010.
25. Ibid.
26. *China Times*, November 19, 2010; *Liberty Times*, November 20, 2010.
27. 'LaJust' Sports, a manufacturer of Electronic Protection Gear, was designated by the 2010 Guangzhou Asian Games.
28. Chang, *Critical Communication Theory*, 85.
29. Femia, *Gramsci's Political Thought*, 24.
30. Ibid.
31. Chang, *Critical Communication Theory*, 86.
32. Ibid., 87, 95.
33. *Liberty Times*, November 23, 2010.
34. Chang, *Critical Communication Theory*, 88.
35. Gitlin, *Whole World Is Watching*, 258–9.
36. Hall, "Culture, Media, and Ideology Effect," 346.
37. The Chinese literal meaning of 'swallowed' here refers to 'To accept reluctantly without saying words/complaints'.

38. Yang, "Meaning of Internet Publics," 128–50.
39. Liu, "Rethinking the Role of Public Sphere," 56–7.
40. Sunstein, *Republic.com 2.0*, 49–51.
41. *China Times*, November 24, 2010.
42. Ibid.
43. *China Times*, November 19, 21, 23, 24, 2010; *Apple Daily*, November 19, 20, 21, 24, 2010; *United Daily News*, November 21, 2010.
44. Habermas, *Structural Transformation of Public Sphere*, 189.
45. Habermas, *Theory of Communicative Action*, 10, 22; Huang, "Jürgen Habermas," 133.
46. Lee and Wu, "Taiwanese Taekwondo Star Qualifies for London Olympics."
47. The Taiwanese thought Yang would secure a gold medal at the London Olympics, but she was beaten in the second round. The former Sports Minister Tai Hsia-ling Tai was disappointed with Yang's performance. She commented that the taekwondo athletes were treated as "diamonds" by the government but Yang seemed to not make an effort in the Games. She was asked to step down by the Taiwanese lawmaker Yang Ying-hsiung, as her comment was criticised to be incorrect and inappropriate. For details see *United Daily News*, August 11, 2012; *United Daily News*, August 12, 2012.

References

Althusser, L. *Ideology and Ideological State Apparatuses: Lenin and Philosophy and Other Essays*. London: New Left Books, 1971.

Bairner, A., and D. J. Hwang. "Representing Taiwan: International Sport Ethnicity and National Identity in the Republic of China." *International Review for the Sociology of Sport* 46, no. 3 (2011): 231–248.

Chan, G. "From the 'Olympic Formula' to the Beijing Games: Towards Greater Integration Across the Taiwan Strait." *Cambridge Review of International Affairs* 15, no. 1 (2002): 141–148.

Chang, J. H. *Critical Communication Theory: From Disarticulation to Subject*. Taipei: Li Ming, 2010.

Femia, J. V. *Gramsci's Political Thought: Hegemony, Consciousness, and the Revolutionary Process*. Oxford: Clarendon, 1981.

Ferguson, Niall. *Colossus: The Rise and Fall of the American Empire*. London: Penguin, 2009.

Gitlin, T. *The Whole World is Watching: Mass Media in the Making and Unmaking of the New Left*. Berkeley: University of California Press, 1980.

Gold, T. B. "Taiwan in 2009: Eroding Landslide." *Asian Survey* 50, no. 1 (2010): 65–75.

Habermas, J. *The Theory of Communicative Action*, Vol. 1. Translated by T. McCarthy. Boston: Eacon, 1984.

Habermas, J. *The Structural Transformation of the Public Sphere: An Inquiry into a Category of Bourgeois Society*. Translated by Thomas Burger. Cambridge: MIT Press, 1989.

Hall, S. "Culture, the Media, and Ideology Effect." In *Mass Communication and Society*, edited by J. Curran, M. Gurevitch, and J. Woollacott, 315–348. Beverly Hills, CA: Sage, 1977.

Hill, C. R. *Olympic Politics: Athens to Atlanta 1896–1996*. Manchester: Manchester University Press, 1996.

Huang, R. C. "Jürgen Habermas: Master of Social Critical Theory." *United Monthly* 71, no. 4 (1982): 128–135.

Lee, Yu-cheng and Sofia Wu. "Taiwanese Taekwondo Star Qualifies for London Olympics." *Focus Taiwan News Channel*. Available at http://forcustaiwan.tw/ShowNews/WebNews_Detail.aspx?Type=aSPT&ID=201107030003 (accessed July 3, 2011).

Liu, C. P., and J. S. Tsai. "The President of International Olympic Committee Who Improved the Commonly Called 'Olympic Formula': Juan Antonio Samaranch." *Bulletin of Physical Education* 18 (1994): 47–56.

Liu, H. W. "Rethinking the Role of Public Sphere on Internet: A Phenomenological Perspective." *Mass Communication Research* 97 (2008): 45–81.

Liu, H. Y. "A Study of Signing of Lausanne Agreement between IOC and Chinese Taipei." *Sports Studies* 1 (2007): 53–84.

Sunstein, C. R. *Republic.com 2.0*. Princeton: Princeton University Press, 2007.

Yang, Y. J. "The Meaning of Internet Publics: Publics, Public Sphere and Deliberative Communication." *Chinese Journal of Communication Research* 14 (2008): 115–167.

Yu, J. W., and J. A. Mangan. "Dancing around the Elephant: The Beijing Olympics – Taiwanese Reflections and Reactions." *The International Journal of the History of Sport* 25, no. 7 (2008): 831–835.

From Honeymoon to Divorce: Fragmenting Relations between China and South Korea in Politics, Economics – and Sport

J.A. Mangan[a], Sun-Yong Kwon[b] and Bang-Chool Kim[b]

[a]*Strathclyde University, Glasgow, UK;* [b]*Department of Physical Education, Seoul National University, Seoul, Republic of Korea*

> This is an analysis of two East Asian Nations, South Korea and China, and a descent from growing friendship to growing friction in economics, politics and sport – with sport as an analogue of fragmentation and the Guangzhou Asian Games as an analogous illustration of crescive tension between the two nations in economics, politics and sport in the twenty-first century.

In this article – an exploration of declining relationships between South Korea and China – the Guangzhou Asian Games will be considered as an analogue for a wider set of associations, political and economic: in short, an allusive exemplar. Interaction through sport will be held up as a mirror reflecting increasing fractious contact between the two close neighbours with incidentally, in the distant past, a bitter history of *direct* military confrontation and in the recent past, a crescive bitter history of *indirect* confrontation.

The history of Korea is commonly divided into three periods: traditional (2333 BC–1910), colonial (1910–1945) and modern (since 1945):

> In the first phase of Korean history, it is believed that Gojoseon (2333 BC–1122 BC) was the first united kingdom founded by Dangun circa 2333 BC in Liaoning Province in Manchuria – later its capital was moved to Asadal, Pyeongyang in North Korea ... This ... unified kingdom did not last long ... *Gijajoseon was invaded and colonized by the Han dynasty of China in 108 BC. This Chinese imperial domination of the northern part of Korea lasted nearly for 400 years.*[1]

Later:

> in the sixth century, after the period of Chinese colonization three kingdoms came into being in the territories formally occupied by the Goguryeo in the north, Baekjae in the southwest and Silla in the southeast of the peninsula. Allied Silla with Chinese Tang Dynasty unified the peninsula circa 668 AD. Silla's unification of the peninsula brought about the popularization of Chinese culture.[2]

Resonances associated with both moments are still heard in South Korea. The South Korean people have long memories. China remains a looming political threat. The threat is now hegemonic, not colonial.

Mutual Accord and Mutual Benefit: Two Modern Dynamic East Asian Economies

The coming together of the economies of South Korea and China for mutual benefit is recent. Even with China's implementation of an open-door policy in the late 1970s,[3] a lack of formal diplomatic Sino-Korean relations meant that trade was limited and had to be conducted indirectly via Hong Kong or Japan. Direct Sino-Korean trade only started in 1992 after the establishment of formal diplomatic relations. A new chapter of bilateral economic relations commenced. Sino-South Korea trade annually increased, and in 2003, China became Korea's most important trading partner. Substantial trading is facilitated by geographical proximity, China's massive market opportunities and rapid economic growth. Sino-South Korea trading has emerged as a crucial factor in determining the significant shift in Sino-South Korea relations and has significantly affected the unstable, hostile relationship between the two Koreas – South and North.

A set of carefully orchestrated events contributed to the transition from political coolness and economic competition in the 1980s to political warmth and economic cooperation in the 1990s. These events were associated with the 10th and 11th Asian Games, in Seoul and Beijing respectively, which came in the wake of a confluence of geopolitical factors (the end of the Cold War, the end of Sino-Soviet split) as well as domestic factors (zero-sum diplomacy with North Korea and Taiwan, mutual economic complementarities), all of which inclined Seoul and Beijing to improve relations.[4]

> The two summer Asiads were scheduled to be held in 1986 in Seoul and in 1990 in Beijing. For Seoul, the Games were effectively a dress rehearsal for the 1988 Olympics ... Seoul wanted to ensure maximum participation for the Olympics after the boycotts in 1980 and 1984, so the effort started with ensuring maximum participation at the 1986 Asiad from countries across the Cold War divide. The organizing committee lobbied China to send a large delegation. The plan was for the Chinese officials and athletes to come to Seoul, perform well in the competition, and generally have a good time. Through this experience, broadcast throughout Asia, the Asiad could build goodwill and change Chinese and South Korean popular perceptions, which were largely antagonistic.[5]

The orchestration worked smoothly with the result that the Chinese were won over:

> China ended up having the largest delegation at the Games. The Chinese team performed well, tallying the most gold medals (ninety-four) and coming in second in the total medal count (to the South Korea hosts). Visiting athletes and officials praised the Koreans' hospitality and friendliness. Visiting dignitaries, moreover, returned to China with a newfound respect and interest in Korea's modernization.[6]

The green light was given to portray the new nation of South Korea, attractively – and positively – by the Chinese authorities. As one commentator reported:

> Chinese government-run media outlets gave glowing commentary on the way Korea had combined Western modernity with Confucian traditions. The Communist Party journal *Hongqi* (Red Flag) and the prestigious literary journal *Renmin Wenxue* (People's Literature) were awash with lengthy observations of the Seoul Asia.[7]

The Chinese media was flattering, praising 'the neatness and modernity of Seoul, the bustling South Gate market, the majesty of Kyungbok Palace, the modern facility of *Chungang Ilbo* (a major South Korean newspaper), and the beautiful students at Ewha Women's University'.[8]

An affluent image of South Korea in general, and Seoul in particular, was projected in significant contrast to the poverty-stricken North Korea and its capital. The Northern government was incensed. *No matter*. What did matter was that both South Korea and China had taken 'an important step in building political goodwill to complement the burgeoning economic interactions taking place at the time'.[9]

There was mutual advantage. Both had sound economic reasons for improving political relations:

> China badly needed South Korean capital and technology and was intrigued by the South Korea's model of economic development, which focused on capitalist export-oriented growth without giving up political control. This 'strong state' model of development practiced by Korea in the 1970s and 1980s offered much to Deng's modernization program. Conversely, the South Korea saw in China cheap labor and a large export market, particularly as it faced growing protectionist sentiment in traditional markets like the United States. Improved economic relations would benefit both countries in terms of trade – the South Korea from the import of Chinese mineral resources (coal, petroleum) and agricultural and fishery products, and China South Korean electronics, consumer goods, and textiles.[10]

An economic 'honeymoon' between the two nations resulted. Like most 'honeymoons', it was to be short. To consolidate relations, South Korea fully supported the Beijing Asian Games four years later. Indeed, in doing so, it went out of a geopolitical limb! And:

> against the climate of international opinion, [helped] support Beijing's preparations for the Games. While the United States, Japan, and the European Union imposed sanctions, the Roh [South Korean] government displayed a pronounced ambivalence to the international campaign against China and tried to use the opportunity to expand political and economic cooperation.[11]

South Korea 'lavished every manner of assistance on Beijing'[12]: financial, technical, logistical *and* political. No stone was left unturned in its effort to woo the Chinese into a long-term economic 'marriage':

> President Roh personally lobbied Asian leaders, many of whom he had just hosted for the Seoul Olympics, to avoid ... a boycott of Beijing's Asian Games because of Tiananmen. More than 22,000 South Korean tourists came to Beijing for the Games. The Korean conglomerate Hyundai and other carmakers donated more than 400 vehicles to China for the transport of athletes and officials at the Games. The South Korea provided assistance to Chinese tourist industries that had been adversely affected by Tiananmen, and Korean companies provided over $15 million in advertising revenues. Three major *chaebol* conglomerates in Korea, Samsung, Lucky-Goldstar and Daewoo each spent between three million to five million U.S. dollars on advertising in China, and one estimate put total South Korea government and private sector support of the Chinese Asian Games at about US$100 million.[13]

China had a hugely successful Beijing Asian Games. Its athletics excelled. In part with Seoul's earlier assistance, the Chinese could unfurl a banner at the end of the Closing Ceremony proclaiming their wish to host the Olympic Games.

The beneficial consequences of close earlier cooperation were immediate. Thus, while:

> South Korea's help was not solely responsible for these developments, it was extremely successful in conveying political intentions in a way that normal diplomacy could not. The Republic of Korea and China established trade offices shortly after the conclusion of the 1990 Games, which then made normalization a foregone conclusion less than two years later.[14]

Beijing 1990 was *not*, however, as hugely successful as Guangzhou 2010, which saw China crush the rest of Asia. By 2010, the Chinese sport juggernaut had gathered purposeful momentum.

The Chinese Economic Miracle and the South Korean 'Pay-Off'

The past 30 years have seen China become the current East Asian regional hegemonic power, built on its economic, military and soft power, which continues to increase. In 2009, China surpassed Germany as the largest global exporter, and 2010 marked China's ascendance as the world's second-largest economy, surpassing Japan.[15] More importantly, currently it is the biggest holder of foreign reserves and it may supplant the USA even as soon as 2025 as the world's largest economic power.[16] In terms of its economic size, China is considered a global superpower: as yet its military power must be considered only as regional.[17] It is some distance away from being a dominant hard power nation on par with the most powerful military nation in the world.

In terms of 'soft power' politics, it is closing the gap more swiftly, especially in sport. The Beijing Olympics, which saw the USA toppled from the top of the gold medal table by China, was a masterpiece of global 'soft power' presentation. The Guangzhou Games was a masterclass in regional 'soft power' presentation: a statement of dominance. As a public relations exercise, however, it may have been a bad miscalculation. The rest of Asia *'losing face' as considerably as it did* may not have been good regional 'soft power' politics.

Be that as it may, South Korea had enough reasons to celebrate at the Guangzhou Games, achieving second place and impressive performances by its athletes,[18] but especially an economic association with China on the back of careful successful support for China at both the earlier Asian Games. China has been South Korea's number one trade partner since 2003 and is currently South Korea's biggest importer ($134.32 billion) and exporter ($80.785 billion). South Korea's exports to China vividly show how much South Korea's economy depends on China. Economically, China is Seoul's closest business partner. More than 32,000 Korean firms have branches or are doing business in the country, and the number of Korean visitors to China exceeded 6.1 million in 2012.

Support for the Chinese at the Seoul and Beijing Asian Games was clearly a sound investment! South Korea has benefited economically from having such a massive market, China – right on its doorstep! Trading with China significantly helped Korea's fast recovery after the recent global financial crisis in 2008.[19] China's labour-intensive and processing industry has been a locomotive for its economic growth, whereas South Korea industries have been based on capital- and technology-intensive industries. Trade frictions, however, resulting from anti-dumping measures, food-safety concerns and decreasing Korean foreign direct investment to China have forced Sino-South Korea trade into deceleration since 2005.[20] Moreover, Lee Myung-bak's administration policy shift to revitalise South Korea's relationships with the USA and Japan to promote South Korea as a 'Global Korea' has further decelerated bilateral trade.[21] Most importantly, China's ability to develop high-quality key exports, from clothes to consumer electronics, has intensified competition between the two countries domestically and internationally, changing their relationship from one of actual benefit to one of potential threat.

The economic 'honeymoon' period is most certainly over. The relationship is increasingly that of a 'marriage of convenience'. Of course, South Korea's economic dependence on China continues to expand and deepen. It is interesting to note how South Korea's trade dependence both on China and the USA for the past two decades has changed. In 1991, South Korea's trade dependence on China was 2.9%, while its dependence on the USA was 24.42%. South Korea's relative dependence on the two powers was conspicuously reversed over the past two decades. In 2009, the USA accounted for just 9.71% of South Korea's trade while China 20.53%. With this change in trading partners, the effects on economics and politics need to be briefly examined. South Korea still maintains a strong alliance with the USA and has intensified a 'strategic and cooperative partnership' with China. The challenge is that South Korea must devise both hedging and engagement strategies to deal with a rising China, while intensifying the strong alliance with the USA because it still has to deal with North Korea. Nevertheless, South Korea's increasing economic dependence on China will substantially reduce the scope and range of strategic choices available in dealing with China, thereby threatening South Korea's relative political independence. From an economic perspective, retreat from China now is no longer an option for South Korea and must be managed with realism, caution and care.

Assets: Human, Academic, Tourist and Cultural – Stressing Regional Identities?

South Korea and China non-political contact has steadily increased: a developing exchange in human resources, academic interaction and cultural programmes. Since diplomatic relations were initiated in 1992, the number of international students has steadily increased in both countries. In China, the number of South Korean international students constitutes the highest percentage of international students. Tourism started to expand in 1994 with South Koreans and Chinese obtaining the right to travel freely between countries.[22] In South Korea, there has been an increase in the number of studies on various aspects of Chinese culture. In addition, academic exchanges are actively conducted via symposia, for example on economic issues.[23] Exchanges are also commonplace now in the area of Arts.

While all this is admirable, the point should not be lost that through these exchanges the perception of a nation can be carefully controlled – officially at least. These exchanges are one element of 'soft power' politics, with both advantages and disadvantages in the absence of a common political framework in which to operate.

Debits: Future Economies and Past and Present Histories

In South Korea, China's rise has been referred to as a 'double-edged sword' presenting a promise as well as a threat.[24] The South Korean export market benefits from China's high growth rate. However, China is a global powerhouse, and is increasingly a dominant force in world markets, benefiting from strong price competitiveness and economies of scale. As China makes further pushes into major export markets, South Korea will be increasingly hard-pressed and, as a result, China is very likely to pose a threat to South Korea's economy.[25] And economic prosperity takes precedence over cultural engagement.

China's status in both regional and global economics will hinge on the proposed objectives in terms of political and economic models. To change its status from a global factory to a global market, first, China has to maintain its sociopolitical stability and, second, it has to successfully implement and maintain a policy for intensive internal growth. If the Chinese market evolves into a global market, it will cause substantial changes in the economic situations of many countries. Increasing economic involvement in a Chinese market will deepen and widen China's positive economic and political influence globally. As noted, this, in turn, will impact South Korea.

As is well known, certainly in Asia, historically, South Korea, located between China and Japan, has suffered much from both countries. Japan, long viewed as the greater threat, has experienced much South Korean 'bashing'. However, with the rise of China, Japan 'bashing' seems to have been replaced with a growing fear of China and even with China 'bashing'.[26] Factors, such as the historical and territorial 'spats' between the two countries, have both affected international relations and trade. With recent product-safety issues and resulting undercurrents of negative public sentiment, the consequent bilateral trade frictions should not be overlooked. Then, following the March riots in Tibet, the Olympic torch passed through Seoul on April 27, 2008 in an atmosphere of high tension with protests similar to those which accompanied the torch relays in other cities around the world. Pro-Tibet demonstrators and Chinese students studying in South Korea universities both held demonstrations during the torch relay in Seoul which sparked violent clashes between Chinese and South Koreans. The contrasting political systems were dramatically emphasised.[27]

The North Korea Factor, Chinese Arrogance and American Friendship

China's mutual economic interests with South Korea have *outweighed* its long-standing ideological and political ties with North Korea.[28] When North Korea viewed the Sino-South Korea diplomatic normalisation in 1992 as a betrayal, China's official response was that China's foreign policy on the Korean Peninsula had shifted from 'One Korea Policy' to a 'Two Koreas Policy'.[29] After normalisation between South Korea and China, noted partnerships were built and cooperative relations steadily progressed. Moreover, the vibrant economic relationship and expanding grass-roots interactions continued to justify closer political ties between the two countries. From a 'friendship and cooperative relationship' in 1992 to a 'cooperative partnership relationship' in 1998 under President Kim Dae-jung, then to a 'comprehensive cooperative partnership' in 2003 during the Roh Moo-hyun administration,[30] and further to a 'strategic cooperative partnership' announced during Lee Myung-bak's inaugural visit to Beijing in 2008 as the new president of South Korea,[31] political and economic relations between the two countries have not only deepened but also broadened – despite setbacks outlined above.

Regarding such cooperation between the two countries together with the China–South Korea diplomatic relations' 20th anniversary in 2012, it can be said that relationships – despite being occasionally problematic – have been *relatively* successful.[32] In formal aspects, friendly Sino-South Korea relations have dramatically developed and in all areas mutual cooperation and development have been noticeable, especially in those involving trade. As already mentioned, since 2011 China has been the number one trading partner and the number one export market in South Korea making South Korea the third-largest trading partner after the USA and Japan.[33]

From an ideological, political and historical perspective, however, China remains emotionally attached to North Korea. This results from the Korean War,[34] where hundreds of thousands of Chinese soldiers, including the eldest son of Mao Zedong, lost their lives fighting for the communist North against South Korean and United Nations allied forces.[35] To date, there are still no accurate estimates, but available estimates show that the Chinese casualties were larger than those of North Korea, South Korea and the USA combined. To this day, the Military Museum in Beijing proudly displays flags of the USA and South Korea that was captured over 60 years ago.[36] Consequently, there is growing scepticism in South Korea about China's role as a mediating power with North Korea amid a continuing series of problematic events:

> WikiLeaks files have raised recent suspicion on China's view on both Koreas. In a leaked account dated on April 30, 2009, Dan Piccuta, deputy chief of mission at the U.S. Embassy in Beijing, stated that a Chinese official had suggested to him that the U.S. needs to have bilateral talks with North Korea or even trilateral ones *without* involving South Korea. This was taken as an insult by some of the media in South Korea, since unification with North Korea is seen as an internal, domestic problem.[37]

> In addition, a string of recent incidents have damaged China's reputation as a trustworthy friend. At the G20 Seoul Summit on Nov. 12, 2010 a Chinese reporter irritated Barack Obama as he kept insisting on asking questions even though Obama himself wanted to talk with a South Korean reporter first. Then, the Chinese reporter shocked every South Korean in the room by saying he was representing the whole of Asia.[38]

Furthermore, the Asian Games did little to erase such arrogance in view of the 199 gold medals China won![39]

Furthermore, despite their ups and downs, South Korea and the USA have maintained a solid partnership based on their security alliance since the Korean War. While there has been opposition to America's presence and anti-American sentiment from time to time, in terms of overall friendship, South Korea is one of the closest partners of the USA in the Asia-Pacific region.

In summary, South Koreans are beginning to distrust China after the country's ambivalent attitude towards the current inter-Korean conflict.[40] South 'Koreans are feeling uncomfortable with China's double standard on the Korean Peninsula and signs of its growing unilateralism'.[41] Relations with the USA have benefited.

Political Provocation and Chinese Political Impotence: The Sinking of South Korea Navy Ship *Cheonan* and Shelling of the Yeonpyeong Island

On November 23, 2010, North Korea fired scores of artillery shells at the South Korean island of Yeonpyeong, killing 4 (2 soldiers and 2 civilians) and wounding 26 (16 soldiers and 10 civilians), destroying several houses and starting numerous fires in one of the most serious clashes between the two countries in decades. North Korea claimed it was a response to earlier shells fired by South Korea – which the South acknowledged had been fired, but as an exercise, and not into North Korean territory. This attack coupled with recent revelations about the North's nuclear capabilities and escalating threats and counter-threats have raised tensions in the region.

These recent events have been proclaimed as the most serious in decades, a product of tensions that have been coming in waves since the sinking of the *Cheonan* earlier in 2010. The immediate response of the international community was one of outrage at the action by North Korea, although while the USA pledged their support, it made it clear that it would seek a diplomatic solution in keeping with President Lee Myung-bak's call for restraint. North Korea's long-term protector, China, refused to place the blame on either of the Koreas.

North Korea's bombardment of Yeonpyeong Island was a direct attack on South Korean soil and included a civilian residential area. This Yeonpyeong attack occurred just as the city of Guangzhou was hosting the Asian Games, part of China's ambitious effort to enhance its regional image! Interestingly, the Yeonpyong incident did not provoke responses in events between athletes and teams from the two Koreas at the Games. This is clear from the following:

> Yang Chun Song of North Korea and Kim Dai-sung of South Korea competed for the 1/8 final men's Freestyle 66 kg wrestling competition at the 16th Asian Games in Guangzhou on November 24, 2010. The bout between the two athletes comes one day after North Korea rained a deadly artillery barrage on the Yellow Sea island of Yeonpyeong that belongs to South Korea. Yang Chun Song of North Korea won the match.[42]

There was no political animosity, expressed by either athlete. This self-control typified the meetings between South and North Koreans. Political self-restraint was the order of the day.

North Korea's two attacks demonstrate that, ultimately, China has very limited influence over North Korea's behaviour and, furthermore, North Korea is acting with absolutely no concern for China's circumstances. The artillery attack on Yeonpyeong not only embarrassed China, both domestically and abroad, but may have also prompted China to reassess the North Korean leadership. For China, North Korea represents a buffer against the South Korea–US–Japan alliance, and thus from a strategic viewpoint it cannot be abandoned. This is the reason why China continues to provide support despite its discomfort about North Korea's nuclear weapon programme. However, if North Korea continues to exhibit unpredictable and uncontrollable behaviour, for China it may become nothing but a 'costly structure'. This may cause China to become more keenly aware of the need to transform the North Korean leadership into one that is more pro-China and easier to control. In the meantime, North Korea's independent self-willed actions work to the advantage of South Korea.

Nevertheless, 'the honeymoon period' of Sino-South Korea relations, which began with the first-ever summit meeting of President Roh Moo-hyun and President Hu Jintao on November 19, 2004, can be said to be over. By way of a reminder, in this summit, they agreed to foster South Korea–China relations and share mutual concerns over issues of common interests, and later, to further develop Korea–China relations into a 'comprehensive, cooperative partnership'. After President Lee Myung-bak took office in 2008, South Korea and China seemed to have agreed on common grounds for cooperation. During the summit meeting prior to the Beijing Olympics in May 2008, President Lee and President Hu Jintao upgraded the bilateral relationship to the status of a 'strategic cooperative partnership' to widen bilateral cooperation beyond two-way diplomacy to encompass future-intended issues.[43]

Unlike the shocked reaction of South Korea and Japan,[44] China's response to *Cheonan* was almost indifferent. China initially saw the *Cheonan* sinking as a mere inter-Korean incident and demonstrated irritation over South Korean efforts to internationalise the issue by taking it to the United Nations Security Council.[45] China repeatedly called for 'calm and restraint'[46] in dealing with the *Cheonan* sinking and did not directly condemn North Korea for its inexcusable action. Chinese leaders persistently reiterated their commitment to approach the matter 'in an objective and fair manner'.[47] This clearly exposed China's passive attitude towards North Korean provocation in the region. The Chinese Vice Foreign Minister Cui Tiankai, for example, stated that the shelling was an 'unfortunate' incident and that the tragedy should be dealt with appropriately to safeguard peace and stability on the Korean Peninsula.[48] China regarded the shelling of the South Korean Navy corvette *Cheonan* as a local conflict between South Korea and North Korea. China's reaction revealed that it did not want the incident to develop into an international problem, but considered it a parochial one.[49] Furthermore, China was reluctant to accept the conclusion of an international investigation that *Cheonan* was sunk in a North Korea torpedo attack.[50] South Korea and China do not share the same attitudes with regards to military provocation in the region. China is playing down the danger that North Korea is in the region.

China took up a similar posture after the shelling of Yeonpyong Island. In a statement after the shelling, Chinese Foreign Ministry spokesman, Hong Lei, urged the involved sides to act in a manner 'conducive to peace and stability' on the Korean Peninsula.[51] Moreover, he urged *both* parties to keep calm. Following China's reaction to the North Korean shelling, President Lee urged China to be more responsible in dealing with issues on the Korean Peninsula during a meeting with the Chinese State Councillor Dai Bingguo.[52] This firm rebuke made very clear the South Korean official's displeasure with China on the issue,[53]and was the clearest indication of political disenchantment with China.

After the *Cheonan* and Yeonpyong incidents caused by North Korea, South Korean society underwent a significant change of attitude towards its neighbouring nations. According to the 2010 Unification Awareness Survey conducted by the Institute for Peace and Unification Studies at Seoul National University,[54] South Koreans revealed an expected wariness towards North Korea. The survey revealed increased South Korean warmth towards the USA. South Koreans now regarded China as the main party responsible for the deterioration in South–North relations and viewed China as a potential ally of North Korea if a war between the two Koreas was to occur.[55] The rapprochement of the 1990s was a redundant memory.

Ambivalence, Contradictions and Ignorance: South Korean Perceptions of the Chinese

According to a survey in South Korea and Northeastern Asia,[56] conducted by the Northeast Asian History Foundation in 2010, 46% of the respondents said that they did not like China, and only 10% said they liked China.[57] In a 2012 survey by the East Asia Institute,[58] a non-profit and an independent research organisation in South Korea, 8 out of 10 Koreans responded that the next leader of Asia will be China. However, 70.5% replied that they would feel revulsion if China became the Asian leader.[59] In short, there is a sensible recognition of the potential of China in the future, but, simultaneously, many South Koreans feel uneasy at the prospect.[60]

De facto, China's influence cannot be ignored. However, Koreans do not have a clear understanding of the country. An editorial in *Kyunghyang Shinmun*[61] stated that South Koreans still have misconceptions about and prejudices towards China. The newspaper conducted a national survey of 200 college students; only 17.5% students knew who the President of China was and more than 45% of the students were not well disposed towards the Chinese. In contrast, the Chinese appear to have a more positive view of South Korea. During an interview held in Beijing, 20 college students correctly named the President of South Korea, and were familiar with Samsung Electronics, LG and Hyundai Motors. Why are there these national differences? Dr. Inhee Han, a Chinese Studies professor at Daejin University, has argued that 'Most Koreans still think of China as an underdeveloped country where the life styles and level of consumption are lower than in South Korea. To understand China correctly, the first step is by removing these prejudices'.[62] Admittedly, these are small national samples but are they indicative of a more widespread polarisation? And what of the South Korean media? How does it view the Chinese? In general, it is also characterised by ambivalence, ignorance and bias. According to a *Kyunghyang Shinmun's* editorial:

> It is aware of, and admires, China's strenuous economic growth and is aware of its huge potential but it reports negatively on China as an unsophisticated country emphasizing underdeveloped aspects. This negative view has recently weakened, but there remains a sense of superiority in South Korean thoughts and attitudes toward the Chinese.[63]

Chinese wealth displayed at the Guangzhou Games is ignored.[64] Perhaps it is time for a new South Korean charm offensive replicating the 1990s!

The Guangzhou Asian Games: Cumulative Consequences and the South Korean Media

South Korean interest in the 2010 Guangzhou Asian Games was considerable. During the 16 days of the Asian Games, KBS 2TV and MBC TV broadcast – live and highlights – 113 programmes and a total coverage of 181 hours and 15 minutes.[65] South Korean advertising revenues were the highest in the history of South Korean coverage of the Asian Games.[66] One reason, perhaps *the* reason, was the excellent performances of South Korean athletes. South Korea came second in the medal table and its athletes won 232 medals: 76 gold, 65 silver and 91 bronze.

It has been claimed that 'South Koreans see China as a big country and Chinese as small people, whereas, Chinese see Korea as a small country and Koreans as big people'[67]:

a disparaging and dismissive *and* dangerous view, if true! While South Koreans have a positive image about China, they have a tendency to belittle the Chinese people.[68] In contrast, the Chinese see Korea as a lesser country, but have positive perceptions of Korean citizens.[69] The negative South Korean perception of the Chinese is related to the history between the two countries, a fear of Sino-centrism and a sense of Korean superiority. This negativity is also based on the production of fake products, blatant dumping and violations of human rights.[70]

Arguably, South Korea is living in a Fool's Paradise. It sees its prosperity grow, it views its democratic freedom as a symbol of superiority and it persuades itself that it can ignore the Chinese – not least because it shelters, in the last resort, under the American military umbrella. Perhaps it is time for an injection of geopolitical realism. Perhaps the Guanzhou Asian Games will provide it: glittering metropolis, state-of-the-art facilities, technological modernity and dominant Chinese.

Early official comments by some South Korean businessmen and diplomats were positive. Kim Jang-Hwan, the South Korean consul general in Guangzhou, for example, was upbeat. He hoped for increased trade links between South Korea, Guangzhou and Guangdong, the region. 'Guangzhou is a city not very well-known to the majority of South Koreans, compared to Beijing or Shanghai', Kim noted, 'Guangzhou has been serving as a China base for many South Korean companies. By hosting Asiad, the city will make itself even better known to the South Korean people', he added, 'Guangzhou, along with Shenzhen, a major Chinese economic hub, is among the most populous and important of all cities not only in its province, Guangdong'.[71] It should be noted that

> Samsung, the famous Korean company, first supported the Asian Games as a local sponsor during the 10th Asian Games held in Seoul in 1986 and continued as a local sponsor for the 12th Asian Games held in Hiroshima in 1994. In 1998, Samsung became an official partner of the Bangkok Asian Games and was a multicategory sponsor at the Busan 2002 and Doha 2006 Asian Games. As the only global company sponsoring the event, Samsung's sponsorship categories for Guangzhou 2010 included audiovisual equipment, home appliances, mobile telecommunications and digital cameras.[72]

Consequently, 'Building on the success of our worldwide sponsorship of the Olympic Games and Beijing 2008 in particular, we are honoured to be a Prestige Partner of the Asian Games', said Kwon Gyehyun, Head of Worldwide Sports Marketing at Samsung.[73] He added, 'Samsung is committed to China and thrilled to contribute to the success of Guangzhou 2010 with our innovative technologies and products, while bringing happiness to the people of Guangzhou'.[74]

The South Korean media, however, did not display either optimism or generosity. Comments can be broadly summed in the epithets: unsophisticated, tasteless and inelegant. It pointed out that the 'epic' Opening Ceremony of the 2008 Beijing Olympic Games flaunted China's superpower status and its international economic strength, and although the Guangzhou Organising Committee promised not to replicate the scale of the Beijing Olympics, as expected, typical of the Chinese people,[75] the Opening Ceremony was a masterpiece of excess without comparison again showing China as an international superpower and once again, China's obsession with scale.[76] China, once known as one of the world's mightiest countries, suffered from nineteenth-century humiliation, and today regains 'face' by showing the world that once again it is *a* mighty country. The ostentatious display of the Opening Ceremony was intended to make clear China's unstoppable rise.[77] The Chinese Guangzhou Opening Ceremony is a burden for the Incheon organisers (the next host in 2014).[78] It is an open challenge to do better!

> The Opening and Closing Ceremonies demonstrated China's position as one of the G2 ('The Group of 2' – the United States and China). It presented itself via the Ceremonies an economic powerhouse showing the world how that China has grown. Furthermore, Ceremonies made it clear that Guangzhou was to be compared favourably with 2008 Beijing. The Asian Games Committee at Incheon is preparing, a very different Games in marked contrast to the monstrous scale of the Chinese Asian Games.[79]

This was the gist of South Korean media comment: unflattering, unimpressed and exasperated.

It would seem for the South Korean media that any vestiges of the 1990s South Korean 'honeymoon' have disappeared without a trace. It is bent on 'divorce' proceedings! There were further dismissive and uncomplimentary media comments. With 1.5 million applicants and 590,000 accepted Games volunteers, there was considerable competition to become a volunteer. This ensured high quality even though there was no financial compensation. The volunteers worked hard eight hours a day.[80] However, the *Moonhwa llbo* stated that the majority of the volunteer college students had difficulty communicating in English, the global language.[81] And, when these volunteers were asked for information about the Asian Games, most gave incorrect answers. Not only that, but these volunteers also controlled broadcasting interviews.[82] The Korean press stressed that the lack of class in the 'Chinese' Asian Games was only too obvious.[83]

Furthermore, the South Korean media did not miss the opportunity to find fault with Chinese despotic actions taken to ensure a smooth and successful Games. It reported that to achieve the 'perfection' of the Opening and Closing Ceremonies, the residents living in the areas surrounding Haisinsa were forced to leave their homes. The Chinese government regulated store opening and closing hours and the streets were 'cleaned up'. According to one citizen, 'With the Asian Games taking place here, the hours that the stores are open are impractical and furthermore, people are even restricted from smoking on the streets'. He added 'There are people watching all over the place, it feels like jail'.[84] The Incheon Organising Committee got in on the act. 'Forcibly relocating more than 20,000 citizens in order to get ready for the Opening Ceremony is something you can only see in a socialist country'.[85] Another newspaper editorial added, '[civic] Order was forcibly ensured ... because of the Asian Games. Like they say there is nothing impossible in China. But, it's hard to just smile and welcome the experience'.[86]

The South Korean media did not end its fault-finding after drawing attention to authoritarian actions affecting shops, stores and restaurants. It next turned its attention to 'self-satisfied' government officials and their claims that the Games were a turning point in civic pride as a result of successful public planning.[87] In fact, it observed that regarding the construction of roads and buildings in preparation for the Games, there were many problems.[88] It went on to further remark that during the Games the subway was free with unfortunate consequence for tourists. It was packed with local people making it almost impossible for tourists to use it comfortably and easily. And the media did not fail to report that 'free travel' was withdrawn after only one week![89] It also found fault with the manners of Chinese drivers. One conclusion drawn was: 'You can build stadiums and facilities in a short time but you cannot instill civic consciousness in a day'.[90]

The Chinese Gold Medal Monopoly: Overkill?

The South Korean media, while recognising China as a sporting superpower, was concerned about China's medal monopoly. Forty-five countries participated in Guangzhou 2010. Most of the medal winners came from three countries, China, Japan and South Korea. China was way out ahead. At Doha 2006, China had its most gold medals (165), while South Korea had 58 and Japan 50. At Guanzhou 2010, China crushed both Japan and South Korea mercilessly and destroyed the remaining 42 nations.[91] In a South Korean nationwide TV news report, a reporter remarked, '...there was a Chinese black hole sucking in all the gold medals ... the true meaning of the Asian Games festival, attracting the attention of 4.2 billion Asians, now could be diminishing'.[92] For China, there are grounds for considering that Guangzhou was a public relations disaster – at least outside China, and perhaps inside China too. Some Chinese appear to have appreciated this. *Xinhua News Agency* declared that 'Chinese gold medals are a reason for disaster ... Ruling over all the gold medals will give other Asian countries a sense of alienation; in the long term, this will not be a good thing for China'.[93] It also added, 'We need to get amateur and college athletes to compete in the next Games'.[94] The South Korean media regarded the *Xinhua* editorial as an unusually candid statement.

In South Korea, the medal pre-eminence of China resulted in increased dislike for China.[95] The accord of the 1990s appears to be disappearing rapidly. South Korea needs China economically, but likes China less and less![96] And perhaps the Chinese reciprocate. According to one South Korean entrepreneur in China, 'Following diplomatic relationship with Korea and China 20 years ago, there was opportunity in China, but now it's become an impossible environment in which to start a business'.[97] And he added, '...among the Chinese there are insulting words when describing Koreans, like "Xiao-fang-zi – small arrogant Korean"'.[98]

Conclusion: From 'Honeymoon to Divorce'?

In summary, a previously harmonious view of China has been transformed within South Korean media. Increasingly, the rise of China as a global political, economic and sports superpower is seen as a threat as much as an opportunity. The following media reports represent and summarise this change:

> ...the Guangzhou Games was different from Beijing ... With the rapid growth in the economy and industry, China has become the world's second economic powerhouse and a G2 member. The rapid development of China's economic power could be observed on the faces of the common Chinese people attending the Opening and Closing Ceremonies. They expressed China's unstoppable strength and power on the way to becoming the world's biggest superpower.[99]

> Even though South Korea has achieved more than expected at the Games in China, an uncomfortable feeling still lingers.[100]

> With China leaving the rest far behind, and exceeding expectations, I felt dispirited and perplexed.[101]

> In the past 20 years, Zhonggou has changed to China, Peking to Beijing, and Deongshaoping to Teng Hsiaoping, this shows how the pronunciation has changed among South Koreans, which can be seen as reflecting the changing attitudes of Korea citizens. Not only in sport, but in the growth in China economically, we need to revise our perceptions of China....[102]

The unease in these comments reflects a wider South Korean unease! Relations between South Korea and China have shifted from sweet to sour.

Notes on Contributors

J.A. Mangan, Emeritus Professor, University of Strathclyde, FRHS, FRAI, FRSA, RSL, D.Litt. is Founding Editor of *The International Journal of the History of Sport* and the series *Sport in the Global Society* and author of the globally acclaimed *Athleticism in the Victorian and Edwardian Public School, The Games Ethic and Imperialism* and *'Manufactured' Masculinity: Making Imperial Manliness, Morality and Militarism* and author or editor of some 50 publications on politics, culture, and sport.

THE ASIAN GAMES: MODERN METAPHOR FOR 'THE MIDDLE KINGDOM' REBORN

Sun Yong Kwon teaches at Seoul National University, Seoul, Korea. His research interests include social, cultural, and historical aspects of sport and leisure, sport policy and development, and sport in international relations.

Bang-Chool Kim teaches at Seoul National University of Education, Seoul, Korea. His current research interests include sports history and various issues in professional sports. He is currently a member of School & Youth Commission, International Association of Athletics Federations.

Notes

1. Ok, *The Transformation of Modern Korean Sport*, 24 (emphasis added).
2. Ibid.
3. Chairman Mao Zedong died at the age of 82, on September 9, 1976, and the end of the Cultural Revolution was followed by China's official declaration of its 'Open-Door' policy in 1978 when Deng Xiaoping took power. Xiaoping announced the official launch of his modernisation programme that aimed to modernise China's industry and boost its economy by introducing capitalist market principles. In 1979, diplomatic relations were established between the USA and China, and it was in 1992 that the diplomatic normalisation was established between China and South Korea.
4. Cha, *Beyond the Final Score*, 93. Cha is among the most penetrating of commentators on the relationship between politics and sport in East Asia. This part of the present article draws on his perceptive insights.
5. Ibid.
6. Ibid., 94.
7. Ibid.
8. Ibid.
9. Ibid.
10. Ibid., 92.
11. Ibid., 95.
12. Ibid.
13. Ibid.
14. Ibid., 96.
15. "Joongguk, Machimnae Miguk-do Jechyutda ... Sangpum Mooyeok 'Segye Numbeo Won' [China leaving the US behind, 'World's Number One' merchandise trading volume]" (*Maeil Business Newspaper*, February 11, 2013).
16. Ibid.
17. Cho, "China's Rise and the Emerging New Regional Order," 53.
18. According to *Yonhap News*, 'South Korea accomplished both of its much-publicised goals. It won 76 gold medals, more than the projected total of 65, and it outdueled Japan's 48 in the gold medal count. With China expected to run away on home soil, South Korea had from the beginning set out to be the second-best by edging its rival Japan for the fourth straight Asian Games'. See "S. Korea Finished Second, Beats Japan in Medal Tables to Meet Goals" (*Yonhap News*, November 28, 2010).
19. An editorial in *The Korea Times* stated that 'China was Korea's economic buffer zone during the 2008 global financial crisis which originated from the United States'. See "Korea–China Relations: Soul-Searching Needed for Mending Fences" (*The Korea Times*, August 24, 2011).
20. Zhou, *Sino-South Korean Trade Relations*, 7–10.
21. Lee Myung-bak administration's foreign policy was significantly different in its relations with the USA, Japan, China and North Korea from the previous progressive administrations of Kim Dae-jung and Rho Moo-hyun. In contrast with both predecessors' active engagement approaches to North Korea, Lee Myung-bak had a relatively low priority for improving inter-Korean relations and upheld a cautious and defensive, rather tougher policy approach to the North. Lee Myung-bak also clearly indicated that his top priority in foreign policy was to improve strategic relations with the USA and Japan. Lee Myung-bak's openly stated intention was to restore and revitalise the South Korea–US alliance based on the established friendship with the USA, and he also emphasised his desire to have 'future-oriented' relations with Japan, even setting aside conflicting history issues to consolidate South Korea–Japan relations. Lee Myung-bak's high priority on strengthening political relations with the USA

and Japan made China and North Korea uneasy and uncomfortable. With the strategic focus on consolidating the South Korea–USA and South Korea–Japan relations, Lee Myung-bak's foreign policy initiative, 'Global Korea', was promoted to increase the visibility and influence of South Korea on the global stage. See Snyder, "Lee Myung-bak's Foreign Policy."

22. Kim, "The Situation and Social Influence."
23. Lee, "Practices and Prospects of the Korea–China."
24. Ju, *Yangnal-ui Kal, Joongguk Gyungje*; "S. Korea's Uncertain Path with China," *The Korea Times*, May 26, 2008.
25. See "Joong Sungjang Deo-neun Bangilil A-nya … Han Gyungjaengryuk Wihyub Simhwa [Growth of China, not a welcoming factor … A threat to Korea's competitiveness]" (*Yonhap News*, February 19, 2013); Lee, *Joongguk-ui Boosang-e Ttareun WooriGyungje Wihyub Yoin*.
26. "Hatred to Take Toll on Biz, Trade and Tourism," *The Korea Times*, August 27, 2012; Kang and Suh, "A Research on the Korean Prospects," 9; Jang, "The First Step for the Future," 5.
27. "Olympic Torch in Seoul: Despite Problems, Flame Should Be Kept Alight," *The Korea Times*, April 24, 2008; "Olympics Highlight Seoul–Beijing Emotional Dispute," *The Korea Times*, August 8, 2008; "Korea Promises Firm Action Against Chinese Protestors," *Chosun Ilbo*, April 30, 2008.
28. Snyder, *China's Rise and the Two Koreas*, 1.
29. Ibid.
30. The Sino-South Korea diplomatic relations officially began in 1992 as a 'friendship and cooperative relationship', which is the elementary level of China's bilateral diplomacy policy. It was with the Kim Dae-jung administration in 1998 that China defined, for the first time, the Sino-South Korea relations at the level of 'partnership'. China was conscious of North Korea in maintaining a '*cooperative* partnership relationship' with Kim's administration. It was with the Roh Moo-hyun administration in 2003 that China established an upgraded '*comprehensive* cooperative partnership' with South Korea.
31. Kim, "20 Years of South Korea–China," 212.
32. Byeon, "Northeast Asia in G2 Era," 80.
33. Kim, "20 Years of South Korea–China," 212.
34. The Korean War began on June 25, 1950, when North Korean forces launched an invasion of South Korea. The United Nations' multinational force engaged and drove the North Korean troops past the 38th Parallel and almost to the Yalu River that divides the border between North Korea and China. China entered the war on the side of North Korea, justifying its engagement as a necessary response against 'American aggression in the guise of the UN'.
35. "China-Skepticism Spreads by Leaps and Bounds," *The Korea Times*, December 2, 2010.
36. Ibid.
37. Ibid.
38. Ibid.
39. Ibid.
40. "How to Mend Ties Between S. Korea and China?" *The Korea Times*, November 1, 2010.
41. Ibid.
42. "Tension in the Koreas," *The Boston Globe*, November 24, 2010.
43. The summit was held on May 27. President Lee highlighted that 'the strategic bilateral relations indicate that the two countries will expand cooperation from trade to other fields, including diplomacy, regional security and North Korea policies'. See "Seoul, Beijing Upgrade Partnership," *The Korea Times*, May 27, 2008.
44. According to *The Japan Times*, Japanese Prime Minister Yukio Hatoyama denounced the sinking of the Korean warship that Seoul had blamed on North Korea by saying: 'Our country strongly supports South Korea … North Korea's action is inexcusable and, along with the international community, we strongly condemn it'. See "Hatoyama Slams North Over Cheonan Sinking," *The Japan Times*, May 21, 2010.
45. Snyder and Byun, "Cheonan and Yeonpyeong," 76.
46. "China Again Calls for Restraint, Calm Over South Korea Warship Sinking," *Xinhua News Agency*, June 10, 2010.
47. "China to Make Objective, Fair Judgment on S. Korean Warship Sinking: Wen," *Xinhua News Agency*, May 28, 2010.
48. "Seoul Vows Retaliation After Confirming N.K. Torpedo Sank Warship," *Yonhap News*, May 20, 2010.

THE ASIAN GAMES: MODERN METAPHOR FOR 'THE MIDDLE KINGDOM' REBORN

49. "China Signals Displeasure with Cheonan Reaction," *Chosun Ilbo*, May 19, 2010.
50. See "China Shows Calm Response to Seoul's Release of Sunken Ship Findings," *Kyodo News*, May 20, 2010; "China Falls Silent on Eve of Cheonan Probe Announcement," *Chosun Ilbo*, May 20, 2010; "Japan, China Differ Over Cheonan Sinking," *Chosun Ilbo*, May 17, 2010; "China Returns U.S. Criticism over Sinking of Korean Ship," *New York Times*, June 29, 2010.
51. "China Expresses Concern over Alleged Exchange of Fire Between DPRK, South Korea," *Xinhua News Agency*, November 23, 2010.
52. "Lee Meets Chinese Envoy over Yeonpyeong Attack," *Chosun Ilbo*, November 29, 2010; "China Moves in Response to Yeonpyeong Attack," *Joongang Daily*, November 29, 2010.
53. "Time for China to Show Some Global Responsibility," *Chosun Ilbo*, November 25, 2010.
54. Park et al., 2010 Unification Awareness Survey.
55. Over 50% of the respondents answered that China will help North Korea in the event of war, compared to 38.4% in 2009 and 29.4% in 2008. Less than 5% of the respondents answered that they feel most close to China, a decrease by more than 5% points since 2007, while more than 70% answered that they feel most close to the USA, an increase by more than 17% since 2007. The survey was conducted after the sinking of *Cheonan* and before the attack on Yeonpyeong Island.
56. Northeast Asian History Foundation, *History Awareness Survey*.
57. "Joonggukin Silta 46%, Banil Gamjung-eun ↓," [Dislike the Chinese 46%, reduction in the anti-Japanese sentiment.] *Newsis*, November 9, 2010.
58. Lee, *Faltering Korea–China Relations*.
59. Ibid., 15.
60. Kang and Suh, "A Research on the Korean Prospects," 17.
61. "Joongguk, Joonghwaro Dolaoda: Woori-nun Neul Saesang-ui Joongsim Ei-ut-da [Sino-centric China returns: We have always been the center of the world]" (*The Kyunghyang Shinmun*, February 7, 2011).
62. Ibid.
63. Ibid.
64. See "Glittering Guangzhou."
65. "Guangzhou Asian Geim Gwango Panmae 183 Eok-won ... Yeokdae Choedae Suik," [Guangzhou Asian Games advertising sales 18.3 billion won ... highest profit ever.] *Herald Economy*, December 1, 2010.
66. Ibid.
67. Min, "Korea–China, Change of Perception," 87.
68. "Hatred to Take Toll on Biz, Trade and Tourism," *The Korea Times*, August 27, 2012; "Hangukin Doomyungjoong Hanmyung-eun Joongguk Sileohanda," [One of two South Koreans hate the Chinese.] *Herald Economy*, November 30, 2012; "Joonggukin Silta 46%, Banil Gamjung-eun ↓," [Dislike the Chinese 46%, reduction in the anti-Japanese sentiment.] *Newsis*, November 9, 2010; Kim, "The Situation and Social Influence."
69. Koh, "Joongguk-ui Hanguk-e Daehan Insik," 124; Min, "Korea–China, Change of Perception," 87.
70. Min, "Korea–China, Change of Perception," 89.
71. "Asiad Likely to Boost Trade Ties between S. Korea and Southern China," *Yonhap News*, November 11, 2010.
72. Ibid.
73. Ibid.
74. Ibid.
75. "42 Eokmyeong-ui Asiain-ui Nun-gwa Gwi-ga Guangzhou-ro Mol-ryeot-da," [4.2 billion Asian eyes and ears set on Guanzhou.] *Asia Business Daily*, November 12, 2010.
76. Ibid.
77. "Joongguk Global Pa-wo Jaepyun-Ui Joongsim," [China, the center of reshaping global power.] *Asian Business Daily*, November 18, 2010.
78. "Guangzhou-wa Bigyodoella ... Incheon Asian Geim 'Chobisang'," [Compared to Guangzhou ... An 'emergency' for the Incheon Asian Games.] *Maeil Business Newspaper*, November 19, 2010.
79. "Asiain-ui Chukje, Incheon Asian Geim Bongyeok Jumhwa," ['Asian Festival' lighting up the preparation for Incheon AG.] *Yonhap News*, November 27, 2010.

THE ASIAN GAMES: MODERN METAPHOR FOR 'THE MIDDLE KINGDOM' REBORN

80. "Gudenil Mada An-neun '59 Man-myung Jawon Bongsajadeul'," [590 thousand volunteers' dedication, even getting down for dirty work.] *The Kyunghyang Shinmun*, November 19, 2010.

81. "Guangzhou Asian Games/Hyunjang-e-seo – 59 Mman-myung Jawon Bongsaja – Jilboda Yang?" [Guangzhou Asian Games/from the venue – 59 million volunteers, quantity over quality?] *Moonhwa Ilbo*, November 17, 2010.

82. Ibid.

83. See Ibid.; "'Wonderful Guangzhou' Gichi-E Sok Alneun Simindeul," [The slogan, 'Wonderful Guangzhou', worries Guangzhou citizens.] *Maeil Business Newspaper*, November 25, 2010; "Guangzhou Asian Games/Hyunjang-e-seo – Gyotong Sisul 'Geummedal' … Simin Uisik 'Nomedal'," ['Gold Medal' for transportation facilities, 'No Medal' for civic consciousness.] *Moonhwa Ilbo*, November 16, 2010; "Nasa Pajin Joongguk Haengjeong/Hanguk Ibchonsik-e Jeongjak Hanguk-eo-neun Eopgo…" [Loose screws in Chinese administration/no Korean at the welcoming ceremony for the Korean National Team's admission to the athletes' Village….] *Hankook Ilbo*, November 11, 2010; "Muodeunji Ganeunghan Joongguk," [Anything possible in China.] *Seoul Sinmoon*, November 12, 2010.

84. "'Wonderful Guangzhou' Gichi-E Sok Alneun Simindeul," [The slogan, 'Wonderful Guangzhou', worries Guangzhou Citizens.] *Maeil Business Newspaper*, November 25, 2010.

85. "Guangzhou-wa Bigyodoella … Incheon Asian Geim 'Chobisang'," [Compared to Guangzhou … An 'emergency' for the Incheon Asian Games.] *Maeil Business Newspaper*, November 19, 2010.

86. "Muodeunji Ganeunghan Joongguk," [Anything possible in China.] *Seoul Sinmoon*, November 12, 2010.

87. "Simindeul Salme Umcheongnan Byunhwa," [Enormous change in citizens' life.] *Busan Ilbo*, November 27, 2010.

88. "Guangzhou Asian Games/Hyunjang-e-seo – Gyotong Sisul 'Geummedal' … Simin Uisik 'Nomedal'," ['Gold Medal' for transportation facilities, 'No Medal' for civic consciousness.] *Moonhwa Ilbo*, November 16, 2010.

89. Ibid.

90. Ibid.

91. " < 2010 Sports Big Event > Guangzhou Asian Geim," [<2010 sports big event > Guangzhou Asian Games.] *Yonhap News*, December 22, 2010.

92. "Hwaryeohague Mak Naerin 42 Eok Chukje … Asian Geim 3-dae Keywod," [Dazzling Closing Ceremony of 42 billion's festival … the top 3 key words of the Asian Games.] *Maeil Business Newspaper*, November 27, 2010.

93. "Yeogi-neun Guangzhou – 'Geum Sakseuli' Joongguk Jasung-ui Moksori," [From Guangzhou: China's self-reflection on its gold sweep.] *Moonhwa Ilbo*, November 17, 2010.

94. Ibid.

95. See "Hwaryeohague Mak Naerin 42 Eok Chukje … Asian Geim 3-dae Keyowd," [Dazzling Closing Ceremony of 42 billion's festival … the top 3 key words of the Asian Games.] *MBN News*, November 27, 2010; "Jiāyóu'-ui Mooseoun Him," [Fearful power of Jiayou.] *News Chonji*, November 30, 2010; "Asiain-ui Chukje, Incheon Asian Geim Bongyeok Jumhwa," ['Asian Festival' lighting up the preparation for Incheon AG.] *Yonhap News*, November 27, 2010; "Joongguk Sasang Choedae 'Geum Janchi'," [China's record size 'Gold Feast'.] *Kukmin Ilbo*, November 18, 2010; "Yamang-ui Asian Geim … Joongguk-ui Norimsu?" [The Asian Games ambition … China seeking for the perfect chance?] *Maeil Business Newspaper*, November 17, 2010.

96. See "How to Mend Ties Between S. Korea and China?" *The Korea Times*, November 1, 2010; "China-Skepticism Spreads by Leaps and Bounds," *The Korea Times*, December 2, 2010; "Korea–China Relations: Soul-Searching Needed for Mending Fences," *The Korea Times*, August 24, 2011; "Han-Joong Guangye Galdeung Dangbungan Jisok," [Korean–Chinese relations, conflict continues.] *Yonhap News*, December 25, 2010; "Hyanghu Han-Joong Guangye Deouk Ac-hwadoel Gut," [Korean–Chinese relations worsen even more.] *Newsis*, May 2, 2012; "Gyuljungjuk Soonganmada Buk Dudun … 'Naengontang' Guangye Banbok," [Supporting N.K at each crucial moment, 'cold pot' relations continue.] August 20, 2012.

97. "[Han-Joong 20 Nyun, Joongguk-eul Dasi Bonda] Wangseobang 'Xiaofàngzì Hangukin' Doerae Yatbone," ([20 years of Sino-South Korea relations, reviewing China] The Chinese look down on 'Xiao-Fang-Zi Korean'.) *Asia Business Daily*, March 28, 2012.

98. Ibid.
99. "Jiāyóu'-ui Mooseoun Him," [Fearful power of Jiayou.] *News Chonji*, November 30, 2010.
100. Ibid.
101. Ibid.
102. Ibid.

References

Byeon, Jong-heon. "Northeast Asia in G2 Era and Korea–Chinese Relations." *The Quarterly Journal of Defense Policy Studies* 28, no. 3 (2012): 79–108.

Cha, Victor D. *Beyond the Final Score: The Politics of Sport in Korea.* New York: Columbia University Press, 2009.

Cho, Young-nam. "China's Rise and the Emerging New Regional Order in East Asia." *Joongsoyungu (China and Russia Studies)* 34, no. 2 (2010): 44–68.

Jang, Soo-hyun. "The First Step for the Future of Sino-South Korea Relations." *Chindia Journal* 55, no. 3 (2011): 4–5.

Ju, Won. *Yangnal-ui Kal, Joongguk Gyungje* [Double-edged sword, China's economy]. Seoul: Hyundai Research Institute, 2012.

Kang, So-Yon, and Woon-Seok Suh. "A Research on the Korean Prospects of China as a Leading Nation in Asia." *Korean–Chinese Social Science Studies* 10, no. 1 (2012): 1–22.

Kim, Do-hee. "The Situation and Social Influence of Cultural Interchange Between Korea–China." *Hyundae Joongguk Yeongu (Journal of Contemporary China Studies)* 9, no. 2 (2008): 313–341.

Kim, Heung-kuo. "20 Years of South Korea–China Relationship and Its Prospects." *The Korean Journal of Area Studies* 29, no. 3 (2011): 211–240.

Koh, Sung-bin. "*Joongguk-ui Hanguk-e Daehan Insik* [The Chinese perception of South Koreans]." *National Strategy* 12, no. 4 (2006): 105–134.

Lee, Chi-hoon. *Joongguk-ui Boosang-e Ttareun WooriGyungje Wihyub Yoin* [China's growth factors threatening Korea's economy]. Seoul: Korea Center for International Finance, 2013.

Lee, Joon-tae. "Practices and Prospects of the Korea–China Cultural Exchange." *Academy of Asian Studies* 7 (2001): 113–139.

Lee, Jung-nam. *Faltering Korea–China Relations with the Emergence of the G2 Era*, EAI Asia Security Initiative Working Paper 26. Seoul: The East Asia Institute 2012.

Mangan, J.A., J. Dong, and D. Lu "'Glittering Guangzhou': The 2010 Asian Games – Local Rivalries, National Motives, Geopolitical Gestures." *The International Journal of the History of Sport* (2013): Forthcoming.

Min, G. S. "Korea-China, Change of Perception After Diplomatic Relations." *East Asia Brief* 7, no. 3 (2012): 87–90.

Northeast Asian History Foundation. *History Awareness Survey in Korea, Japan and China.* Seoul: Northeast Asian History Foundation, 2010.

Ok, G. *The Transformation of Modern Korean Sport: Imperialism, Nationalism, Globalization.* Elizabeth, NJ: Hollym International, 2007.

Park, Myung-gyu, Byung-ro Kim, Won-taek Kang, Sang-sin Lee, Jung-lan Park, and Eun-mi Jung. *2010 Unification Awareness Survey.* Seoul: The Institute for Peace and Unification Studies, 2011.

Snyder, Scott. *China's Rise and the Two Koreas: Politics, Economics, Security.* London: Lynne Rienner, 2009.

Snyder, Scott. "Lee Myung-bak's 'Foreign Policy: A 250-Day Assessment'." *Korean Journal of Defense Analysis* 21, no. 1 (2009): 85–102.

Snyder, Scott, and See-Won Byun. "Cheonan and Yeonpyeong: The Northeast Asian Response to North Korea's Provocations." *The Rusi Journal* 156, no. 2 (2011): 74–81.

Zhou, Shengqi. East Asian Institute Background Brief No. 508. *Sino-South Korean Trade Relations: From Boom to Recession.* Singapore: East Asian Institute, 2010.

Rivalries: China, Japan and South Korea – Memory, Modernity, Politics, Geopolitics – and Sport

J.A. Mangan[a,b], Hyun-Duck Kim[c], Angelita Cruz[c] and Gi-Heun Kang[d]

[a]Strathclyde University, Glasgow, Scotland, UK; [b]Cairns Institute, Cairns, Australia; [c]Keimyung University, Daegu, South Korea; [d]Kyung-Hee University, Seoul, South Korea

> Sport is an effective modern means for revealing a country's political preoccupations and geopolitical concerns. For China, Japan and South Korea, the pre-eminent countries in the recent Asian Games, sport has become a sharp tool for promoting nationalism and national identity. There is a history of bitter rivalry between these countries, not least, due to Japan's occupation of Korea and the Second Sino-Japanese War, the largest Asian war in the twentieth century. Consequently, a prominent characteristic of Korean and Chinese nationalism is anti-Japanese antipathy. This essay examines China–Japan–Korea rivalry through global sports events hosted in Asia during the past decade cumulating in the Guangzhou Asian Games. Here, the focus is on the use of these events as manifestations of resentment and revenge arising out of historic rivalries. This use may well grow in intensity as these nations grow in wealth, confidence and power as the EAST ASIAN EPOCH comes closer. This essay is the first to draw attention to the tripartite politics of sport as confrontation in the region's past, present and future.

Part 1

Preliminary Consideration

This is a preliminary consideration of confrontation between three modern East Asian nations expressed through modern sport, and in addition, a brief consideration of South Korea's antagonism to the USA viewed by some Koreans as a Western neo-colonial intrusive power rather than a contributor to its democratic freedom.

The central argument here is that the past historical conflict fuels present confrontation in sport and that this will increase in intensity in future as these countries increase in power, prosperity and confidence and seek to project themselves successfully through modern sport – a powerful medium for self-projection.

Critical Concepts

The term 'nationalism', among other things, can represent statism, racialism and ultra-nationalism associated with a state. The term 'state' here is to be understood as a demarcated territory and its people united over time and by a shared language and culture and a sovereign ruling system. 'Statism' here stands for the belief that the power of the state is more important than the freedom of the individual. 'Racialism' may be said to represent here the pursuit of political unity, independence and prosperity of an ethic community. Invoking nationalism to sustain political legitimacy – through sport – the focus of this essay – can be pathological in both intention and outcome. This phenomenon is not unknown in East Asia in the form of 'ultra-nationalism', and this essay is a preliminary explanation of this phenomenon.

In post-war Asia, the relationship between sport and politics has steadily advanced in significance. This is nowhere better illustrated than in the fractious relationship in sport over recent years between the Koreas – North and South following the tragic civil war. However, the political confrontational significance of modern sport in Korea as a pathological manifestation goes back further to the pre-Second World War era of the Japanese imperial oppressor when Korea was a united nation.[1]

The Japanese occupation of Korea furnishes a brutal example of sport as pathological nationalism in the form of sport as a method of conditioning into regimented subjection (see Figure 1).[2] For this reason, among others, it is often argued that sport should be independent of politics. This is a lost cause. Sport is a frequent form of politics. East Asia is no exception to the rule. There is a recent outstanding recent illustration: Beijing 2008 – 'the Geopolitical Games'.[3] Tokyo 1964 and Seoul 1988, incidentally, are not exempt from this rule, albeit to a different practical elemental purpose: Tokyo – the desire to be re-absorbed into the civilised nations of the world following the demise of Japanese Fascism, and Seoul – the desire to make it clear to the nations of the world that South Korea was a new independent and successful nation. Beijing 2008, of course, was an ideological proclamation: Communist China Ascendant and moving impressively and inexorably forwards towards regaining its regional, and perhaps global, status once more as the 'Middle Kingdom'. Guangzhou 2010 was equally a geopolitical proclamation of intent – on this occasion for regional eyes and ears: a reinforcement of the Beijing 2008 message. Brand China was once again marketed through compelling images – this time a 'Glittering Guangzhou' and gold medal of the adorned Chinese athletic.

All states have learnt to utilise modern sports mega-events as political tools. This is now the reality throughout East Asia. It is certainly no secret that sport and politics have been inseparable in the modern era in East Asia as elsewhere.

To return briefly to the consideration of the United Korean nation under Japanese imperial control, Lee Hak-Rae has claimed that the Chosun Sports Council on July 13, 1920, during the early twentieth-century Japanese oppression, was influenced by the national resistance of the March 1st Movement in 1919.[4] He bases this claim on the fact that the annual tournaments between 1929 and 1934 held by the Council were designed to use sport to sustain the people's sense of unity and argues that this demonstrated an attempt to keep alive the oppressed nation's spirit through sport. Nationalism and sport took on a new aspect in the later authoritarian Park Chung-hee regime.[5] Park Chan-seung believes that the dominant feature of the ruthless Park era was statism and claimed that Park's lavish regime combined statism *and* militarism after the Revitalization Reform in October 1972.[6] In the early 1970s, it is a well-known fact that sport was aggressively promoted for political purposes during those years of military dictatorship. Furthermore, significant events during this period, the construction of the Taereung Training Centre, support for the national football team, the Presidential Cup soccer tournament, the emergence of the national gymnastics and physical fitness tests, the creation of professional baseball and football leagues, the Seoul Asian Games and the Seoul Olympics

THE ASIAN GAMES: MODERN METAPHOR FOR 'THE MIDDLE KINGDOM' REBORN

Figure 1. Military related physical activities and training of Korean people during the Japanese colonisation. *Source*: From the collection of Gwang Ok.

during the military regime of Chun Doo-hwan,[7] were the products of dictatorial politicisation.[8]

International performance is frequently regarded as evidence of national superiority and used to demonstrate a nation's powerful political, cultural, social and economic systems. Sport allied to nationalism has been used to not only stress ideological, racial and national superiority, but also on occasion to manifest bitter feelings towards past conquerors and oppressors – arguably nowhere more intensely than in Asia. And the reason, it has been suggested that 'Sport...matters more in Asia because the turbulent histories that still the nations there. Historical animosities translate readily into political disputes there'[9] – and these animosities carried over into sport.

The Concept of '(the Complex)'

In psychology, a 'complex' ('ideenkomplex' or 'affect circumplex') is defined at one level as personal resentment towards a specific subject.[10] If a 'sport complex' is to be regarded as a similar mental and emotional state, it can be argued that sport is related in this way to communities, nations and races, as well as individuals. The concept of a 'sport complex', it is suggested, can be utilised as an explanatory tool in the specific context of modern sport. Can it be found in East Asia? Does it have a regional identity? Does it overlap with nationalistic, ethnic, political, economic, cultural and historical 'complexes' – superior and inferior? The answer given here is unequivocal. It does. It can be a manifestation of all or some of these things. In the modern East Asia, mega-sports events in particular, at times, chances for clashing political relations are higher than for harmonious ones. They may even be a substitute for ultimate aggression: in short, 'war without weapons'.

'Sports complex' can be an 'inferiority complex' or a 'superiority complex'. Either way, it can be a demonstration of 'covert' or 'overt' racial, ethnic and national animosity. This is not to suggest that success in sport is not a source of apolitical community and individual delight, euphoria and excitement but to recognise and acknowledge that it has both 'bright' and 'dark' potential.

> Sport is a mirror in which nations, men and women and social classes now see themselves. The image is sometimes bright, sometimes dark, sometimes distorted, sometimes magnified. This metaphorical mirror is a source of exhilaration and depression, security and insecurity, pride and humiliation, association and disassociation. As sport has grown to a gargantuous size, progressively replacing religion in its power to excite passion, it has come to loom larger and larger in [people's] lives.[11]

And loomed larger and larger, it must be added, in the calculations of nations in their struggles for status, self-pride and self-image – *and the settling of old political scores*.

Part 2

Colonisation, Postcolonisation, Consequences and Complexes

The postcolonial presence of 'sports complexes' can be usefully examined by focusing on three East Asian nations: China, Japan and South Korea.

South Korea and Japan: Resentment, Revenge and Sport

Despite South Korea's impressive economy, the world's 15th largest economy on the basis of gross domestic product, close nations have even more impressive economic records, namely China and Japan. In the case of Japan, South Korea also arguably has an inferiority complex, linked to some recent state history. Studies of postcolonial Korea invariably refer not only to Japan's direct political colonisation of Korea prior to 1945, but also to the indirect economic 'colonisation' of South Korea following the later civil war between South and North and incidentally to American 'neo-colonialism' in recent years. In consequence, as will be made clear shortly, South Korean resentment towards the three pacific powers is sometimes expressed through the medium of modern sport. Furthermore, China has impacted on Korea throughout its history. Korean resentment towards these three pacific powers as a result today is often expressed through modern sporting opportunities.

The patriotic zeal of South Koreans rises dramatically whenever the nation competes against Japan, the USA and China on sports fields and in sports arenas. A bitter historic legacy in the case of Japan is revealed by symbolic expressions used when South Korea meets Japan: 'Shatter Fuji Mountain', 'Overthrow Japan' and 'Overcome Japan' (Figure 2).

In the 1960s and 1970s, professional boxing, wrestling and soccer provided opportunities for revengeful expressions of postcolonial hostility. Victory was an important part of national self-assertion, satisfaction and recrimination, and revenge made was all the sweet in view of a postcolonial Japanese economic 'imperialism' which replaced the

Figure 2. Statement of memory: after winning against Japan during the 2006 World Baseball Classic, several Korean players plant flags on the pitcher's mound. *Source*: http://viewfrom103.blogspot.kr/2006/03/world-baseball-classic-will-empire.html

political variety. The arrival in East Asian of sports mega-events – the Olympic Games, the Asian Games and the Soccer World Cup – has greatly increased opportunities for many of the open display of a legacy of loathing: redemptive moments of national psychological reconstruction.

The decision to hold the 1988 Olympics in South Korea instead of Japan played a crucial role in enhancing the country's sense of distance from Japan's humiliating past oppression. Pride in actually extending this distance reached a new peak when South Korea became host partner with Japan for the Korea–Japan Soccer 2002 World Cup, soared *even higher* then when the South Koreans beat the Japanese in the 2006 and 2009 World Baseball Classic (WBC).[12]

A legacy of loathing is spelt out with emphatic clarity in this frank observation:

> The history of the 2002 World Cup cannot be separated from the history of imperialism in East Asia, albeit that imperialism has characterized not so much the relationship between the West and the East as the relationship between Japan and Korea. For South Korea, there was in the offing a clear opportunity to redress its humiliating past at the hands of Japan and the Japanese.[13]

Finally, it should not be overlooked that South Korea (like China)[14] has past and present territorial grievances with Japan which have inflamed South Korean *sensibilities* – Park

Jung-woo became a South Korean hero in the London 2012 Olympics for political reasons. The footballer in the eyes of his nation scored a spectacular political goal:

> South Korea was pitted against rival Japan in the bronze medal contest. It was a physical match with seven yellow cards drawn on the two teams. After South Korea defeated Japan 2 to nil, Park's teammates celebrated, waving a rather large South Korean flag. But winning was not enough for Park. He took off his jersey and then grabbed a sign and hoisted it over his head for the world to see. The sign read "Dokdo is our land," referring to a territorial dispute over two islets that sit between Korea and Japan in the East Sea (Sea of Japan).[15]

Park's timing was perfect, his impromptu signage followed only hours after the president of South Korea paid a visit to the islands (now occupied by South Korea). The unprecedented visit prompted the government of Japan to recall its ambassador from Seoul. The Japanese national legislature then prepared a rare joint resolution decrying ROK president's actions as an 'illegal landing' on Japanese territory. A letter of protest was presented to the South Korean government, which the ROK refused to open. The Koreans tried to return the letter to the Japanese government, which refused to receive it.[16] His national awards and rewards were nakedly symbolic – informal and formal: The picture of Park holding his Dokdo sign went viral on the web, and the footballer became a national hero. He was selected for his nation's World Cup team for the first time. Coaches, in making the selection, said that he was a strong midfielder who could cover a lot of ground, but from a Korean perspective, how could they not select him? Park was accorded other privileges as well. All men in Korea are required to do military service, but for athletes, an Olympic medal exempts one from such service. Technically, Park had not yet been allowed to receive his bronze medal,[17] but the Korean government accorded him this privilege nonetheless.[18] As it has been put succinctly, when the Koreans play the Japanese, *it is never just about sport.*

In addition, in hosting the Korea–Japan 2002 Soccer World Cup, South Korea ostensibly, and certainly to its own satisfaction, demonstrated to the world its equal status alongside Japan in the Western Pacific. The co-hosting of international events by a developing country and a developed country, and involving a county that had recently conquered other regional countries, provided an immense political lift to South Korean morale, suggesting as it did that South Korea and Japan were for once politically comparable.

The South Korean fierce and unwavering encouragement of the national team was expressed with acute intensity during the two recent World Baseball Championships of 2008 and 2009. The qualifying matches in 2008 were played in Tokyo, and the main rounds in the USA. South Korea beat Japan sparking off frenetic celebrations. Postcolonial patriotic euphoria exploded again throughout South Korea in 2009 with further successes against Japan. Beating Japan at baseball provides an excitement with a unique flavour rooted in the postcolonial paying off of old scores than victory in any other popular sports, such as football or basketball. Judo matches versus Japan in the Olympics and the Asian Games for obvious reasons also tend to have high value attached to them. East beats East at their *own* sport. A measure of the significance to South Korean of victories over Japan may be gauged from media reports. Japanese defeats at the hands of South Koreans in Judo, Volleyball and the Marathon in the 1994 Hiroshima Asian Games were reported as 'The third Sweeping Victory in Hiroshima' referring to earlier military defeat of Japan by Korea in the Japanese invasion of Korea in 1592 (Figure 3).[19]

Both Bong-Ju and Hwang Young-Cho were icons of revenge-realisation representatives of a remembered resolution in a dark moment in Korean history.

Anti-Japanese feelings reached boiling point during the 2010 Vancouver Winter Olympic Games. South Korea in a bid to win its first gold medal in the history of Olympic

Figure 3. Korean marathon stars, Lee Bong-Ju (left) and Hwang Young-Cho (right), both raised their arms after triumphant gold medal wins in the 14th Busan Asian Games and 1994 Hiroshima Asian Games marathon races, respectively. *Source*: http://image.search.naver.com/search.naver; http://mjse.multiply.com/journal/item/292/Hwang-Young-Cho-A-Run-for-Korea

skating was successful. The taste of victory was made special due to the fact that the rival in the final was Japanese and a former world champion (Figures 4 and 5).[20]

South Korea and the USA: 'Neo-Colonial Resentment'

In South Korea, resentment towards the USA although simmering for decades had rarely been seen openly in sport before the 2002 South Korea–Japan World Cup, although some South Korean spectators had cheered for the former Soviet Russia in a basketball match versus the USA which was considered by many South Korean as a neo-colonial expression of anti-Americanism. In the 2002 South Korea–Japan World Cup, anti-American neo-colonial exasperation was undisguised when South Korea met the USA in the qualifiers in the middle of several contentious domestic issues involving the USA including the presence of the US military,[21] the environmental pollution related to the US Army[22] and above all the deaths of two middle-school students killed accidentally by American soldiers (Figure 6).[23]

The match, which brought matters to a head in a sports encounter, ended in a draw. However, a South Korean team's ceremonial ritual afterwards was interpreted as a satire on the behaviour of the American 'occupier', and the resentment spilled over into sports. The USA had openly become a controversial issue in South Korea.[24] As there were no matches between South Korea and the USA in the main draw, however, further expressions of anti-Americanism did not occur (Figure 7).

Baseball in the future could be the fuse to set off an explosion of further anti-Americanism, especially if South Korea can defeat the USA in the WBC series. To humiliate America, the home of baseball by defeating it at the highest level would be the most complete example of 'putting one over' an increasingly resented 'occupying force',

Figure 4. Kim Yu Na rejoiced after receiving her score and setting a new world record for both short and free skate programmes. *Source*: http://www.csmonitor.com/World/Olympics/Olympics-blog/2010/0226/Kim-Yuna-record-score-gives-Vancouver-Olympics-their-6.0-moment

its presence seen as new-colonialism by the back door. The wings of the eagle would be momentarily clipped. In this context, it should not be forgotten that baseball above all else, in Japan, is also a potent indirect political assertion vis-à-vis the USA. Japan too feels moments of resentment towards a western conqueror and a once neo-colonial occupier.[25]

Figure 5. Skating rivals Kim Yu Na of Korea and Mao Asada of Japan. *Source*: http://english.chosun.com/site/data/html_dir/2010/05/10/2010051001297.html

THE ASIAN GAMES: MODERN METAPHOR FOR 'THE MIDDLE KINGDOM' REBORN

Figure 6. *Note:* Civil organisation hosts a memorial service for two South Korean teenaged girls who were killed by a US military vehicle on June 13, 2002 in Yangju, Gyeonggi Province. Since then, major candlelight protests have been held in Seoul and large cities nationwide against negotiations for South Korea–United States Free Trade Agreement policies and other administrative policies made by the government. *Source*: http://english.hani.co.kr/arti/english_edition/e_national/293278.html

South Korea and China: 'Sports Complex' as Inferiority Complex?

China is viewed uneasily, not unreasonably, by South Korea. Its vast size, its vast population and not least, its momentous economic rise besides which even the South Korean performance seems limp, increasingly produced in the South Korean people ambivalence, admiration and anxiety. In the past, at times, 'the Middle Kingdom' has

Figure 7. Korean soccer players performed a ceremonial dance that was interpreted as a satire against the USA after a goal during the 2002 World Cup qualifying round. *Source*: http://www.youtube.com/watch?v=4um2LtvjWhE

directly dominated the Korean nation: 'the peninsula's history – that is, its geography – had too often been bleak. There had always been a more powerful regional player, a nation on a power ascent of its own, eager to dominate Korea'.[26] In regional history that 'player' has been on occasion, China.[27] In future, it may well exert indirect dominance: economic and military. However, South Koreans have feelings of *both* inferiority and superiority. They are aware of their individual higher living standards, greater general personal wealth, wider availability of educational provision especially in higher education facilities and above all perceived advantage in terms of personal freedom due to their democratic political system. Nevertheless, they have 'anti-colonial' moments of fierce exhilaration when they defeat their huge neighbour – in sport. History casts a long shadow.

A salient example: when South Korea's basketball team defeated the Chinese during the basketball finals of the 2002 Pusan Asian Games, the victory was compared to the collapse of the Great Wall.[28] The triumph of the South Korean Yoo Seung-min over a Chinese in the men's singles table tennis final in the 2004 Athens Olympic Games was greeted with national delight tinged with anti-imperial colour. Victories against China in sport represent freedom from the past threat of bondage by the gigantic and powerful China as well as the assertion of a small national over a large nation providing a boost to national morale. Meanwhile, South Korea's successes against China in football help South Koreans to cope with a more general inferiority complex caused by China and allow them a 'postcolonial' and 'anti-colonial' perception that South Korea is bravely facing up to China rather than allowing China to intimidate it (Table 1).

'Given that China promises to be so inordinately powerful and different, it is difficult to resist the idea that in time its rise will herald the birth of a new international order'.[29] In this world order increasingly organised around China, South Korea's success in sports in which China has superior skills, or in a popular global sport such as football, allows South Korea to feel confident that the relationship with China will not be invariably one-sided.

Sport in South Korea can also be understood as South Korea's attempt to strengthen the identity of the nation during the present globalisation. In the global era, it has become commonplace for the concept of a single ethnic nation to weaken in, for importance, for multi-ethnicity and multiculturalism to emerge in many countries and for labour migration

Table 1. Reverse domination: Korea versus China results for the last 20 years.

Year and host country	South Korea	China	Round	Final result
1990 Beijing, China	Win (2-0)	Loss	Preliminary round	South Korea: third place
1994 Hiroshima, Japan		Did not meet		China: second place; South Korea: fourth place
1998 Bangkok, Thailand		Did not meet		China: third place
2002 Busan, South Korea		Did not meet		South Korea: third place
2006 Doha, Qatar		Did not meet		South Korea: fourth place
2010 Guangzhou, China	Win (3-0)	Loss	Round of 16 finals	South Korea: third place

Source: Korea versus China soccer match results for the last two decades sourced from http://www.ocasia.org/Index.aspx.

Table 2. Korean medal performance in the Asian Games as sources of reassurance.

Year	Gold	Silver	Bronze	Total	Rank
2010	76	65	91	232	2
2006	58	52	82	192	2
2002	96	80	84	260	2
1998	65	46	53	164	2
1994	63	56	64	183	3
1990	54	54	73	181	2

Source: http://www.ocasia.org.

trends to make crossing borders as common as changing jobs. When globalisation is understood as the process through which a neo-capitalistic world order is constructed with China at its centre, South Korea, which could once again become part of a new Chinese hegemony, will increasingly face challenges to its independence, indirectly if not directly, and thus, face threat to a sense of its own distinctive identity. In an identity crisis like this, the South Korean people are reassured by the achievements and successes of athletes: iconic symbols of nationalism and participate in the process of modern globalisation and the emergence of the new Asiatic world order with more confidence (Table 2).

The recent performances of South Korea athletes in the Guangzhou Asian Games were, therefore, a considerable boost to South Korean confidence vis-a-vis China but also vis-a-vis the other Asian nations. South Korea sent a message in all these countries but especially to its North East neighbour that South Korea can and will stand tall in East Asia: Sport was an assertive symbolic statement of national purpose and intent: intensity of confrontation in sport as capability with a deeper metaphorical meaning.

China and South Korea: Sports Complex as 'Superiority Complex'?

Chinese resentment towards South Korean athletes was witnessed not only at the 2008 Beijing Olympics but also at the 2010 Guangzhou Asian Games. Arguably, it has been the outcome of irritation that a small, local nation has had the audacity to challenge the much larger local neighbour. There is not space here to consider fully this Chinese expression of exasperation in all its political moments and all its manifestations – but an incident in Guangzhou will serve as further evidence of extensive, aggressive and even violent Chinese chauvinism.

During the 2010 Asian Games, Yang Shu-chun of Chinese-Taipei was expelled from the Taekwondo competition because she apparently installed two extra sensors on the heel of her socks.[30] The negative reaction to the South Koreans was probably provoked by a Game technician, a South Korean, who discovered the illegal sensors, and the officials from the World Taekwondo Federation (WTF), who were also South Koreans who banned the athlete for 3 months. Her coach also received a 20-month suspension.[31] As a result, Chinese particularly from Chinese Taipei burned South Korean flags, hacked the WTF website and smashed, as well as boycotted, imported products from South Korea in protest at the disqualification of Yang (Figure 8).[32]

There was a precedent for such aggressive behaviour, and serious confrontations related to sports incidents occurred prior to and during the 2008 Beijing Games. Rehearsal footage of the Opening Ceremony was leaked by a broadcasting station in South Korea infuriating the host nation.[33] This incident produced an outburst of ill-feeling towards South Korea, leading to reprehensible actions in various sports venues throughout the

THE ASIAN GAMES: MODERN METAPHOR FOR 'THE MIDDLE KINGDOM' REBORN

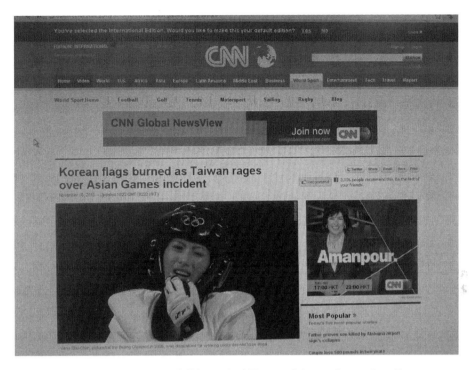

Figure 8. Yang Shu-chun, Cause of Chinese Anti-Korean violence. *Source*: http://www.monster-island.net/2010/11/so-this-is-what-it-feels-like-to-be-on.html

Games. In archery, for example, the South Korean women had to deal with vindictive distractions including whistling blowing and booing from the Chinese spectators.[34] This is merely the tip of the iceberg (Figure 9).[35]

It is perfectly reasonable to suggest that acerbic and sour relations between China and South Korea's longest term have a political dimension. To what *extent* Chinese protests are government inspired and directed must be conjectured, but Chinese support for North Korea – a fellow communist country – in its struggles with South Korea possibly predisposes the Chinese to less than warm feelings towards South Korea and its people: It is unwise to forget history with specific reference to the Korean conflict.

> In fact, Chinese concerns were much broader and were perhaps not very different, *mutatis mutandis*, from those of the United States. If the United States could decide that South Korea was within its security perimeter – in spite of apparently having ruled this out – and send troops to defend a pro-Western government there, might not China, which had given a series of increasingly explicit warnings on the subject, also see North Korea as being within its security perimeter and be willing to defend its interests with force? It seems remarkable in retrospect that so little attempt was made to understand the Chinese position.[36]

Japan and China: Antagonism and Sport

Acts of bitterness between Japan and China expressed at sports venues are well documented in the East Asia media and covered on occasion by the world's media.[37] The historical sources of – China and Japan – a long and deep animosity between the two great East Asia nations are well known, but the Nanjing Massacre is arguably the most powerful and painful memory of many that will not fade in Chinese consciousness.[38] The

Figure 9. Chinese outbursts against Korea during the 2008 Beijing Olympics. *Source*: http://image.search.naver.com/search.naver

consequence is that whenever a sports event is staged between the two countries, there is always a high probability of expressions of overt hatred. For instance, Chinese fans insultingly booed the Japanese team while their national anthem was being played, burned Japanese flags, shouted profanities and sang patriotic songs during the 2004 Asian Football Cup.[39] They did the same at the East Asian Cup Final in 2008.[40] Between no two other East Asian nations is sport the stimulus to such extreme enmity. Sports meetings between these regional counties, on occasion, appear to fully justify the famous (some say infamous and others say realistic) statement by George Orwell: 'Serious sport has nothing to so with fair play – it is bound up with hatred, jealousy, boastfulness, and disregard of all the rules!'[41] There is also no sign of rapprochement between the two nations: popular or political (Figures 10 and 11).

The recent tension between China and Japan over the Senkaku/Diaoyu islands is yet another – and very recent – example of politics carried over into sport.[42] The Chinese badminton team, for example, cancelled their participation in the Yonex Japan Open in September 2012. This decision was confirmed by the Japan Badminton Association Vice-Chairman, Yoshio Sekine, although he did not elaborate on the reason for the team's withdrawal.[43] The timing was hardly fortuitous (Figure 12).

In the case of the recent Tour of China in September 2012, the race organisers expelled the Japanese Cycling team. In the Tour of Beijing in 2012, the Japanese team was excluded.[44] It is uncertain whether the Chinese organisers themselves purposely ejected the Japanese or whether an influential governmental body instructed them to do so in retaliation to the Japanese government's inflexibility over the islands.[45]

In retaliation for these Chinese actions, the Japanese Figure Skating Team might withdraw from the Grand Prix series event held in Shanghai in November 2012. The Cup of China, which is the third stage of the 2012–2013 ISU Figure Skating Grand Prix season, in November, might not see the presence of the Japanese if the Chinese organisers cannot guarantee their security as a result of the two nations' controversial islands dispute and the rage it provokes in China (Figure 13).[46]

THE ASIAN GAMES: MODERN METAPHOR FOR 'THE MIDDLE KINGDOM' REBORN

Figure 10. After the controversial Asian Cup 2004 final match win of Japan against host China 3-1, Chinese soccer fans burned Japanese flags as a sign of protest while others sang anti-Japanese songs and chanted 'Kill! Kill! Kill!'. *Source*: http://www.washingtonpost.com/wp-dyn/articles/A40260-2004Aug27.html; http://www.chinaexpat.com/2008/07/28/chinas-soccer-blues.html/

Provocation comes in various guises and disguises. During the Japanese bid for the 2016 Summer Olympics, the Tokyo Bid Committee focused on three elements in order to obtain the support of International Olympic Committee (IOC) officials. They included the close proximities of the sports venues, their impressive existing facilities and ecological

THE ASIAN GAMES: MODERN METAPHOR FOR 'THE MIDDLE KINGDOM' REBORN

Figure 11. 2008 East Asian Cup Final between China and Japan. *Source*: http://cn.yimg.com/gallery/sports/200802210739148249748824749.jpg

and energy advantages. Although the members of Committee did not openly criticise the 2008 host, there was a clearly implicit criticism of China in the way Japan publicised and promoted their bid by contrasting their country with China and its shortcomings in 2008.[47] Few actions could be more inflammatory given that many consider Beijing 2008 the most spectacular, expensive and successful Games in Olympic history: epideictic in political purpose.

There has been only space here for fragments of evidence regarding the use of sport events between China and Japan as a surrogate as yet for ultimate violent action. And there is no sign that the surrogate will lose its symbolic meaning: Quite the opposite. As China grows stronger in sport as demonstrated so emphatically at Guangzhou in 2010 and Japan grows weaker, the former will become more delighted and the latter more depressed: Both attitudes are catalysts for future confrontation.

There is every possibility that rejoicing will become even louder on the one hand and despair will become even deeper on the other. Without question, sport is as much an agent of disharmony as harmony in international relations binding past, present and future with sport as the glue: Past military defeats, present geographical disputes, future economic unbalance and a nascent geopolitical reorientation of power could eventually result in further open demonstrations of hostility in sports arenas. This hostility will become sharper as the West declines in power and its 'colonial' and humiliations are replaced by an Eastern renaissance and the hegemonic struggle between China and the other nations of the region is once again resumed. There will be no western distractions. The East will face up to the East. And through sport, the Great Global Obsession of the twenty-first century, nations *will assess themselves and their worth* in confrontation with their neighbours in part through their athletes, through medals and through cups. China, Japan and South Korea will engage in regional struggle on sports fields and in sports arenas – with fresh intensity – for national self-confidence, self-pride and self-satisfaction.

Figure 12. Citizens of both China and Japan carry national flags and protest signs during their respective rallies in front of the Japanese Embassy in China (top picture) and Tokyo (bottom picture) about an island dispute known as the Diaoyu in China while it is called Senkaku in Japan. *Source:* http://www.japantimes.co.jp/news/2012/08/19/national/chinese-protest-against-japans-arrest-of-activists-who-traveled-to-senkaku-islands/#. UTSbiTBTDMs. http://www.pbs.org/newshour/rundown/2012/09/island-dispute-escalates-strains-between-china-and-japan.html

Part 3

Conclusion: East Confronts East

Memory is as sharp in East Asia as elsewhere in the world and,

> Memory has a special power. Memory, it has been written, resembles a film with sharply focused images, with the set tidily arranged and brightly lit and the script learnt and unchangeable. The memory of war is one of the most significant ways of shaping national identity: images of sacrifice, heroism, mourning and loss provide symbols of unity in suffering, in sadness, in valediction. Sport, and the memory of sport, while of a different order of individual and collective experience, also has the power to shape national identity.[48]

Figure 13. Political issues carried over to sports. *Source*: http://au.eurosport.com/cycling/china-withdraw-from-japan_sto3428432/story.shtml

And sport itself has a special allure:

> Sharply focused memories of sporting moments – played or watched – are among the most frequently recalled and infrequently forgotten. Such 'poetic' images enjoyed in pensive mood are rooted in particular places and perhaps, above all, in particular things: 'images which are the life of poetry cannot be raised in any perfection but by introducing particular objects.'[49]

More than this, sporting memories give communities the security of belonging. Sport is a powerful means of creating, sustaining and reinforcing imagined communities – making the imagined concrete. It sustains the collectivity in hope and despair, happiness and sadness, pleasure and pain. For many, it has replaced religion as the opium as the masses. This is as true for East Asia as anywhere on earth. But sport has yet another contribution to make to the masses and their rulers – its role in the contemporary shaping of national identity, allegiance *and* antagonism. This cannot be ignored:

> Sport reinforces antagonism bred on memories of 'battles long ago', defeats deep in the past and victories recorded in history books, and as such exacerbates antipathy, fuels hostility and extends dislike. Sport can be sublimated warfare kept alive repeatedly year after year, in 'conflicts without casualties' in national stadiums keeping vivid past conflicts with casualties and perhaps contributing to future conflicts with casualties![50]

And perhaps for this good reason

> the team spirit inherent in all international sports gives scope to a number of truly valuable patterns of social behaviour which are essentially motivated by aggression, and which, in all probability, have evolved under the selection pressure of tribal warfare at the very dawn of culture.[51]

There has been no shortage of statements about sport as an ameliorative means of accord between nations. IOC pronouncements have been replete with them. Indeed, sport is frequently depicted as a positive force in international relations, not just in preventing potential conflict but also acting as a means to bring states and their people closer together.[52]

Merely two illustrations:

> Article 11 of UNESCO's 1978 International Charter of Physical Education and Sport reads: Through cooperation and the pursuit of mutual interests in the universal language of physical education and sport, all people will contribute to the preservation of lasting peace, mutual respect and friendship and will thus create a propitious climate for solving international problems' (UNESCO 1978). The Olympic Charter talks of 'building a peaceful and better world' and the Olympic movements' current 'peace through sport' initiative sets out a vision of being able to 'build a better world by promoting the Olympic Truce and using sport to forge friendship among athletes, young people and communities.'[53]

For the sake of balance, it is sensible to see all that

> The 1988 Seoul Summer Olympic Games provides a dramatic depiction of the close relationship between politics, geopolitics and sport. The Games followed decades-long ideological inimicality between democracy and despotism. Korea, North and South, was for a time an ideological crucible of confrontation. Moreover, the Seoul Summer Olympic Games held on the Korea Peninsula – itself a horrific symbol of Cold War conflict – came hard on the heels of two earlier politicised Games: Moscow, 1980 and Los Angeles, 1984, in which only about half 'the Global Village' participated which made a nonsense of the Olympic Movement's ideals of the universality of involvement.[54]

Without any doubt, it is time for a fuller consideration of sport as a means of aggressive confrontation between nations.[55] The discussion here offers evidence for this of fresh substantiality. The argument presented here constitutes an interpellation of possibly too many plots of pontifications.

Reprise: national, political, cultural and emotional animosities expressed through sport have been briefly explored in three East Asian nations: China, Japan and Korea: paradigmatic exemplars in an East Asian setting. A deeper and fuller enquiry is planned for the future. Self-evidently, there is insufficient space available here to do complete justice to the subject.

Concluding Comments

It has been argued that 'The most important function in sport lies in furnishing a safety value for that most indispensable and at the same time most dangerous form of aggression ... collective military enthusiasm!'[56] This may be true but the reverse is equally true throughout history – Asian history and world history sport has been used as a preparation for war.[57] It has also been argued with the best of intentions that 'as the twentieth century devises yet more total means of mass destruction, it is not too fanciful to discern an instinct for self-preservation in the popular passion for representative sport. A kind of warfare perhaps. But war without weapons.' It has earned a rejoinder:

> What is more to the point is that war will continue to serve sport and sport to serve war well beyond the twentieth century. Sport will serve anti-militarism far less well,[58] and provoked an acerbic comment: [The] close and continuing relationship between sport and war should not be hidden behind the pious platitudes of officials, administrators and functionaries of regional and global sports organisations uttered at the reception of another international sports event at which they appear yet again in the majority to clasp each other hands with shining eyes and express their delight at the healing balm of modern sport.[59]

The reality: relationships express as open dislike – even manifest hatred – throughout recent decades have characterised sport involving China, Japan and Korea. This is certainly *part of the story of engagement and this part is a legacy of the past.*

THE ASIAN GAMES: MODERN METAPHOR FOR 'THE MIDDLE KINGDOM' REBORN

> In Asia [more particularly East Asia] today, moreover, leaders of nations will refuse to meet with one another because of controversial historical actions or statements. Both China and South Korea's presidents refused to meet with Japanese Prime Minister Junichiro Koizumi in 2006 because Koizumi paid respects at Yasukuni Shrine, which is a memorial commemorating Imperial Japan's war dead. A long string of diplomatic disputes over insensitive statements by politicians or because of controversial history textbooks have afflicted Japan–Korea and Japan–China and Korea–China relations. Westerners are often astounded by how much history remains alive in Asia.[60]

And the result,

> Sport acts as an outlet for releasing pent-up historical resentments in ways that cannot be expressed through regular diplomacy. To put it bluntly, Japan's imperial past in Asia causes most former colonies to view every match with Japan as a historical grudge match.[61]

Prophecy is a risky business, especially in history: 'History is not an exam question. It is chaotic, contradictory and complicated.' It has been described as 'messy, unpredictable, contradictory, transitory' and has also been said with succinctness, 'Too often mess is the quiddity of history'.[62] Yet prophecy here will be attempted with the conviction of reasonable certainty: China, Japan and Korea (South) will become more affluent, more confident and on occasion, more combative towards each other in the twenty-first century. Possibly, a portent of things to come is contained in the recent headline of a respected western national newspaper. It announced with reference to the Diaoyu/Senkaku islands stand-off: *Japan and China Heading for Military Clash*.

Below it an East Asian analyst Yang Xuetong stated with regard to the region, 'In terms of the [regional] economy, China and the US are partners . . . in terms of security they are rivals . . . When China narrows the [military] gap it will scare the US!'[63] It will also scare Japan and South Korea. The islands dispute may not result in a military clash – some argue that China is not yet ready and is biding its time: militarily, a still sleeping dragon.

> China has been spending increasing amounts of money on its military, which has been modernized into an impressive fighting force. This is and should be a source of concern to its immediate neighbors and countries with which it has ongoing border disputes. But the build-up of the PLA is not just about having the ability to project force abroad, the Chine regime still thinks of itself as needing to ensure that China is not attacked...And at least as significantly, it also sees having a powerful military as crucial for maintaining control at home . . . [64]

Nevertheless, the islands dispute has heightened tension in the region and is far from finished. As America grows geographically *and* regionally politically weaker, China grows geographically and regionally politically stronger. Japan and South Korea (and other regional nations – not least India) watch with ever increasing anxiety.

Against this backdrop, the Guangzhou Asian Games become a *modern metaphor* for China's increasing wider dominance. *The Middle Kingdom is Reborn*. And against this backdrop, sport will be increasingly one demonstrative means of defining regional nation against regional nation – *psychologically*, as well as politically, economically, culturally and socially: optimistically, a possible surrogate – a war without weapons seen on 'playing fields' not battlefields. Realistically, even on these 'playing fields', one thing will not diminish in the foreseeable future, national antipathy – one nation to the other. Indeed, it may well increase as a wide struggle beyond sport as the Far East develops for resources to sustain new standards of living. That is the prophecy reiterated. Time holds the answer.

> 'The Great Game', in which world powers struggled a century ago for control of oil in Central Asia, may well recur in the coming century. When states are rivals for control of scarce natural resources, military conflicts will be harder to avert.[65]

East Asia, no doubt in due course, will have its local 'Great Game!'

CODA

To conclude with three pronouncements and two questions:

> Civilizations geographically distant from one another might trade amicably with one another, allowing the gradual emergence of an international division of labour. But it was just as possible for one civilization to make war on another, for the same base motives that had actuated man in prehistoric times: to expropriate nutritional and reproductive resources. Historians, it is true, can study only those human organizations sophisticated enough to keep enduring records. But no matter how complex the administrative structure we study, we should not lose sight of the basic instincts buried within even the most civilized men. These instincts were to be unleashed time and again after 1900.[66]

and,

> History does not stop. It continues, as evolving technologies interact with the unalterable human animal and old conflicts are given new twists. Governments may be better informed than they have ever been, but they are not any wiser and if politicians and their advisers believed the boom could go on forever it was because they had lost any sense of history.[67]

and again,

> The War of the Worlds remains science fiction. The War of the World is, however, historical fact. Perhaps, like Wells' story, ours will be ended abruptly by the intervention of microscopic organisms like the avian influenza virus, which could yet produce a worse mutation and pandemic than that of 1918. Until that happens, however, we remain our own worst enemies. We shall avoid another century of conflict only if we understand the forces that caused the last one — the dark forces that conjure up ethnic conflict and imperial rivalry out of economic crisis, and in doing so negate our common humanity. They are forces that stir within us still.[68]

Will global sport via the Olympic Games and the like, and regional sport via the Asian Games and the like stimulate, repress or be the forces that stir within us still? Is this a rhetorical question?

Acknowledgements

The authors wish to thank Professor Gwang Ok for permission to use photographs in his possession and Marcus P. Chu for skilled support with presentational preparation.

Notes on Contributors

J.A. Mangan, Emeritus Professor, University of Strathclyde, FRHS, FRAI, FRSA, RSL, D.Litt. is Founding Editor of *The International Journal of the History of Sport* and the series *Sport in the Global Society* and author of the globally acclaimed *Athleticism in the Victorian and Edwardian Public School, The Games Ethic and Imperialism* and *'Manufactured' Masculinity: Making Imperial Manliness, Morality and Militarism* and author or editor of some 50 publications on politics, culture, and sport.

Hyun-Duck Kim is a professor in the College of Physical Education at Keimyung University in South Korea. His main research interests focus on managerial issues of sport organization in Asia and how these influence the economy and society.

Angelita Cruz works in the College of Physical Education at Keimyung University. She explores topics concerning Eastern and South Eastern sports.

Gi-Heun Kang works in the Department of Taekwondo at Kyung-Hee University in South Korea and his research interest is in the area of sport consumer behavior.

Notes

1. Kim, *Research on Korean Nationalism*, 54–55.
2. Lee, "What is Nationalism," 3–13.

THE ASIAN GAMES: MODERN METAPHOR FOR 'THE MIDDLE KINGDOM' REBORN

3. Lee, "Minjokjueui and Nationalism," 100–103.
4. Park, "Relationship," 94–95.
5. Lee, "Korean Sport History," 243–262.
6. Park, "The Origin of Stateism," 199–246.
7. Chung, "The Return," 125–145.
8. Ibid.
9. Cha, *Beyond the Final Score,* 23.
10. Song, "Sport and Politics," 131.
11. Mangan, *Prologue, Sport in Europe.*
12. Although Korea did not win the championships in both occasions, the fact that they won more games 2-1 in 2006 and only lost during the 2009 final match was considered "victories" for the whole nation.
13. Close and Askew, "Globalization and Football."
14. See Cha, "'Winning is Not Enough'." Cha's essay is an incisive comment on the politics of sport in the region. His *Beyond the Final Score: The Politics of Sport in Asia* is equally penetrating.
15. Ibid.
16. Ibid.
17. Withheld by the IOC for violating the Olympic spirit and infringing the ruling on political statements.
18. Cha, "'The Asian Games and Diplomacy'."
19. In the Marathon event, two Koreans won the gold and bronze medals courtesy of Hwang Young-Cho and Kim Jae-Ryong, respectively, while Japan got the silver. Similarly in Judo, from the seven gold medals won by South Korea, six of them battled against Japanese judokas.
20. South Korea's Kim Yun Na won her first Winter Olympic Games gold medal and also the first medal in figure skating for the country. She received the highest scores in both the short and free skate programmes defeating Mao Asada of Japan who landed second place.
21. Paik, "Korean Village Could be First."
22. *Green Korea United.* Accessed October 24, 2012. http://green-korea.tistory.com/52
23. *ROK Drop,* "GI Flasback: The 2002 Armored Vehicle Accident." June 13, 2008. http://rokdrop.com/2008/06/13/gi-myths-the-2002-armored-vehicle-accident/
24. Koh, Andrews and White, "Beyond the Stadium," 315–329.
25. In the space available in this essay, this issue will be left for another occasion and another essay.
26. Mangan and Ok, "Seoul'88 – Media, Politicians, Public," 22.
27. China's invasion of Korea happened during the Qing Empire in 1627 and 1637.
28. The Korean basketball squad won against China via overtime and their first Asian Games championship in 20 years. The team managed to win the game even with the powerhouse Chinese players led by walking "Great Wall" centres Yao Ming, Menk Bateer and Wang Zhizhi.
29. Jacques, *When China Rules the World,* 16.
30. *The China Post.* "Asian Games Marred by Controversy." November 18, 2010. http://www.chinapost.com.tw/taiwan/national/national-news/2010/11/18/280379/p1/Asian-Games.htm
31. Arirang, "Taiwan Calls for Restraint."
32. CNN, "Korean flags burned"; Mack, "Taekwon-NO! Controversy."
33. Chang, A. "Some Secrets out about Olympics Opening Ceremony" (*USA Today*, July 31, 2008). http://usatoday30.usatoday.com/sports/olympics/beijing/2008-07-31-opening-ceremonies-leak_N.htm
34. *The Korea Times.* "Anti-Korean Sentiment Seoul, Beijing Should Boost Understanding and Friendship." August 21, 2008. http://www.koreatimes.co.kr/www/news/opinon/2008/08/202_29759.html
35. At the baseball stadium, the Japanese team received loud cheers, whereas the Korean opponents were greeted with jeers by the Chinese fans who watched the game. The same thing happened at the women's table tennis competition.
36. Cooper, *The Breaking of Nations,* 92.
37. Zhe, T. "Take Soccer Back to School, Says 'Godfather' of Beijing Soccer" (*China Daily*, August 21, 2011). http://www.chinadaily.com.cn/sports/2011-08/21/content_13157472.htm
38. See Gendercide, http://www.gendercide.org/case_nanking.html.

39. See "Anti-Japanism at sporting events," http://en.wikipedia.org/wiki/Anti-Japanese_sentiment_in_China.
40. Ibid.
41. George Orwell Quotes, http://www.george-orwell.org/l_quotes.html.
42. *New Straits Times*, "Biejing Marathon Bars Japanese Amid Island Row: Report." November 10, 2012. http://www.nst.com.my/latest/beijing-marathon-bars-japanese-amid-island-row-report-1.169579
43. O. Shine, "Chinese Miss Japan Open as Diplomatic Row Rages" (*Reuters*, September 18, 2012). http://www.reuters.com/article/2012/09/18/us-badminton-japan-china-idUSBRE88H0DL20120918
44. See Tour of Beijing official website, http://www.tourofbeijing.net/teams/.
45. VeloNation, "Japanese riders and Personnel out."
46. A. Himmer, "Figure Skating: Japan Considers Cup of China Pullout" (*Reuters*, September 23, 2012). http://www.reuters.com/article/2012/09/23/us-figure-skating-japan-china-idUSBRE88M04D20120923
47. Kelly, "East Asian Olympics."
48. Mangan, *Militarism, Sport, Europe*.
49. Ibid.
50. Ibid.
51. Ibid.
52. Bridges, *The Two Koreans*.
53. See UNESCO, "International Charter."
54. Mangan and Ok, "Seoul'88 – Media, Politicians, Public," 27–28.
55. In the case of Asia, Victor Cha is obligatory reading, especially his writings mentioned earlier.
56. Ibid., 281.
57. Ibid., 283.
58. In the case of Asia, Victor Cha is obligatory reading, especially his writings mentioned earlier.
59. Ibid., 824.
60. Cha, "Winning is Not Enough," 9–10.
61. Ibid.
62. Mangan, *Prologue, Sport in Europe*.
63. *The Daily Telegraph*, September 20, 2012, 22.
64. Wasserstrom, *China in the 21st Century*, 17–18.
65. Gray, *False Dawn*, 218.
66. Ferguson, "The War of the World," XIV.
67. Gray, *False Dawn*, XII.
68. Ferguson, *The War of the World*, 64.

References

Arirang. "Taiwan Calls for Restraint over Asian Games Taekwondo Controversy." November 22, 2010. http://www.arirang.co.kr/News/News_View.asp?nseq=109324&code=Ne2&category=2

Bridges, B. *The Two Koreas and the Politics of Global Sport*. London: Global Oriental, 2012.

Cha, V. "The Asian Games and Diplomacy in Asia: Korea–China–Russia." *International Journal of the History of Sport*. doi: 10.1080/09523367.2013.782537.

Cha, V. *Beyond the Final Score: The Politics of Sport in Asia*. New York: Columbia University Press, 2011.

Chung, J. Y. "The Return of the Sports Republic: Sports and the June 1987 Uprising." *Critical Review of History* 78 (2007): 125–145.

Close, P., and D. Askew. "Globalization and Football in East Asia." In *Football Goes East*, edited by Wolfren Manzenreiter and John Horne, 243–256. New York: Routledge, 2004.

CNN. "Korean Flags Burned as Taiwan Rages over Asian Games Incident." November 18, 2010. http://edition.cnn.com/2010/SPORT/11/18/asian.games.china.taiwan/

Cooper, R. *The Breaking of Nations: Order and Chaos in the Twenty-First Century*. London: Atlantic Books, 2003.

Ferguson, N. *The War of the World: History's Age of Hatred*. London: Penguin Books, 2006.

Gendercide. Accessed December 21, 2012. http://www.gendercide.org/case_nanking.html

Gray, J. *False Dawn: The Delusions of Global Capitalism*. London: Granta Books, 2009.

THE ASIAN GAMES: MODERN METAPHOR FOR 'THE MIDDLE KINGDOM' REBORN

Jacques, M. *When China Rules the World: The Rise of the Middle Kingdom and the End of the Western World*. London: Allen Lane, 2009.

Kelly, W. "East Asian Olympics, Beijing 2008, and the Globalisation of Sport." *The International Journal of the History of Sport* 28, no. 16 (2011): 2261–2270. doi: 10.1080/09523367.2011.626679.

Kim, D. S. *Research on Korean Nationalism*. Seoul: Olem Publications, 1996.

Koh, E., D. L. Andrews, and R. White. "Beyond the Stadium, and into the Street." In *East Plays West: Essays on Sport and the Cold War*, edited by S. Wagg, and D. Andrews, 315–329. London: Routledge, 2007.

Lee, Gyu-Ho. "Minjokjueui and Nationalism." *The Unified Korea* 21, no. 8 (1985): 100–103.

Lee, H. R. "Korean Sport History during the End of Japanese Colonization Era." *Journal of East Asian Cultures* 15, no. 1 (1989): 243–262.

Lee, K. W. "What is Nationalism?" *The Academy of Korean Studies* 17, no. 2 (1994): 3–13.

Mack, L. "Taekwon-NO! Controversy at Asian Games Heats Up." About.com. November 19, 2010, http://chineseculture.about.com/b/2010/11/19/taekwon-no-controversy-at-asian-games-heats-up.htm

Mangan, J. A., ed. *Militarism, Sport, Europe: War Without Weapons*. London: Frank Cass, 2003.

Mangan, J. A., ed. *Prologue, Sport in Europe: Politics, Class, Gender*. New York: Taylor and Francis, 1999.

Mangan, J. A., and G. Ok. "Seoul'88 – Media, Politicians, Public: Confrontation, Cooperation and Democratic Consequences." *The International Journal of the History of Sport* 29, no. 16 (2012): 2276–2292.

Park, H. S. "Relationship between International Sport Activity and Social Integration – Possibility and Limitation." *Korean Journal of International Studies* 42, no. 2 (2002): 93–110.

Paik, K. "Korean Village Could be First Casualty of US Military's 'Pacific Pivot'." *Earth Island Journal*. October 29, 2012. http://www.earthisland.org/journal/index.php/elist/eListRead/korean_village_could_be_first_pacific_pivot_casualty/

Park, C. S. "The Origin of Stateism in Korea." *The Journal of Korean History* 117 (2002): 199–246.

Song, Byung-Rok. "Sport and Politics: Lessons of the West-East German Sports Exchanges on the Integration of Two Koreas." *Zeitschrift der Koreanisch-Deutschen Gesellschaft fuer Sozialwissenschaften* 14, no. 2 (2004): 131–151.

UNESCO. "International Charter of Physical Education and Sport." http://www.unesco.org/education/educprog/eps/EPSanglais/EVENTS_ANG/international_charter_ang.htm

VeloNation. "Japanese Riders and Personnel out of Tour of China Due to International Tensions." September 16, 2012. http://www.velonation.com/News/ID/12870/Japanese-riders-and-personnel-out-of-Tour-of-China-due-to-international-tensions.aspx#ixzz2AdGW3STP

Wasserstrom, J. *China in the 21st Century: What Everyone Needs to Know*. New York: Oxford University Press, 2010.

Guangzhou 2010: Singapore at a Global Crossroads

Peter Horton

School of Education, The Cairns Institute, James Cook University, Queensland, Australia

> This essay is an analysis of the reality of Singapore's Asian Games' aspirations and achievements and the responses to the challenges it faced in Guangzhou in 2010. How did 'Team Singapore' respond to the challenges that they met at what represented a crossroad in their sporting history at which they met the vehicle carrying China's sporting and soft power products. How did they react and were the effort, industry, hyperbole and not insignificant government financial outlay and policy initiatives worth it? The analysis constitutes a critique of articles relating to the Guangzhou Asian Games of 2010 that appeared in the three major English language newspapers in Singapore, *The Straits Times*, *The Sunday Times* and *The New Paper* before, during and after the Games. From the analysis, major themes emerged which characterised the environment of elite sport in Singapore and revealed that it is very much part of the nation's inimitable social, political and diplomatic schema; sport, as with all other socio-cultural institutions in Singapore, has not and does not evolve accidentally.

Introduction

> Singapore's authoritarian-capitalist regime has its own peculiar political arrangements that mesh with its economic policies. By combining a sense of national insecurity and dread of the unknown with the fear of government retribution, Singapore's ruling party has implemented a special form of 'Asian democracy' that can be identified as phobocracy. The rule-by-fear government of the People's Action Party (PAP) regime judiciously combines a western democratic vocabulary with a particular set of traditional values that it claims are unique to Asia.[1]

This review of the newspaper articles on the Asian Games of 2010 was undertaken mindful of the widely held belief that the press in Singapore has long been regarded as an extension of the authoritarian control of the People's Action Party (PAP) government's information network and is seen as being subject to the strict controls that the government imposes upon the media.[2] Whether the 'phobocracy' of 1998 still operates today is highly contestable, Singapore, however, is still governed by a definitive form of 'Asian democracy'.[3]

The three newspapers embraced in this review and all other newspapers and magazines in Singapore are still engaged in what has been referred to as 'Third World development journalism' where the media is expected to give aid and assistance to the 'great tasks of nation building ... building a political consciousness, (and) assisting economic development'.[4] Early in Lee Kuan Yew's rule, he placed draconian restrictions on the media, which were claimed to be protecting the nation from pro-Communist activists. The media was governed by the Official Secrets Act, and there was a ban on many overseas publications, ranging from *Mao's Little Red Book* to the *Playboy Magazine*.[5] In 1998, Prime Minister Goh Chok Tong was still exhorting the media to do their duty by supporting the government's nation-building efforts, unifying the nation through supportive editorial comment.[6]

Singapore's third Prime Minister, Lee Hsien Loong,[7] won a 'mere' 60% of the vote in the election in 2012 and now faces a 'challenge (to) the nation's paternalistic leaders and their "autocratic light" style of governance'[8] via a wave of mute political activism. Confronted by the need to jockey the media he now faces challenges emanating from the social media revolution and the ever-growing online-media access, though the government still assiduously vets all media output, which has for over two decades left the populace, as Joshua Kurlantzick maintains, virtually 'tongue-tied'.[9] Central to this is the fact that the dominant newspaper publisher is Singapore Press Holdings (SPH), a government-linked print media monopoly, has since 1996 controlled all English, Chinese, Malay and Tamil newspapers.[10] It is thus not surprising that all of these exhibit exemplary levels of self-censoring with all domestic news particularly political commentary following the PAP line.[11] Cherian George, an ex-*Straits Times* journalist, suggested that not only has the press-media been centralised and mainstreamed, but also it has been totally marginalised.[12] George describes this situation succinctly, suggesting that this arrangement actually 'facilitates the government's freedom *from* the press'[13] rather than promoting the liberal democratic ideal of the freedom *of* the press.

Apart from the legal constraints placed upon the release of specific political information and of course in regard to the publication of material that would have national security repercussions, the force of law exerted upon making anti-government or anti-Singaporean comments or statements that are deemed to be contrary to the implicit nation-building role the media in Singapore is obligated to exhibit is ironically enshrined in Article 14 (1) of the Constitution of the Republic of Singapore, which guarantees Singapore citizens the rights 'to freedom of speech and expression, peaceful assembly without arms, and association',[14] while Article 14 (2) outlines the contexts in which these rights can be revoked.[15] It is here that fragility of the freedom of speech, assembly and association in Singapore can be detected. If it is deemed by the government or their agents that at any time the 'security of the Singapore or any part thereof' is under threat such rights can be revoked by laws imposed by Parliament.[16]

Lee Kuan Yew's authoritarian power still casts a long shadow over Singapore's governance[17] and consequently any commentary on the performances and conduct of the nation's athletes, the national sporting bodies and, even by association, the related government ministers in such a politically sensitive context as the Asian Games, particularly when it is being hosted by Asia's most geopolitically powerful nation, China. It goes without saying that all journalists have to exert restraint and to carefully phrase any reference to their hosts. From the initial review of the articles from the major English language newspapers addressing the Guangzhou Asiad three themes emerged that illustrate not only Singaporean attitudes, values and its sporting ideology but also the media's linkage to the politico-economic institutions that form a hegemony where little is left to chance.

Considering the geopolitical sensitivity of the relationship between Singapore and China, an interpretation of text that directly discusses China's performance as hosts sets the scene for this analysis. Eternally Team Singapore faces intense media scrutiny at mega-sports festival; the team and officials suffer an inevitably high level of pressure with expectations and grandiose predictions often rampant. This hangs over the team like the sword of Damocles and all know of the likely consequence of failure. This was most evident in Guangzhou and for some the blade was felt even before the team left for China. The final theme is the discussion of individual successes and failures and the team's collective performance. There were a few 'Golden' moments but predictably there were more 'brickbats than bouquets' and many were aimed at team officials and managers.

China, Guangzhou, the Games: Singapore's View

For China, the Guangzhou Asian Games of 2010 represented a further extension of its massive campaign to internationalise the nation and to assert its status in Asia. It also served to further establish China's position as the hegemon of Asian sport, firstly by its hosting, organising and presenting of what was, unquestionably, the most lavish and best organised Asian Games ever[18] and secondly with the Chinese team's outstanding performance. The Guangzhou Asiad was heralded throughout Asia and beyond. A majority of competitors and managers from the visiting national teams concurred that these were indeed the most extravagant Asian Games ever though they will probably 'never be this big again'.[19]

At the global crossroads before the dragon's lair, Singaporean journalists were mindful of the potential disasters and predictably the initial flurry of articles ahead of the Opening Ceremony was positive, and in both *The Straits Times* and *The New Paper*, the Asiad was characterised as being China's '3rd blockbuster project',[20] following the Beijing Olympic Games of 2008 and the World Expo, also in 2010 in Shanghai. Much was made of the extravagant preparations, the extent of the infrastructure improvements and the new sporting facilities, which as the Public Relations Director for the Guangzhou Asian Games Organising Committee, Sun Xiuqing,[21] pointed out were 'mainly located in the district and country level cities or colleges, where there was a lack of sports facilities'.[22] This seemingly excellent decision, one that ticked the 'sustainability box', spreading the infrastructure legacy to the provincial areas of Guangdong, was to raise the ire of Singapore's Chef de Mission, Low Teo Ping, as he was annoyed that he had to travel so far to the various outlying venues. Though in one of his final interviews, he conceded that though they 'were far apart ... they were well thought about beforehand, located in different townships'.[23] Throughout the Games Low Teo Ping was to make some ill-considered statements and eventually became a victim of Team Singapore's 'less-than-stellar showing at these Asian Games'.[24]

In her opening report in *The Straits Times* Ling Chang Hong also pointed out that as she toured the city before the opening ceremony, 'there appeared to be little of the panic seen in New Delhi before last month's Commonwealth Games, which were plagued with problems including delayed construction and corruption scandals'.[25]

The New Paper On Sunday launched its coverage of the Guangzhou Games with an excellent lead article that informatively foreshadowed the up-coming Games. It outlined the efforts Guangzhou had made 'sprucing' the city up and in creating yet another opportunity for China to 'showcase' itself by staging a 'spectacle of Olympic proportions'.[26] An accompanying article also presented a balanced, informative and comprehensive discussion of China's favouritism in upcoming table tennis competitions whimsically entitled, 'Solid GREAT WALL'.[27] Upon closer examination it was noted that both articles were taken from Associated Press (AP) and probably via Reuters Beijing office. Two days later, the somewhat 'polite' coverage in *The New Paper* soon gained some bite, with Lim Say Heng's first 'Games Diary' being headed, 'Strike one, Guangzhou',[28] in which he criticised the 'hour long bus rides' to and from the venues and volunteers who smiled like 'Stepford Wives'[29] but were unable to provide any worthwhile information. He was also irritated by the annoying mix-ups with the interview schedules.[30] It would seem that Lim Say Heng's industry was not however daunted, as he virtually single-handedly, with the help of AP, produced all the reports for *The New Paper* from Guangzhou.

The plaudit-like initial reports from *The Straits Times* and *The Times on Sunday* were polite and 'politically correct'. Lin Xinyi in her commentary on the power of the Chinese team and the ambitious though, as it turned out nearly spot-on predictions that the 'hosts can break the 200-gold barrier'[31] was not just being obsequious as she continued with a similarly deferential review of South Korea's and Japan's medal prospects. In her final reflection, *The Straits Times*' China Bureau Chief, Peh Shing Huei, acclaimed that 'The Real Winners [*sic*] in Guangzhou' was 'Brand China'. Peh suggested that China's dominance did not end in the sport arenas; China had also won the contest in the commercial arena saying 'the country's commercial brands have been wiping the floor with their advertisements and endorsements'[32] and she maintained that, as domestic companies had secured 88% of the Games' sponsorships, Brand China had a virtual monopoly of the event's sponsorship.[33] This reaped over ¥3 billion or S$585 million, or five times the amount earned at the 2006 Doha Asiad.[34] It appeared that domestic companies in China that were previously reluctant to sponsor such sporting festivals were now more aware of their marketing potential; the prospect of winning 200 gold medals and being hosts may well have been rather persuasive.

Singapore at Guangzhou: Expectations, Predictions, Actual Belief

The ambitions that the host city and nation had for the Guangzhou Asian Games are well outlined and discussed throughout this volume, which emphatically demonstrates the significance of this mammoth production for the global superpower in-waiting: but could it be equally as important for the sporting minnow, Singapore? What were the aspirations and the expectations of the sporting community, the people and, of course, the politicians in Singapore? The analysis of this theme focused on specific examples of the eventual performances of the team, individual athletes and team officials as they rose or crashed in the face of the challenges, expectations and responsibilities precipitated. Why, it may be asked, were expectations so high? This possibly stems from the fact that Singapore, for its size and population, is an amazingly successful and economically powerful Asian nation. Driven initially by Lee Kuan Yew, much of this success derives its elitist attitude and the attendant national trait of meritocracy that Lee instilled into the nation.[35] Singapore expects success, but international sporting success thus far remains an unfulfilled, if not vainglorious aspiration.

As in many 'developing' nations in the twentieth century, sport in Singapore has acquired an important role in the creation of a sense of national identity. However, in Singapore, the actual reality of this ambition in terms of the government's perspective, despite their much-heralded support, has long been considered as being somewhat ambivalent and most idiosyncratic.[36] The growing profile of sport as a feature of public diplomacy via cultural outreach of those nations with serious aspirations to be 'associated' with major developed nations now seems to one of the rites of passage into the inner sanctum; to enter, developing nations need to demonstrate that they are actively engaged in international sport, particularly mega-sports festivals such as the Olympic Games.

Despite its conservative attitude, the Singapore government has robustly invested in the development and support of its elite athletes. In the late 1990s, it established the Multi-Million Dollar Award Programme (MAP)[37] to support the nation's top athletes so that they could train without personal cost and importantly, it included an incentives scheme for medal winners with prizes ranging from a $1 million for an individual Olympic gold medal to $10,000 for an individual gold medal at the SEA Games.

In July 2001, Prime Minister Goh Chok Tong announced his ambition to see Singapore become one of the 'Top-Ten' Sport Nations in Asia by 2005.[38] A major element of this plan was the Singapore Sports School, which Prime Minister Goh opened in 2004. It cost S $75 million to build and was designed to allow elite school-aged athletes to maintain their sporting ambitions while studying; in the standard school environment this is impossible. Its stated mission is to nurture 'Learned Champions With Character for the 21st Century'.[39] The School's greatest success thus far is the 'Queen' of Singapore swimming, Tao Li, who going into the Guangzhou Asian Games had been a student at the school since 2005. Having migrated from China (Wuhan) in 2002 as a 13-year old and with her international success she has long borne the brunt of national sporting expectation. She was unquestionably Singapore's highest profiled athlete at Guangzhou and the pressure of national and personal expectation was no doubt immense. Indeed, in 2010 although now a Singapore citizen she still seemed to be a victim of a 'love–hate' relationship with the press and Singaporeans in general.

Rohit Brajnath, a senior journalist, opened his article in *The New Paper* covering Tao Li's gold medal win in the 50 m butterfly, rather sardonically entitled, 'Gold ... finally', expressing the increasing tension as the nation waited for some success. In the opening paragraph, he delved into Tao's personality and even hairstyles creating an ambiguous tone:

> Tao Li is a young woman of delightful statements. If she isn't making one with her peroxide blond hair, she is with her electric swimming. Either way, it is hard to look away.
>
> Not everyone likes the spotlight. Some freeze in its glare. Tao Li looks like she wishes they'd turn up the lights a bit brighter.[40]

Later Brijnath more positively describes her character to applaud her effort:

> It was the sort of day when you never want to leave the stadium, for you're never quite sure when it will happen again.
>
> It was Tao Li's sort of day when everyone in Asia just had to look at her. It was also a day when Prime (her coach) said: 'I've told her, take on the world now, not just Asia.'[41]

Brajnath pointed out that as the final was getting underway, '... She articulated ... with a sign she makes after her races, which involves two horizontal fingers aimed across her eyes'. In response to her gesture, in a churlish letter to the Forum page in *The Straits Times*, a Mr Lim Fah Kiong, though applauding Tao Li's gold medal, said he believed that 'She tainted the victory with an uncalled for gesture ... Singapore athletes should behave appropriately and with pride when representing the country'.[42] One wonders, knowing the level of editorial control exercised by the government-run SPH, how and why this chivvying letter was published.

In *The Straits Times*, Leonard Lim applauded Tao Li's 'magnificent' effort suggesting that with the swim she had 'slayed two demons' – getting the 'underperforming' Singapore team its first Gold and the doubt of her poor form going into the Games.[43] Lim also illustrated a sense of the pressure Tao Li was under citing her response when asked how she compared herself to star table tennis player, Li Jiawei, herself a Chinese recruit in 1995, 'I think I am also a national treasure now. I did not disappoint Singapore, and I did not disappoint myself.'[44] Lim closes quoting Chef de Mission Low Teo Ping, who following Tao Li's win, promptly imposes further pressure upon her, 'I almost stood up on my chair to cheer ... Now, for London 2012!'[45] Unfortunately, Tao Li performed poorly in London coming twenty-sixth in the heats of the 100 m and though she won through to the semi-finals of the 100 m butterfly she failed to qualify for the final coming eleventh. Singapore was ranked seventh-fifth on the medal tally winning just two bronze medals.[46]

Performances, Brickbats and Bouquets, Excuses

The team's effort began indifferently as typified by the disqualification of the men's 4 × 200 m freestyle relay team, where in the final the lead swimmer was adjudged to have moved forward to take his mark before the whistle-signal had been given.[47] No medal was lost as they came in fourth; however, this came on the heels of a bureaucratic disqualification the previous month in the Commonwealth Games in New Delhi, where the same team was disqualified because a team manager had not submitted the entry form on time. Thus, again athletes and management immediately created a disruptive sense of ineptitude in Guangzhou. Leonard Lim was less than charitable with his criticism of the officials in Guangzhou with their execution of the subsequent appeal process, which appeared to have not followed protocol.[48] Performances remained indifferent until Tao Li's tenacious victory, yet it would appear that the trend to micro-politics in the critique of the team's performance was soon to assume elements of *realpolitik*.

Sailing has a 'special' place in the sport culture of Singapore with competitive sailing and the attached elitist subculture with the original Singapore Yacht Club purported to have been founded in 1826.[49] Through the island-nation's modest history in sport, sailing has brought Singapore a significant level of success; it is also the haunt of some strong-willed and politically powerful individuals. The reports from Guangzhou from the twenty-first and twenty-second of November were replete with commentary on what amounted to a 'bonfire of vanities', as major players in Singapore sport administration, all with a strong association with the sport of sailing, entered into a 'War of Words'.[50] Lim Say Heng in his article in *The New Paper on Sunday* outlined the spat that erupted over the selection process of the keelboat crews for Guangzhou.[51] Despite winning two gold, a silver and four bronze medals at these Asian Games, the sailors failed to follow up on the gold they won in the keelboat class in Doha in 2006. Low Teo Ping, the Chef de Mission and the immediate past-president of 'SingaporeSailing', suggested publicly that '... Our keelboat team should have done better, the selection process contributed to the results'.[52] Low certainly had a point as the sailors had won five gold, three silver and two bronze medals in Doha with one of the gold medals coming in the keelboat class. However, his comments were immediately rebutted by the newly appointed president, Dr Ben Tan, sporting icon and national hero,[53] who, in turn, blamed it 'on the lack of appropriate preparation by Low's team'[54] as he was the immediate past-president; Tan added that the association 'did nothing until this year (2010) ... we did not prepare for the keelboat at all'.[55]

Following this report, the Chef de Mission was 'slammed' by Singapore's highest-profiled sports administrator, Ng Ser Miang,[56] who immediately swung his support behind Ben Tan. Ng Ser Miang openly rebuked Team Singapore's leader, in a very direct manner saying, 'Mr Low's outburst cast aspersions on the new leadership of SingaporeSailing and demeans the achievements of our sailors, who have given their best for the country – whether they win medals or not'.[57] Ng Ser Miang is a past supremo of sailing himself *and* is Vice-President of the International Olympic Committee (IOC): he is also Singapore's Ambassador to Norway and is thus not without influence.

Leonard Lim, in his column 'At the Games',[58] further condemned Low Teo Ping by quoting another well-connected sailing administrator Brigadier-General (Ret.) Dr Loh

Kok Hua[59] who insisted that the new system of selection was 'objective and robust' and less open to 'subjective individual opinions of coaches'.[60] Doyen of Singapore sport journalism, Godfrey Robert, writing in *The New Paper*, summed up the *contretemps* with the title of his reflections, 'Timing of feud befuddled me'[61] in which he maintained that Ben Tan and Low Teo Ping had performed poorly in their particular roles and asked, 'Why engage in finger-pointing now, when the die is cast?'[62] He suggested that neither combatant can be exonerated and that both were to be blamed for the poor performance.[63] This suite of incidents, reactions and responses and the outcome illustrate the nature of the hegemony at work in Singapore and it is very apparent in the reports of the homecoming that Singapore's performance at Guangzhou was less than spectacular, as Deputy Prime Minister and President of the SNOC Teo Chee Hean[64] ominously suggested as he greeted the team at Changi airport.[65]

Pertinent to the analysis of the journalistic coverage and the nature of the critique of Team Singapore's performance in Guangzhou it is important to note that Ng Ser Miang is also a non-executive director of the SPH,[66] which as mentioned previously, has the absolute control of the press in Singapore: so all journalists would have been respectfully mindful of Ng Ser Miang's heavy involvement in sport and the media.

Games, Sets and Mismatches

The final salvo of articles naturally concentrated on unpacking the overall performance of the team. Leonard Lim in *The Straits Times* in his final report from Guangzhou entitled 'Excel or Just Take Part?'[67] called for Singapore to 're-look who it sends to the Asian Games'.[68] He suggested, naively, that 'Singapore may need to tweak its policy and send only those capable of excelling to the Asian Games'. However, in *The New Paper*, Lim Say Heng suggested that Singapore could have returned with more medals considering the near misses.[69] He neither made the point that there is always a need to 'blood' the next generation of athletes at this level of competition. In Lim Say Heng's article, he implied that the upper echelons of sport administration in Singapore assumed no responsibility for Team Singapore's below-par performance in Guangzhou. SNOC Secretary-General, Chris Chan[70], said he was puzzled as to why they did not win more gold medals saying that many of the sports and individuals had performed well leading up to Guangzhou. He placed the blame squarely at the feet of the national sports associations urging those that performed poorly should 'go back and ask themselves what is it that they are not doing enough of, that others are catching up?'[71] Chan negatively added, ' . . . Still, it makes me wonder, given the recent best-ever performance at the Commonwealth Games, [why] have we gone down the drain?'[72] He wondered why his athletes had not peaked for Guangzhou. A very significant point that seems to have been lost completely throughout the discussion of Team Singapore's performance in Guangzhou, though it was touched upon by Chris Chan, was that a significant proportion of the team had just returned from the sapping environment of New Delhi where they had competed so well in the Commonwealth Games before departing for Guangzhou. Most had less than a month to re-energise before leaving for the overwhelming enormity of Guangzhou. All their physical and psychological 'batteries' would have been seriously depleted; though admittedly not all would have doubled up, but it must have been a factor for athletes such as Tao Li, however, this was not mentioned in a single report.

In true Singaporean style, the press debate on Guangzhou 2010 drew to a close with issues about money. Front and centre and overwhelming Leonard Lim's final 'At The Games' report in *The Straits Times* was the prize list for Guangzhou 2010, crassly entitled,

'Asiad 2010 money makers'.[73] The full list appeared from Tao Li, who topped the list winning with S$300,000 to Yu Mengyu, who received S$32,000 for winning a team silver medal in table tennis. Closer inspection of the table shows an anomalous situation concerning the distribution of prize money from the MAP scheme. *Straits Times* correspondent, Terrance Voon unveiled the 'glitch', which meant that Tao Li would have received less money for two individual gold medals than for the individual gold and silver medals she did actually win.[74] A second individual gold medal for some inexplicable reason was deemed, by the administrators, to be worth only S$70,000, while a silver medal warranted S$100,000. Scurrilously, once this was discussed in Voon's initial article, suspicions surfaced. The Swimming Association's Secretary-General, Oon Jin Gee, felt it necessary to state that '... I'd give our athletes the benefit of the doubt that they would give their best for Singapore and not throw a race or contest because of money'.[75] Once exposed and the details published in *The Straits Times* it drew an immediate response from the SNOC Secretary-General Chris Chan, who the next day, declared that '... This mistake won't happen again ... from now on the gold medals will definitely be worth more than a silver medal, [but added] at least marginally'.[76] Admitting the oversight, he was able to save some face by cautioning the athletes as to the fact that '... We cannot assume the status quo will remain for the awards. It all depends on our sponsors, and whether we can attract more companies to sponsor sports'.[77]

Chan's almost threatening comment implied that future support for elite sport may be in doubt if athletes and administrators continued to perform so indifferently. However, the next day, with these foreboding words still echoing in the ears of aspiring and now fearful athletes, miraculously Voon reported the arrival of a new sponsor for elite sport and the SNOC, cable-broadcaster StarHub, which, as part of their efforts to 'push into local sports' gave a donation-cum-sponsorship of S$800,000 to elite sport.[78] And, in the lead photograph, posing accepting the preliminary cheque from StarHub Chief Operating officer Tan Tong Hai, was SNOC's Vice-President and Vice-President of the IOC Ng Ser Miang: that is, after all, the way things happen in Singapore.

Conclusion

The analysis of the themes emerging from Singapore's press coverage of Guangzhou 2010 suggests that the media in Singapore remains firmly locked in the mode of 'development journalism'[79] with the national agenda still central in all publications. In this discussion, each theme resonated with the voice and presence of the PAP government. What was stressed and what was not stressed or ignored was there or not by design, not by journalistic flair but political intent.

When Lee Kuan Yew was facing the threat of Communism in Singapore the expression 'riding the tiger'[80] was banded around in the media, now they face the prospect of 'Riding the Chinese Dragon'.[81] Singapore's media knows, understands and avoids both excessive fawning and overt criticism of China. It is suggested, however, that China looks to Singapore and covets its economic model[82] but wonders how one could match Singapore's ability to retain its soft-authoritarian hold on the people and yet still run an incredibly successful western liberal economy. Commentary on the Guangzhou Asian Games considered in the first thematic analysis illustrated that the acclaim in the press of Guangzhou's and China's achievements represented typical Singaporean journalism, which has a propensity for 'navel gazing and inherent introspection'.[83] This may well be a coping mechanism (possibly SPH induced) to offset the negativity the indifferent performances of the nation's athletes would likely engender.

THE ASIAN GAMES: MODERN METAPHOR FOR 'THE MIDDLE KINGDOM' REBORN

A particularly restrained applause was apparent in general, but specifically in regard to, as J.A. (Tony) Mangan so per lucidly depicted, the 'symbolic demonstration of wealth, confidence, capacity and power exuded by the Chinese and China in the holding of these ostentatious Games'.[84] It is suggested that this was, however, a manifestation of Singapore's nimble and lithe hedging foreign policy at work.[85] As Tan maintains Singapore is able to 'hedge' against China because it can as a consequence of its economic strength, geopolitical standing and because it *has* to, being sandwiched between two powerful Muslim neighbours, Indonesia and Malaysia.[86] The significance of this becomes apparent when it is remembered that Singapore is often referred to regionally as the 'third China'.[87]

The reports from the staff-reporters from *The Straits Times* and *The New Paper* and their Sunday versions demonstrated a polite level of acclaim of both the massive infrastructure developed by Guangzhou, the lavish opening and closing ceremonies and the 'Gold-fest' of China's athletes. China was seen to be 'way ahead' of their rivals and 'Brand China' was deemed to be the 'real winner' in Guangzhou, though Lim Seng Heng[88] did manage to illustrate that there were flaws in China's overall performance. The lack of an obsequious tone from the, in the main, young squad of journalists from Singapore could well reflect the fact that they are familiar with such munificence in infrastructure and development; for that is all they have known in their lives, and of course this would be the tone their 'leaders' would want projected. Though the author is armed with an embedded perception of the nature of Singaporean journalism and its commitment to the national agenda, it is believed that the reporting of the 2010 Guangzhou Asian Games with the omniscience of characters from the 'inner sanctum' of the PAP was still very cautious but the enthusiastic and very supportive tone of the, in the main, young squad of journalists from Singapore could well reflect the fact that they are well versed and familiar with the requirement for self-censoring and their nation-building roles which are typical of the journalism of Third World developing nations. What has become apparent is that as China, with its two systems of governance, moves to a 'softer' form of authoritarianism Singapore remains steadfast in its.

Notes on Contributor

Peter Horton is a Senior lecturer in the School of Education at James Cook University and Fellow of the Cairns Institute.

Notes

1. C. Lingle, "Singapore and Authoritarian Capitalism" (*The Locke Luminary*, 1 (Summer, 1998), Part 3. Available at: http://www.thelockeinstitute.org/journals/luminary_v1_n1_p3.html, accessed March 15, 2012).
2. Bokhorrst-Heng, "Newspapers in Singapore," 559.
3. Ibid.
4. Hatchten, *The World News Prism*, 73.
5. Bokhorst-Heng, "Newspapers in Singapore," 565.
6. Ibid., 560.
7. Lee Hsien Loong (born, 1952) the current prime minister of Singapore is Lee Kwan Yew's eldest son. In 1983, he became the youngest-ever Brigadier General in the Singapore Armed Forces and was elected as an MP in 1984. After rapid rise in politics in 1990, he became deputy prime minister in Goh Chok Tong's government. He took over as PM when Goh retired in 2004. See "The Son Rises; Singapore" (Singapore's Lee Dynasty) (Lee Hsien Loong), *The Economist* (US), July 24, 2004, available at http://www.highbeam.com/doc/1G1-119711620. html, accessed October 15, 2012.
8. Jacobs, "As Singapore Loosens Its Grip."

9. See Joshua Kurlantzick, "Love My Nanny," 69–74.
10. Bokhorst-Heng, "Newspapers in Singapore," 564.
11. See Lee and Willnat, "Political Communication in Singapore," 93–111.
12. George, "Singapore: Media at the Mainstream and the Margins," 175.
13. Ibid.
14. *Freedom of Expression and the Media in Singapore*, Baseline Studies in Southeast Asia, London: Article December 19, 2005, 16–17.
15. Ibid.
16. Ibid.
17. K. Sundby, "Lee Kuan Yew" (*New York Times*, Updated: August 6, 2010), available at http://topics.nytimes.com/top/reference/timestopics/people/l/lee_kuan_yew/index.html, accessed December 12, 2012.
18. English.Eastday.com. "'Best ever' Asian Games Lowers Curtain," November 28, 2010 09:18, available at http://english.eastday.com/e/101128/u1a5576261.html, accessed June 21, 2012.
19. Manuel Silvereio (AOC) cited in, P. Simpson, "Guangzhou Pulls Out All the Stops Hosting Biggest Sports Event" (*South China Morning Post*, Sunday, January 10, 2010), available at http://www.scmp.com/article/703222/guangzhou-pulls-out-all-stops-hosting-biggest-sports-event, accessed October 23, 2012.
20. Ling Chang Hong, "All fitted out for the Asian Games," A14.
21. Sun Xiuqing was also the Vice Chairman of the Guangzhou Development District.
22. Ibid.
23. L. Lim, "China Signs Off With a Flourish" (*Sunday Times*, November 28, 2010, 53).
24. T. Voon, "No Free Ride, DPM Teo Warns Athletes" (*The Straits Times*, November 29, 2010, B10), available at http://www.singaporeolympics.com/news20101129.php, accessed December 4, 2012.
25. Chang Hong Ling, "All Fitted Out for the Asian Games" (*The Straits Times*, November 8, 2010, A14).
26. Associated Press, "Another China Showcase" (*The New Paper on Sunday*, November 7, 2010, 43).
27. Associated Press, "Solid GREAT WALL: Chinese Paddlers to Dominate on Home Soil" (*The New Paper on Sunday*, November 7, 2010, 43).
28. Lim Say Heng, "Strike One, Guangzhou" (*The New Paper*, November 15, 2010, 42).
29. Ibid.
30. Ibid.
31. Lin Xinyi, "China Way Ahead of Rival," A1.
32. Peh Shing Huei, "The Real Winners in Guangzhou: Brand China" (*The Sunday Times*, November 28, 2010, 52).
33. Ibid.
34. Ibid.
35. See Barr and Kuan, *The Beliefs Man Behind the Man*, 97–136.
36. See Horton, "Shackling the Lion," *passim*.
37. Information regarding the scheme is available at http://www.singaporeolympics.com/mmdap.php.
38. "S'Pore Sport Targets Top-10 Spot in Asia" (*The Straits Times Interactive*, July 1, 2001), no longer available, accessed July 3, 2001.
39. See "Singapore Sports School", available at http://www.sportsschool.edu.sg/, accessed July 17, 2012.
40. Rohit Brajnath, "Gold Finally" (*The Straits Times*, November 19, 2010, A1).
41. Ibid.
42. Lim Fah Kiong, "Her Two-Fingered Retort was Unnecessary," (Letter to the Editor, *The Straits Times*, November 24, 2010, A33).
43. L. Lim, "Tao Li, Silences Naysayers" (*The Straits Times*, November 19, 2010, 9).
44. Ibid.
45. Ibid.
46. See "The London Olympics Medal Tally", available at http://london2012.olympics.com.au/medal-tally, accessed February 4, 2013.
47. L. Lim, "Relay Team Disqualified Again" (*The Straits Times*, November 16, 2010, B11).
48. Ibid.

49. The club's insignia proudly heralds its founding as 1826 and the Royal Singapore Yacht Club's history, available at: http://infopedia.nl.sg/articles/SIP_1646_2010-02-12.html, it thus suggests that the club was established then, though the first regatta did take place until 1834. Accessed October 31, 2012.
50. Say Heng Lim, "War of Words" (*The New Paper on Sunday*, November 27, 2010, 58).
51. Ibid.
52. Ibid.
53. See "Benedict Tan," (*Singapore's Sports Museum, Hall of Fame*, available at http://www.s portsmuseum.com.sg/heroes/hall_of_fame/benedict_tan.html, December 10, 2012.
54. Say Heng Lim, "War of Words," 58.
55. Ibid.
56. See "Ng Ser Miang, Singapore Sailing Federation," available at http://www.sailing.org.sg/aboutus/exco.php, accessed December 10, 2012.
57. Ng Ser Miang, cited in, L. Lim, "Ser Miang Slams Head of Asian Games Team" (*The Straits Times*, November 22, 2010, A5).
58. L. Lim, "At The Games" (*The Straits Times*, November 22, 2010, B9).
59. Loh Kok Hua represented Singapore at the 1975 South East Asia Peninsular (SEAP) Games and the 1993 SEA Games. He served in the Singapore Air Force for 29 years and retired from his last held position as Brigadier General in 2002. See "Singapore Sailing Federation" available at: http://www.sailing.org.sg/aboutus/exco.php, accessed December 10, 2012.
60. Ibid.
61. G. Robert, "Timing of Feud Befuddles Me" (*The New Paper*, November 22, 2010. 45).
62. Ibid.
63. Ibid.
64. Rear-Admiral Teo Chee Hean has been a Member of Parliament since 1992, prior to this he was Singapore's Chief of Navy from 1991 to 1992.
65. Terrance Voon, "No free ride, DPM Teo warns athletes."
66. Reuters-Markets, "Singapore Press Holdings Ltd," available at http://www.reuters.com/finance/stocks/companyOfficers?symbol=SPRM.SI, accessed December 12, 2012.
67. L. Lim, "Excel or Just Take Part?" (*The Straits Times*, November 27, 2010, C23).
68. Ibid.
69. Say Heng Lim, "Time for Soul Searching" (*The New Paper*, November 27, 2010, 60).
70. SNOC secretary-general Chris Chan now seats Asia's sports' governing body, the Olympic Council of Asia, as a vice-president. He is a former lieutenant-colonel in the Singapore Armed Forces and previously was chief executive of football's S-League. See "Chris Tan, Association of National Olympic Committees – ANOC," available at http://www.en.acnolympic.org/acno/fiches/cno.php?id=171&l=en, accessed December 10, 2012.
71. Ibid.
72. Leonard Lim, "Excel or Just Take Part?" C23.
73. "Asiad 2010 Money Makers" (*The Straits Times*, November 27, 2010, C 23).
74. T. Voon, "Payout Puzzle" (*The Straits Times*, November 29, 2010, B10).
75. Ibid.
76. T. Voon, "Incentive Glitch to be Fixed Next Year" (*The Straits Times*, November 30, 2010, 20).
77. Ibid.
78. T. Voon, "Athletes Get $800k From StarHub" (The Straits Times, December 1, 2010, 22).
79. Hatchten, *The World News Prism*, 73.
80. See Ministry of Information and the Arts, "Riding The Tiger: The Chronicle Of A Nation's Battle Against Communism" (DVD). Singapore: Ministry of Information and the Arts, 2001, ISBN: SB#: 03321 (113).
81. See Sen Tan, "Riding the Chinese Dragon," 21.
82. "China to 'Emulate' Singapore's Economic Model" (*BBC News Asia*, November 13, 2012, availableat: http://www.bbc.co.uk/news/world-asia-20307144, accessed February 4, 2013.
83. Mangan, "Personal Communication," December 11, 2012.
84. Ibid.
85. See Sen Tan, "Riding the Chinese Dragon," 21–2.
86. Ibid.
87. See Sen Tan, "Riding the Chinese Dragon," 35.
88. Lim Say Heng, "Strike one, Guangzhou," 42.

References

Barr, M. D., and Yew Lee Kuan. *The Beliefs Man Behind the Man*. Washington, DC: Georgetown University Press, 2000.

Bokhorrst-Heng, W. "Newspapers in Singapore: A Mass Ceremony in the Imagining of the Nation, Media." *Media, Culture & Society* 24 (2002): 559–569.

George, C. "Singapore: Media at the Mainstream and the Margins." In *Media Fortunes, Changing Times: ASEAN States in Transition*, edited by R. H. K. Heng, 173–200. Singapore: Institute of Southeast Asian Studies, 2002.

Hatchten, W. A. *The World News Prism: Changing Media, Clashing Ideologies*. Ames, IA: Iowa State University Press.

Horton, P. "Shackling the Lion, Sport in Independent Singapore." *The International Journal of the History of Sport* (September/October 2002): 243–274.

Jacobs, A. "As Singapore Loosens Its Grip, Residents Lose Fear to Challenge Authority." *New York Times – Asia Pacific online*, June 16, 2012, available at http://www.nytimes.com/2012/06/17/world/asia/activism-grows-as-singapore-loosens-restrictions.html?pagewanted=all, accessed November 19, 2012.

Kurlantzick, J. "Love My Nanny: Singapore's Tongue-Tied Populace." *World Policy Journal* 17, no. 4 (2000): 69–74.

Lee, T., and Willnat Lars. "Political Communication in Singapore." In *Political Communication in Asia*, edited by L. Willnat, and Aw. Annette, 93–111. Abingdon, Oxon: Routledge, 2009.

Ministry of Information and the Arts. "Riding The Tiger: The Chronicle Of A Nation's Battle Against Communism" (DVD). Singapore: Ministry of Information and the Arts, 2001.

Tan, S. S. "Riding the Chinese Dragon: Singapore's Pragmatic Relationship with China." In *The Rise of China: Responses from Southeast Asia and Japan, Joint Research Series 4*, edited by Tsunekawa Jun, 21–45. Tokyo: National Institute for Defense Studies, 2009.

Guangzhou: The Asian Games and the Chinese 'Gold-Fest' – Geopolitical Issues for Australia

Peter Horton

School of Education and The Cairns Institute, James Cook University, Queensland, Australia

> At the Guangzhou Asian Games, the performances of China's athletes, the officials and the host city of Guangzhou were outstanding. China's journey to the Asian Games in Guangzhou and the accompanying political and sporting machinations throughout are considered in the initial discussion of this essay. The analysis subsequently focuses on Australia's metamorphosis as an 'Asian' nation and the sporting, cultural and diplomatic implications this could have for Australia and China. Would this signal Australia's egress from the Commonwealth Games and the Commonwealth *per se*, thus cutting the British Imperial umbilicus? The presence of Australia at the Asian Games may also enhance the soft power ambitions China has for its engagement in the Asian Games; succeeding in competitions that include a global sports 'heavyweight' like Australia would add kudos to the performances of Chinese athletes. How would Australia benefit from this shift? Considering Australia's geopolitical and economic ties with East Asia would an increased level of sporting engagement with China concomitantly produce cultural, economic and political successes? In the long term, Australia may inevitably become part of the post-colonial East Asian world: the future world of power, wealth and geopolitical influence.

Introduction

The Asian Games, as with all international mega-sports festivals, has since its inception been underpinned as much by politics as by sport.[1] In fact, China's (re)emergence on the global stage in the twenty-first century as an 'international' power was predicated, albeit somewhat mythically, upon its engagement with the USA during the era of 'ping-pong diplomacy' in the 1970s.[2] During this era, the People's Republic of China's (PRC) articulation of the relationship between sport and politics became more adroit and less robust than it had been during the first two decades of its existence when confronted by the International Olympic Committee's (IOC) apparent support of Nationalist China (Taiwan).[3] After the cessation of the final phase of the Chinese Civil War (1927–1950), the War of Liberation (1946–1950) that followed the end of the Second Sino-Japanese War,[4] communist mainland China split from the nationalist governed Taiwan (Chinese Taipei) and the PRC essentially excluded itself from the Olympic Movement from 1950 until 1979.[5]

The analysis of the convoluted machinations of Chinese national politics following the formal cleavage of Taiwan from mainland China in 1949 and the impact this had on the PRC's participation in international sports competitions has mainly focused on the Olympic Games. However, the issues that arose from the era of the 'two Chinas' also led to the exclusion of China from the Asian Games from 1954 to 1970. The Asian Games were first held in 1951 in New Delhi. Following the Civil War during which the Nationalists had 'taken' China's affiliation to both the IOC and the Asian Games Federation (AGF), the New Delhi Asian Games organisers invited the PRC to take part in the inaugural Asian Games.[6] The PRC, unable to organise a team at such short notice declined and sent only a nine-man delegation to observe. However, international politics immediately undermined the PRC's plans to take part in the next Asian Games and under the pressure of Western powers the AGF withdrew its support for the PRC until 1970, when it returned to the Asian Games 5 years before it was welcomed back into Olympic Movement.[7]

The Asian Games – 'Ever Onward'

The original motto of the Asian Games was 'Ever Onward' and the PRC certainly utilised its involvement to project itself politically and in sport. Its first competitive foray into the Asian Games was in 1974 in Tehran, and this, as Hong and Zhouxiang reflected, proved to be an outstanding sporting achievement; they took 269 athletes and, in claiming 33 gold medals, came third out of the 19 competing nations. More significantly for the PRC, it was a huge diplomatic success.[8] The invitation to the PRC came only after Taiwan's membership of the AGF had been revoked a year earlier in September 1973. China's close relationship with Iran was the basis of the decision to expel Taiwan from the AGF and to welcome in the PRC. This decision was supported by a majority of the member nations, including Japan and Pakistan. This decision proved to be a significant political breakthrough for China, and being in the death throes of the Cultural Revolution, it desperately needed to establish some international credibility. This decision by the AGF was frowned upon by the IOC's President, Lord Killanin, who rather limply commented that sport should be free of political intervention.[9]

The ninth Asian Games was again held in Delhi in 1982 and marked a new epoch in the dynamics of Asian sport and for China it symbolically represented the closure of the ignominious period of the Cultural Revolution. China had 'opened' its political, economic and cultural 'doors' to the world and their take-off to Asian dominance was launched and sport played an important role in this process. The next two Asiads, the 10th in 1986 in Seoul and the momentous 11th held by the PRC in Beijing in 1990, were massively significant multi-sports festivals, serving as dress rehearsals for future Olympic Games. Both were very productive diplomatically with subsequent legacies extending well beyond sport and indeed Asia. In geopolitical terms, each of these events pre-empted an epochal shift in the dynamics of global affairs.

The period from the mid-1980s to 1990s was of major geopolitical importance for the nations of East Asia linked as they were elsewhere to shifts in the Soviet bloc. The seismic events of this era saw the end of one of the history's most prodigious ideo-political systems which set into motion a series of political, economic and cultural changes precipitated by the end of the Cold War. And even though it could be justifiably asserted that the western democratic capitalism led by the USA had won that 'war', it is suggested eventually that the end of the Cold War led to China's emergence as an economic powerhouse, hegemon of Asian sport and the master of soft power politics.[10]

The Asian Games in Seoul (1986) and Beijing (1990) each played diplomatic roles that led to improved levels of diplomatic communication between Asian nations. Victor Cha in his consideration of the normalisation of diplomatic relations between the Republic of Korea (ROK) and the rapidly democratising Soviet Union[11] deliberated upon the extent of sport's role in the realpolitik at work at this time and adjudged that '... The prevailing explanation, of course, is the end of the Cold War'.[12] Throughout China's journey out of the quagmire of world politics during the last three decades of the twentieth century, the embrace of sport as an instrument of public diplomacy and soft power was apparent in a number of productive political interactions. The positive political, diplomatic, cultural and sporting interactions of the ROK and its Asian confrères that emanated from the Asian Games in Seoul in 1986 were in stark contrast to the ongoing festering relationship with its sibling, the Democratic People's Republic of Korea (DPRK); the Korean nations were, as they still are, at war. Importantly, one of the most critical diplomatic ententes to emerge was the ROK's new and mutually productive engagement with the DPRK's sole regional ally, the PRC. As ideologically divergent as they were, both the PRC and the ROK were ruled by 'hard' authoritarian governments and both governments had realised how mutually beneficial a closer geopolitical alignment would be to their futures. The Seoul Asiad provided both with an opportunity to begin the process of normalising their previously problematic relationship. Also, the sport-related public diplomacy strategies that both China and South Korea adopted subsequently led to the growing democratisation of the ROK, and with respect to China, influenced its 'opening up' and the adoption of a unique system of governance: one that merges a socialist polity with a Chinese-styled market economy. Seoul was granted the hosting rights of the Xth Asian Games in November 1981 after having been awarded those of the 1988 Olympic Games in September 1981 and consequently the Seoul Asian Games was literally used as a dress rehearsal for the 1988 Olympics.[13]

The Asian Games Beijing 1990 – Delayed Gratification and Rewards

China's progression from Asian Games host to Olympic host was not as smooth as that of the ROK. The diplomatic climate and global opinion was far more vexatious towards China. The intolerable legacy of the Tiananmen Square Massacre in June 1989 stained China's record sufficiently enough to allow the still-Western dominated IOC to respond in the manner that mirrored desires of the suspicious nations of the West who wanted to stall China's entry into the inner-sanctum of world politics, a move which this 'honour' would certainly have precipitated. China's harsh response to the student demonstration was to see its 'natural' accession to the Olympic throne temporary halted thus allowing Australia to win the hosting rights of the historically significant first Olympics of the new millennium.

The PRC dominated the 1990 Asian Games winning 183 gold medals and its athletes broke one world, 30 Asian and 96 Asian Games records.[14] Even so the Beijing Asian Games was first and foremost a 'political event' orchestrated by the Central government with a very specific purpose in mind, that of cleansing China's image following the Tiananmen Square incident. Though the Beijing Asiad most certainly paved the way for better understanding and engagement between Asian nations particularly between China and the ROK[15] and was organisationally a very efficiently and well-hosted festival,[16] its success was not, however, enough for the Olympic establishment in 1993 to select Beijing to host the 2000 Olympic Games. Although heavily favoured by the President of the IOC, Juan Antonio Samaranch, Beijing failed to win the Millennium Olympic Games losing to Sydney in the final round of voting by just two votes. China thus had to wait almost another decade but ironically, the additional period of economic, social and sports development served them well leading to the amazingly successful 2008 Olympic Games. China, Beijing and its people were far more internationalised and able to offer a host city that in terms of infrastructure development was unparalleled. Its exponential advances economically, its apparent emergent superpower status and its efforts in the global assault on the global financial crisis (GFC) of 2008–2009 also added to the kudos and acclaim it had received for not just the Olympic Games but also the nation's response to the Sichuan earthquake that occurred just three months before the Opening Ceremony in 2008.[17]

In light of the 'success' of the Beijing Games as affirmed by the IOC,[18] the sense of national confidence must have soared. It may well been its response to the GFC, not the sporting or diplomatic victories, which represented China's greatest 'victory' of this period. The re-emergence of the Middle Kingdom (Zhongguo), replete with cultural connotations of the 'soft power' successes, such as the Beijing Olympics and the more steely power that came from its emergence as an economic superpower, placed Zhongguo at the centre of the 'new' global geopolitical dynamic.

Going to London via Guangzhou ...?

China maintained its sporting thrusts on the global stage when it hosted the largest-ever Asian Games in Guangzhou in 2010. But what was the nature of the ambitions China had for the Guangzhou festival so soon after the monstrous public diplomacy achievements that issued from Beijing in 2008? Going into the 2008 Olympics China had used the 2006 Asian Games in Doha to blood its next generation of elite athletes as well as for peaking its established stars.[19] In winning 361 medals including 165 gold medals, the PRC further emphasised its ranking as Asia's leading athletic nation in such international multi-sports festivals. It could be assumed that, as with the 2006 Asiad, the 2010 Guangzhou Asian Games was, in the main, just part of China's team preparation for the London Olympics. However, this is hard to imagine, looking at the extent of the development undertaken at a cost of ¥122 billion (US$18.3), which represented 13% of the Gross Domestic Product (GDP) for Guangzhou in 2009.[20] The Guangzhou Asian Games were focused on provincial as well as on Asia-wide ambitions and were not merely part of the PRC's London Olympic campaign. There was clearly no easing-off from the 'soft power' pedal; however, the vehicle of public diplomacy on this occasion was being steered directly towards Asian destinations and naturally, to the Chinese people, who delight in seeing arch-enemies Japan and South Korea defeated. Domination in such festivals as Macleod observed legitimises the system, the government and the people and inspires patriotism.[21] Macleod added that dominating the contests was not the only way China demonstrated its superiority in Guangzhou, the 'lavish preparations and hospitality show[ed] fellow Asian nations that it is a friendly power whose leadership in the region should be embraced, not feared'.[22] It could also be asked to what extent was the tone and ambiance generated at Guangzhou, particularly, as Husain Al-Musallam, Director General of the Olympic Council of Asia (OCA) said at the official hand-over of the final report to the Olympic Council of Asia in Kuwait on the July 3, 2011, 'the beautiful smiles of the 60,000 volunteers',[23] generated by China to assuage the negativity that emerged from the non-sport-related comments from the Beijing Olympics? Was the ambience created at Guangzhou designed to reclaim some of the public diplomacy ground lost in Beijing as a consequence of the lack of humanity (the human face) exhibited in man-management in the public areas such as the over-zealous actions of the guards accompanying the Flame Relay? It must be said that this was always likely to be a public relations nightmare, let alone political disaster, as it provided a global stage for all manner of anti-China protests.[24] The stoic visages of the security guards and their at times churlish responses to spectators, generally locals on the Olympic Green, also drew criticism abroad.[25]

2010 – A Year of Mega-Festivals and 'Soft Power'

For China, the year of 2010 in 'soft power' terms was, even by their standards, gargantuan. As well as hosting the 16th Asian Games and the Asian Para Games in November and December in Guangzhou, from May to October China hosted the World Expo in the country's richest city Shanghai. Expo 2010 was lavish by any standards; the site was the largest ever, 190 nations had pavilions, the number of visitors, close to 73 million, was a record and not surprisingly the capital outlay was similarly a record, at an estimated US $55 billion, some suggest that with investment on-costs it may have been as much as US $95 billion.[26] The associated wide-spread infra-structure projects and urban renewal efforts have left a significant and tangible legacy to the city and the entire Guangdong Province. Tu Qiyu, Director of the Shanghai Academy of Social Science's urban research centre, stated that as a consequence Shanghai moved up the ranks of world metropolises and importantly he added it was a 'huge education for Shanghai and many Chinese in modernization'.[27]

The Guangzhou Asiad was widely acclaimed as not only the 'largest' ever and a ' huge success', and according to Sheikh Ahmad Al-Fahad Al-Sabah, President of the Olympic Council of Asia, it was the 'best ever' in history.[28] This being so, how then was Guangzhou's Asiad the best ever *for* China? In athletic terms, China 'crushed' its opponents, as the all-important medal tally clearly indicates, and for the Chinese people, the continued dominance over East Asian rivals, Japan and South Korea, was for historical reasons, even more satisfying. With 199 gold medals and 416 overall compared to nearest rivals, South Korea's 76 gold and 232 in total, the PRC confirmed its status as the hegemon of Asian sport; China has led the gold medal tally in Asian Games since 1982 and now had organised not only an amazing Olympic Games in 2008 but the greatest-ever Asian Games. The city of Guangzhou also won 'gold' for the Asian Games as the 'best ever' host city, aided by the vast budget spent directly on venues and associated infrastructure development and renewal. This hard legacy, according to Li Yongning, of Research Institute for International Strategies in Guangzhou, 'helped internationalise and modernise the city'.[29] Although undoubtedly the goodwill and positive exchange were engendered by the hospitality of hosts especially that extended to the heads of state of allies such as, the President of Pakistan, Asif Ali Zardari, who was rich in praise for Guangzhou after attending the opening ceremony, the following day he lauded the Games' hosts saying that 'the Guangzhou Asian Games was a great demonstration of China's soft power to the world'.[30] He went on to discuss the generosity of China's aid to Pakistan in response to the severe floods that had recently impacted upon 20 million of his people leaving 1.5 million homeless and over 1700 dead. China had immediately given US$250 million worth of aid and cash for relief and reconstruction. In a none-too subtle expression of public diplomacy at work, he embellished his thanks with an expression of his hope, 'that both countries would speed up cooperation in agriculture and road construction' and that ' ... Our trade ties will continue to grow with volumes to reach hundreds of billions in the future'.[31]

Chinese Sport, the Changing Face of Sport and Australia

China is rapidly developing and with the march of urbanisation and its continued economic prosperity it is apparent that the neo-bourgeoisie is conscious of the need for physical activity, while the growing middle classes are also seeking a wider range of active leisure pursuits and sport-related tourism experiences, such as snow skiing, water sports, hiking and cycling. Global elite sport is also a growing feature of China's television programming, with football, basketball, tennis and golf from overseas being very popular.

Despite these changes in the nation's sport culture, the traditional draconian system of state recruitment and training institutions, which are fundamental to the Juguo Tizhi system, is likely to prevail beyond 2012.[32] Supporting this notion the Chinese team's performance in London did not reach the dizzy heights of Beijing, although they did come second in the all-important gold medals tally. The post-Games' comments from China's Olympic boss Liu Peng further added to this notion; in a very restrained manner, he described the performance as being 'satisfactory' and added that they had a lot of work to do if they want to make an impact in Rio de Janeiro in 2016. Liu is notorious for 'playing down' the PRC's Olympic expectations;[33] however, he did assertively add that in London, China did win eight gold medals in events in which they had never done so before and had increased their haul of gold in swimming from one to five.

Whether this indicates as Random opines, that the 'Soviet-styled system is under threat',[34] is difficult to assess. However, it should be said that *all* elite athletes worldwide should be treated with dignity and respect as human beings and not merely as means of capital production or as commodities. In regard to China, a wider engagement with sport systems, coaches and athletes from other countries, such as Australia, could serve to enhance the holistic development of their elite sport programmes. By the same token, foreign athletes and their coaches, particularly from Australia, considering their somewhat disappointing performances in the London Olympics, could profit from regular competition and exposure to the dedicated ethos of Chinese athletes. Such a fundamental shift in mind-set would have once been unlikely in Australia but with its ever-growing multi-cultural character, considering the diversity of modern migration patterns, this shift, albeit a difficult one could be achieved; sport does have a propensity to carry and to effect social change. Quoting Lao-tzu, '... A journey of a thousand miles begins with a single step'.[35] It could be suggested that the next step towards China's internationalisation, particularly through sport, could be coupled with a step towards China by countries such as Australia.

China's growing presence and power in the Asia Pacific region have led to it being described as the next 'global superpower'. Whether China should or should not aspire to such a mantle is problematic; perhaps a circumspect realignment and further domestic liberalisation and a continuation of its 'soft power' public diplomacy policies should be a priority of the new the Politburo (PB) and the Politburo Standing Committee (PBSC) when they are finally selected between late September and early November in 2012.[36] It is to be hoped that when the new PB and its PBSC are inducted the three central political reflections of sport in China, as embraced by Hu Jintao in 2008, elite sport, 'sport for all' and the sports industry will remain as priorities. It has been noted that the phenomenon of sport in Asia and the associated sports industry is beginning to dominate the global sports market.[37] Asia's massive population, of approximately 4 billion people, represents 60% of the world's total population, led by the mega-economies of China and India is beginning to impact upon the world's sports economy. The emergent middle classes in both China and India are developing an insatiable appetite for televised elite sport.[38] This growth in the sport–media complex and related competition should keep the door open to further the public diplomacy interface between regional neighbours, near and far, and points to the intriguing proposition of Australia increasing its range of sporting engagement with the PRC as an 'Asian' nation, as the Australian government now describes the nation.[39] Australia's major public diplomacy thrusts are, understandably, directed to its major trading partners in East Asia, China being by far Australia largest two-way trading partner.[40] Though the recent re-invigoration of the US military alliance strategy in the Pacific into which Australia has been 'pivoted'[41] required Australia to promptly state 'that the new arrangement with the United States was not directed at China'.[42] As tenuous as it may seem an elevated level of cultural outreach such as increasing the level of sporting engagement between Australia and China could assuage some of the negativity the ramping up of the Pacific strategic alliance has created.

Australia in the Asian Games: Value, Merit, Implications

In considering the ramifications for sport and the advantages of Australia competing in the Asian Games, it is suggested that this expansion would open up a fantastic high-level competitive opportunity for the nation's elite athletes, both for the potential success it would offer and as part of the developmental progression to an approaching Olympic Games. It would also offer another tier of structured Olympic-style competition for emerging athletes who could gain much needed experience and competition against strong opponents from the region's leading sporting nations including China, South Korea and Japan.

The next Asian Games will be held in Incheon in South Korea in 2014 and will embrace all twenty-eight Olympic sports that will be featured in the 2016 Olympic Games in Rio de Janeiro. However, traditionally the Asian Games support a wider collection of sports that 'vary' from host city to host city expressing both a more 'populist' orientation and specific cultural contexts; for example in Guangzhou, Dragonboat racing was included.[43] The Asian Games are not just about Olympic sports as they offer a wider access to athletes who participate in non-Olympic sports, which in the context of Australia's changing culture and demographics has particular merit. If Australia was to participate in the Asian Games, leading Asian sports nations, China, South Korea and Japan would face stronger competition and the presence of another of the world's sporting powerhouses would offer meaningful competition, particularly in the Olympic sports that Australia so heavily focuses upon, such as swimming, athletics, sailing and cycling. For Australia the renewal of Asia's strength in swimming may also be valuable, while the strong competition and expertise of Asian athletes in gymnastics, diving, boxing, wrestling, weightlifting, taekwondo, archery and women's football and hockey could offer a much-needed lift to Australia's performances in those disciplines.

In light of Australia's geopolitical and geographical location and economic ties with Asia, it is difficult to accept that there should be any resistance to an increased level of sporting engagement with China, though undoubtedly emotive outburst would accompany a major shift, such as competing in the Asian Games rather than the Commonwealth Games. The implications are confronting and are likely to be met with stoic resistance. Though Australia could like Singapore compete in both, there does, however, exist a successful example of Australia competing in a world sporting championship as an 'Asian' nation; since 2006, Australia has been a member of Asian Football Confederation (AFC) and is currently playing the qualifying rounds for the 2014 finals that will be held in Brazil. The decision to apply to join the AFC was a very pragmatic one, because as a member of the lowly ranked Oceania Football Confederation and to progress to the World Cup finals the Oceania winner had to face the third best team from South America: a daunting task.

As we address the final and likely most problematic issue in this discussion, what would be the non-sport specific value and implications for the proposed 'shift' to Asia for Australia's Olympic Sports – programme? Central to this discussion is: what are Australia's geopolitical and socio-cultural positions? what is its identity going to be in the next half century? and how can sport impact upon Australia's sustainability, integrity and regional and, by definition, its global status in the Asian Century?

In the first instance, it is apparent that Australia's future is unquestionably linked to its trading relationships with its Asian neighbours, although evidently trade with China is of paramount importance. In 2011, in all three major indicative categories of, exports to, imports from and total trade, China was Australia's number one trading partner.[44] Australia is thus uniquely placed geopolitically as one of the most highly regarded middle-ranking powers in the Asia Pacific, which is now the most positively dynamic theatres of global economic action considering that the region includes the USA, China and India.

Australia, located literally and politically almost like a geological foundation at the base of the Asia Pacific region, lies most strategically between the two most populated nations on the planet, India and China, and it is suggested, has the potential to play a central role in the creation of a harmonious and balanced geopolitical environment in the wider Asian Pacific region as it can 'speak' on diplomatic, economic matters to all major players in the region. Its own public diplomatic outreach activity, including sport, cultural exchange, aid and education, is a major platform for its own 'charm offensive' and hegemony.

This analysis of the value, merit and the implications of Australia's potential direct engagement 'with' and specifically 'from within' Asia represents a litmus test as to whether Australia will function globally as an 'Asian' nation or as a 'Western' nation in the Asia Pacific region. If Australia was to become affiliated with the OCA and to take part in the Asia Games, it would represent an emphatic declaration of its intent to be part of the region and once accepted, it would enhance its potential to exact a wider and balanced influence in Asian affairs. Australia would also be affiliated with the IOC *via* the OCA and this would substantially add to Asia's status in the Olympic Movement, Australia being a founder member of the IOC and carries a deal of non-aligned political and sporting capital within the Movement. The contemplation of this shift, just as the FFA has done, makes sound geopolitical sense and, as has been argued earlier, it also makes perfect sense in terms of elite sport. The Asianisation of sport is fast approaching on three fronts: Asian athletes, administrators and Asian-conducted events; the Asian sports market with its ever-increasing appetite for the global sports industry and the sports media and Asian money and capital investment by individuals, corporations and government-owned investment funds such as the immensely well-capitalised Chinese Investment Corporation.[45] If this eventuates, Australia would be very well placed to benefit from its position close to the centre of the new power base of sport worldwide.

Predictably, the most vociferous argument that will inevitably be presented in opposition to this proposition will revolve around the threat that this shift would make to Australia's continued participation in the Commonwealth Games and all that this implies in terms of Australia's 'membership' of the (British) Commonwealth of Nations. The fact that both the Commonwealth and Asian Games were set in the same 4-year cycle provided an immediate and insurmountable justification for the bureaucrats and traditionalists to stone wall any such attempt. However, the OCA has decided to move the 2018 Asian Games to 2019, in order to bring them to just a year immediately before the 2020 Olympic Games. Australia has been granted the 2018 Commonwealth Games which will be held in the city of the Gold Coast in South Eastern Queensland. Thus, hypothetically, Australia could compete in both and with both the 2019 Asian Games and the 2020 Olympic Games hosts yet to be selected their schedules could be better integrated. Although Australia 'could' theoretically compete in both festivals, the spectre of funding looms large, it may just allow expense and the lack of funding to again justify the rejection of the notion. Competing in both could well be seen as being philosophically counter-productive to the broader issue of Australia's future place in world affairs and its long-term efficacy, meaning and relevance in matters as important, if not more important than sport. This essay does not attempt to present a 'soft' option. The proposition has been made recognising Australia's 'real' not imagined long-term international, diplomatic, economic and societal future and in the belief that Australia should be realistically driven and so divorce itself, constitutionally, from the UK. This discussion is firmly based on the pragmatic argument that Australia should make the move to compete in the Asian Games and not to change its political allegiance or to deny a major dimension of its multivariate heritage but that it should shift its contextual focus geopolitically, diplomatically, socially and culturally. Competing in the Asian Games does not necessitate the creation of an Australian republic, though it is probably a long over-due development; it is time for this nation to advance to adulthood.

Notes on Contributor

Peter Horton is a senior lecturer in the School of Education at James Cook University and a fellow of the Cairns Institute. He is a member of the editorial boards of *The International Journal of the History of Sport* and *International Sports Studies*.

Notes

1. See Hong and Zhouxiang, "China, The Asian Games and Asian Politics," 98–112.
2. Hong, "Communist China and the Asian Games 1951–1990," 479–92.
3. See Hong and Xiong, "Communist China: Sport, Politics and Diplomacy."
4. For an informative overview of the final phase of the Chinese Civil War, see Lynch, *The Chinese Civil War 1945–1949*.
5. Guttmann, *The Olympics*, 91–4.
6. Hong, "Communist China and the Asian Games 1951–1990," 480.
7. Guttmann, *The Olympics*, 144–5.
8. Hong and Zhouxiang, "China, The Asian Games and Asian Politics," 100.
9. Ibid.
10. See Kurlantzick, *Charm Offensive*, 176–96.
11. See Horton and Saunders, "The 'East Asian' Olympics: What of Sustainable Legacies?" 11–12.
12. Cha, *Beyond the Final Score*, 85–6.
13. See "The Xth Asian Games in Seoul: A Successful Venture," 700–2.
14. Typically, little or no comment regarding this achievement could be found in the Australian media.
15. Cha, *Beyond the Final Score*, 90–3.
16. Xu, "Modernizing China in the Olympic Spotlight," 94–5.
17. See Horton, "Geopolitical Balance Post-Beijing 2008," 2541–2.
18. See IOC, *Final Report of the IOC XXIX Olympiad, Beijing*, 16.
19. Hong and Zhouxiang, "China, The Asian Games and Asian Politics," 109–10.
20. This indicates that Guangzhou's GDP for 2009, which is nearly ¥950 billion, was larger than such as countries Vietnam. See "China to Close Asian Games After Spending More Money Than London Olympics" (*Bloomberg News*, November 26, 2010 12:49 PM GMTþ1000). http://www.bloomberg.com/news/2010-11-25/china-to-close-asian-games-with-budget-topping-london-olympics.html
21. Macleod, Calum, "China Turns to Youth for Asian Games" (*USA TODAY*, accessed June 21, 2012). http://www.usatoday.com/news/world/2011-01-03-asia-games_N.htm
22. Ibid.
23. "GAGOC presents OCA with 16th Asian Games Archive."
24. Hong and Zhouxiang, "The Politicisation of the Beijing Olympics," 158–66.
25. See "Beijing's Bad Faith Olympics." (*New York Times*, August 22, 2008), cited in Nafees A. Syed. "The Effect of Beijing 2008 on China's Image in the United States: A Study of US Media and Polls." *The International Journal of the History of Sport* 27, no. 16–18 (2008): 2863–2892.

26. P. Waldmeir, "Shanghai: Expo has a Transforming Effect" (*Financial Times.com*, October 27, 2010, 10:45). http://www.ft.com/cms/s/0/de3414cc-dfc8-11df-bed9-00144feabdc0.htm l#axzz243TyT1jzBy.
27. "Shanghai's World Expo to Close After Attracting Record 72 Million Visitors" (*Bloomberg News*, October 31, 2010 10:06 AM GMT+ 1000). http://www.bloomberg.com/news/2010-10-31/shanghai-s-world-expo-to-close-after-attracting-record-72-million-visitors.html.
28. "'Best Ever' Asian Games Lowers Curtain."
29. "China to Close Asian Games After Spending More Money Than London Olympics."
30. "Guangzhou Asian Games Shows China's soft power: Zardari" (*People's Daily Online*, November 14, 2010, 10:37). http://english.people.com.cn/90001/90776/90883/7198667.html.
31. Ibid.
32. Hong and Zhouxiang, "China, The Asian Games and Asian Politics," 188.
33. I. Ransom, "Chastened China Sees Tough Road ahead to Rio" (*Reuters*, accessed August 20, 2012). http://www.reuters.com/london-olympics-2012/articles/china/liu-xiang/2012/08/12/chastened-china-sees-tough-road-ahead-rio.
34. Ibid.
35. Attributed to Lao-tzu, who is traditionally regarded as the founder of Taoism. See, "Lao-tzu, The Father of Taoism."
36. For an excellent overview see, Wang and Vangeli, "China's Leadership Succession."
37. See Horton, "The Asian Impact on the Sportisation Process." 518–28.
38. Ibid., 521–4.
39. See *Australia in the Asian Century: An Issues Paper*, December, 2011, 3.
40. "Australia's Trade with East Asia," 7.
41. Fitzgerald, "Australia and China at Forty," 20.
42. Ibid.
43. In Guangzhou, there were 14 additional sports, while in Incheon, there were only 7. The established and idiosyncratically Asian sports of Kabaddi, Sepak Takraw, Karate and Wushu were included, while board games (Chess, Weigi and Xiangi), cue sports (Billiards and Snooker), Dragonboat racing, Cricket (because of the lack of facilities) Softball and Dancesports have been omitted. See "The Olympic Council of Asia."
44. "China–Australia Trade Figures – 2011." Australian merchandise trade with China, 2011:

	Volume	Total share (%)	Rank	Growth (yoy) (%)
Exports to China (A$m)	71,561	27.3	1st	22.5
Imports from China (A$m)	42,144	18.6	1st	7.4
Total trade (A$m)	113,705	23.2	1st	16.4

45. Horton, "Sport in Asia," 131–9.

References

Australia in the Asian Century: An Issues Paper. Australia in the Asian Century Task Force: Commonwealth of Australia, December 2011.
"Australia's Trade with East Asia." Accessed February 5, 2013. https://www.dfat.gov.au/publications/stats-pubs/Australia-trade-with-east-asia-2011.pdf
"'Best Ever' Asian Games Lowers Curtain." Accessed November 28, 2010 09:18. http://english.east day.com/e/101128/u1a5576261.html
Cha, V. *Beyond the Final Score: The Politics of Sport in Asia*. New York: Columbia University Press, 2009.
"China–Australia Trade Figures – 2011." Accessed August 23, 2012. http://www.dfat.gov.au/geo/fs/chin.pdf
Fitzgerald, S. "Australia and China at Forty: Stretch of Imagination." Keynote Lecture, Australian Centre on China in the World, Australian National University, November 12, 2012, 1–30. http://ciw.anu.edu.au/events/2012/fitzgerald/ciwstephenfitzgeraldoration12Nov2012.pdf
"GAGOC Presents OCA with 16th Asian Games Archive." Accessed August 18, 2012. http://www.ocasia.org/News/IndexNewsRM.aspx?WKegervtea2XTZrfkgZyaB+me1e8kUuR
Guttmann, A. *The Olympics: A History of the Modern Games,* 2nd edn. Champaign, IL: University of Illinois Press.

Hong, Fan. "Communist China and the Asian Games 1951–1990: The Thirty-nine Year Struggle to Victory." *Sport in Society* 8, no. 3 (2005): 479–92.

Hong, Fan, and Xiong Xiaozheng. "Communist China: Sport, Politics and Diplomacy." In *Sport in Asian Society: Past and Present*, edited by J. A. Mangan, and Fan Hong, 319–42. London: Frank Cass, 2003.

Hong, Fan, and Lu Zhouxiang. "China, The Asian Games and Asian Politics." *The International Journal of the History of Sport* 29, no. 1 (2012): 98–112.

Hong, Fan, and Lu Zhouxiang. "The Politicisation of the Beijing Olympics." *The International Journal of the History of Sport* 29, no. 1 (2012): 157–183.

Horton, P. "The Geopolitical Balance of the Asia-Pacific Region Post Beijing 2008: An Australian Perspective." *The International Journal of the History of Sport* 27, no. 14 (2010): 2530–66.

Horton, P. "Sport in Asia: Globalization, Glocalization, Asianization." In *New Knowledge in a New Era of Globalization*, edited by Piotr Pachura. Rjekia: Intech Open-Access Publisher. ISBN 978-953-307-501-3. June 2011. http://cdn.intechopen.com/pdfs/17529/InTech-sport_in_asia_globali zation_glocalization_asianization.pdf

Horton, P. "The Asian Impact on the Sportisation Process." *The International Journal of the History of Sport* 29, no. 4 (2012): 511–34.

Horton, P., and J. E. Saunders. "The 'East Asian' Olympics: What of Sustainable Legacies?" *The International Journal of the History of Sport* 29, no. 6 (2012): 887–911.

IOC. *The Final Report of the IOC Coordination Committee: Games of the XXIX Olympiad, Beijing.* Lausanne: IOC, 2008.

Kurlantzick, J. *Charm Offensive: How China's Soft Power is Transforming the World.* Melbourne: Melbourne University Press, 2007.

"Lao-tzu, The Father of Taoism." Accessed July 20, 2012. http://www.chebucto.ns.ca/Philosophy/ Taichi/lao.html

Lynch, M. *The Chinese Civil War 1945–1949.* Oxford: Osprey Publishing, 2010.

"The Olympic Council of Asia." http://ocasia.org/Game/GameParticular.aspx?VKZk7uGbk/C5i kIBubFL4g=

"The Xth Asian Games in Seoul: A Successful Venture." *The Olympic Review*, 700–2. National Committee, Lausanne: IOC, 1986.

Wendland, J. "China Launches Massive Rescue After Sichuan Earthquake." (*People's Weekly World Newspaper*, May 13, 2008, 17:01). http://www.pww.org/article/articleview/13047/

Xu, Xin. "Modernizing China in the Olympic Spotlight: China's National Identity and the 2008 Beijing Olympiad." *The Sociological Review* 54, no. Suppl. 2 (2006): 90–107.

Wang, Zhengxu, and Anastas Vangeli. "China's Leadership Succession: New Faces and New Rules of the Game." European Institute of Security Studies, August 2, 2012. http://www.iss.europa. eu/publications/detail/article/chinas-leadership-succession-new-faces-and-new-rules-of-the-game/.

The Asian Games and Diplomacy in Asia: Korea–China–Russia

Victor Cha

Georgetown University, Washington, DC 20057, USA

In this article, I will look at the impact of sport on relations between states. In particular, I will study the role that sport has played in enhancing (or damaging) diplomacy in international relations. I will look especially at the role that the Olympics and the Asian Olympics have played in promoting diplomatic breakthroughs between countries. My cases focus on the use of sports diplomacy to foster the end of the Cold War in Asia, studying the breakthroughs between Korea, China and Russia. I will then look at the Beijing Games of 2008 and Guangzhou Asian Games of 2010.

You have opened a new chapter in the relations of the American and Chinese people. I am confident that this beginning again of our friendship will certainly meet with majority support of our two peoples.

(Zhou En-Lai to US National Table Tennis Team
Members, April 14, 1971, Great Hall of the People)[1]

With these historic words to a visiting delegation of American ping-pong players by the Chinese premier, a new era opened in Sino-American relations. This rapprochement would have an impact far beyond Asia as the world welcomed the wealth of economic and geostrategic benefits created by the meeting of East and West. Who would have thought that a little white ping-pong ball helped facilitate this sea change in world politics?

In this article, I will look at the impact of sport on relations between states. In particular, I will study the role that sport has played in enhancing (or damaging) diplomacy in international relations. I will look especially at the role that the Olympics and the Asian Olympics have played in promoting diplomatic breakthroughs between countries. My cases focus on the use of sports diplomacy to foster the end of the Cold War in Asia, studying the breakthroughs between Korea, China and Russia. I will then look at the Beijing Games of 2008 and Guangzhou Asian Games of 2010.

Sport and Diplomacy

Sport is more than sport. It is a tool of diplomacy. Sport events can carry a political significance that goes far beyond the final score.[2] This significance is measured not only in terms of status and reputation but also in terms of spurring countries and governments to overcome diplomatic obstacles. Sport offers a symbolic, high-profile, and yet tactful tool for diplomatic statecraft that can accomplish what a standard embassy demarche could not dream of accomplishing. In Asia, where tactfulness, symbolism and subtlety are highly valued, sport has been unusually central to policy, arguably more so than elsewhere in the world.

Sport has been successful at facilitating diplomacy in international relations. At certain times throughout history, sport has helped foster progress in difficult situations when normal diplomacy was ineffective. Sport can create public goodwill or provide opportunities for high-level contacts that might help to spur forward a stagnant diplomatic process. While 'ping-pong' diplomacy in Nixon's opening to China is the most well-known case, there are other interesting cases in Asia that can be discussed. Sport is usually not a sufficient condition on its own to create a breakthrough in diplomacy. But when it is combined with other trends, its uniqueness and timing to accomplish objectives that years of diplomatic demarches could not is shown, Baseball has been used as a tool to improve relations between the USA and Cuba. As far back as 1975, National Security Adviser Henry Kissinger and Secretary of State William Rogers talked with baseball commissioner Bowie Kuhn about replicating with Cuba a baseball version of 'ping-pong' diplomacy with China. In 1999, the Baltimore Orioles and the Cuban national team played exhibition games in the USA and Havana and the event was widely seen as a bilateral effort aimed at thawing relations.

Asian Sports Diplomacy

Two of the little known but most successful cases of sport diplomacy in Asia took place on the Korean peninsula; the 1988 Seoul Olympics and the 1986 and 1990 Asian Games. In each case, the Republic of Korea government utilised the sport event as an effective tool to overcome Cold War barriers with the Soviet Union and China. Though these cases are less well known when compared with ping-pong diplomacy, they represent an effective use of sport to engineer diplomatic breakthroughs that fundamentally changed the geostrategic environment around the peninsula. In the case of the 1988 Seoul Olympics, the ROK used the games to help establish diplomatic relations with Moscow in 1990. And in the case of Asian Games, events surrounding the 1986 Games (hosted in Seoul) and the 1990 Games (hosted in Beijing) gave the two countries the pretext for crossing the Cold War divide despite China's alliance with its communist North Korean brethren.

The 1988 Olympics and Korean Nordpolitik

The establishment of diplomatic relations between the ROK and the Soviet Union in 1990 was widely seen as a breakthrough step in ending the Cold War in Asia. The Soviet Union became the first major power in Asia to have diplomatic relations with both Koreas (China, the USA and Japan did not). The ROK used sport as a diplomatic tool in their larger strategy of 'nordpolitik' or 'northern policy'. Modelled on West Germany's 'ostpolitik', the Korean version, formed under the Roh Tae Woo government in 1988, stated that the ROK would seek normal relations with communist nations on the basis of pragmatism and economic benefits, and not based on ideology. Seoul would do this while maintaining three core policy principles. First, the new foreign policy outreach would be grounded in a stable domestic–political situation at home; second, the outreach would be grounded in strong relations with traditional allies (i.e. the USA) and third, it would be grounded in a strong economy.

Nordpolitik was a clear expression of South Korean confidence at the time.[3] Politically, the country had just gone through a peaceful transition to democracy in 1987. The economy was running at an extraordinary 12% annual growth rate, giving rise to an insurmountable economic gap with its rival North Korean regime. By any measure, the competition of social systems between the two that had raged during South Korea's earlier days of postwar poverty was now over with Seoul emerging the clear winner. In this sense, Roh's nordpolitik declaration of July 7, 1988, was not just about establishing diplomatic relations across the Cold War divide with Soviet bloc countries, but by doing so, also achieving the ultimate diplomatic victory of isolating the North from its communist patrons.

Nordpolitik's stated objective of normalising relations with the Soviet Union was by no means an easy task. There was a history of mutual hostility and non-dialogue between Moscow and Seoul. The Soviet–North Korea defense treaty, tens of millions of dollars in Soviet aid, and ideological support for Pyongyang made Moscow one of the primary patrons of the North Korean threat in the eyes of South Koreas. Similarly, the Soviets saw South Korea as a forward base for US ground, air and naval assets in the region, as well as the third leg in the 'iron triangle' (US–South Korea–Japan) designed to contain them. Non-dialogue and mutual recrimination was the dominant narrative for the relationship. Tensions reached their heights in 1983 when a South Korean civilian airline (KAL 007) was shot down by a Soviet fighter plane, killing over 200 passengers. This tragic incident resulted in the suspension of all bilateral dialogue including non-official private exchanges.

By the late-1980s, however, a series of developments pointed to a potential thaw in relations. In July 1986, Soviet leader Mikhail Gorbachev made a speech in Vladivostok calling for a new engaging role for the Soviet Union in Asia. In an effort to reduce tensions with China, Gorbachev also announced his intention to unilaterally draw down forces on the Sino-Soviet border. In July 1988, Roh announced the new nordpolitik policy and responded to Gorbachev's Vladivostok speech by calling for improved relations with communist countries based on pragmatism and economic gain. Gorbachev responded in September 1988 with a declaration at Krasnoyarsk, in which he explicitly stated his intentions to improve relations with the ROK. These declarations were followed by a series of economic contacts and semi-official political meetings between the two sides from 1988 to 1990. These contacts led to the establishment of trade offices by the South Korean government-backed KOTRA (Korea Trade Promotion Association) and the Soviet chamber of commerce in the summer of 1989. Consular functions were added to these trade offices in February 1990. These burgeoning contacts were finally consummated at the highest level in June 1990 in San Francisco. Presidents Roh and Gorbachev held the first ROK–USSR summit in postwar history and agreed in principle to establish formal relations. Relations were established in September 1990, followed by two additional summits in Moscow (December 1990) and Jeju Island (April 1991) in which the two leaders reaffirmed ties; the Soviets provided a formal apology for the KAL 007 shootdown in 1983; and the two countries inked a major US$3 billion loan agreement.

Sport and Non-Sport Factors

How does one explain the shift from decades of non-dialogue to diplomatic reconciliation in a period of 5 years (i.e. 1986–1990)? And what role did sport play? The prevailing explanation is the end of the Cold War. In South Korea, the end of the Cold War enabled Seoul to improve relations with Moscow without opposition from traditional partners, particularly the USA. Indeed, what facilitated the Roh–Gorbachev meeting in San Francisco in June 1990 was Gorbachev's earlier meeting with President George H.W. Bush in Washington, which effectively marked the end of the ideological hostility between the two superpowers.

An equally important factor lending to ROK–Soviet normalisation was Gorbachev's new political thinking and programme of domestic reform. From Moscow's viewpoint, it was physically a part of Northeast Asia, but had not yet enjoyed the full benefits of the region's phenomenal economic growth. Gorbachev sought to tap into these benefits through a combination of diplomatic initiatives and tension reduction measures. This was the purpose of the 1986 Vladivostok speech. It called for a unilateral withdrawal of Soviet troops from the Sino–Soviet border, reducing tensions with China, and enabling Gorbachev to meet with Deng in May 1989 (a historic visit obscured by the demonstrations in Tiananmen Square).

Of the Asian countries, South Korea was seen as a particularly good fit for Soviet needs. It was a source of consumer goods and could provide foreign capital and technology for the development of Siberia. Moreover, the Soviet hope was that the ROK could play the role that Japan had not. Soviet attempts at eliciting Japanese economic cooperation on Siberia in the 1970s fell flat as a result of uncertainties in Japanese assessments of the economic viability of the projects and the absence of a resolution of the longstanding northern territories issue. Seoul was a particularly good target: There was economic complementarity; there was hope that ROK interest in Siberia might spur Japanese interest and there was the view that outreach to a frontline Cold War state like South Korea might help to remove the stigma faced by Moscow as the region's threatening power.

South Korean incentives for normalising relations derived from the nordpolitik policy of the Roh government and the economic rationales described above. But an equally important motive for Seoul was winning the diplomatic competition with North Korea. Having one of the North's primary Cold War patrons officially extending diplomatic recognition to its archrival in the South was considered the ultimate diplomatic victory in further isolating the North. The Soviets indeed watered down its 'automatic intervention' commitment to the DPRK after ROK normalisation.

Finally, normalisation with the Soviets could pave the way for an ROK seat in the United Nations. Because of Cold War politics and the veto held by the two communist powers on the UN Security Council, the ROK was unable to become a member of the international organisation as a divided country. This constituted a source of great indignation for South Korean foreign policy-makers over the years as it reinforced the notion that South Korea was a 'pariah state' and not truly a member of the international community. Soviet recognition of the ROK removed a major obstacle to the goal of a UN seat, which the ROK finally achieved in 1991.[4]

Wooing the Soviets with Sport

Sport played a critical role in facilitating the breakthrough in Soviet–ROK relations. Sport provided a proximate event; the activities around it provided a way for each side to send clear signals of its interest in improving relations. While the strategic and domestic forces were conducive to an improvement in relations, an event like the Olympics was in many ways the trigger that enabled an accelerated diplomatic reconciliation to progress.

When Seoul won the bid in 1981 to host the games, many thought the lack of diplomatic relations with Eastern European countries and with the Soviet Union would be an inhibiting factor. The USA had just led a boycott of the 1980 Moscow Games, and the Soviets were expected to boycott the 1984 Los Angeles Games. Since the ROK was a frontline Cold War ally of the USA, there were real concerns that Moscow would again choose not to attend the Seoul Games. The ROK government adopted a two-pronged strategy: First, the Seoul Olympic organising committee undertook a full-court press early to win Soviet agreement to participate in the 1988 games. Second, the government used the Games as an opportunity to build goodwill and facilitate high-level meetings to achieve the expressed goals of nordpolitik.

Seoul's courting of the Russians began at the 1984 Los Angeles Games. ROK officials sought out representatives of the Soviet sports ministry, who were in attendance despite the boycott as officers of the international cycling federation, and enthusiastically called for their participation in the 1988 Games. They intimated how the Olympics could grease the skids for South Korean big business conglomerates entering the Soviet market with trade and investments. They pointed to the opening of trade promotion offices between the ROK and Hungary (all facilitated by Daewoo chairman Kim Woo Chung) as an example of the opportunities available to Moscow. Seoul's improving relations with other Eastern European countries put subtle pressure on the Soviets to follow suit. As the ROK moved forward with countries like Hungary in trade relations, they also gained public commitments from governments to attend the Seoul Olympics. This complicated any Soviet contemplation of a boycott because it might not be honored by other satellite countries. Though this was never stated explicitly as a strategy, it was a subtext of Seoul's smile diplomacy toward the Soviets.

As a political gesture intended to thaw relations and display the Asian sense of 'trust', Seoul offered to allow a Soviet ship to call at Incheon port for the duration of the Seoul Games if Moscow preferred its delegation not to stay in Seoul proper. The offer of Incheon was significant not only because it was unprecedented, but also because it was where MacArthur had landed during the Korean War. As a further gesture of 'trust', Seoul asked the Soviet Union to make available certain portions of airspace in conjunction with the Games. This was meant as a sign of willingness on the part of the ROK to move beyond the 1983 KAL shootdown.

The first indicator of the success of the ROK's engagement strategy came in April 1986. Roh Tae Woo, who would later become South Korea's president in 1987, succeeded in bringing 30 Eastern European countries and the Soviets to a preparatory meeting of the Seoul Games. Once the Soviets agreed to participate in the games, the ROK government built as much goodwill as possible. The ROK government allowed a 12,800 ton ship, the *Mikhail Sholokov*, to dock at Incheon harbour for over a month. Prior to the start of the Games, in August 1988 special envoy Park Chul-un carried a private letter to Gorbachev conveying Seoul's desire to seek normalised diplomatic relations.[5] Both the Moscow Philharmonic and the Bolshoi Ballet were invited to perform at the National Theater of Korea, which proved hugely popular among the South Korean public. Nelli Kim, a Soviet gymnast who participated in the 1976 and 1980 Olympics and who is half-Korean, appeared on Korean television for interviews and gymnastic performances. The public's enthusiasm was on full display at the opening ceremonies, when the Soviet delegation entered the stadium to the loudest standing ovation, second only to the Korean delegation.

In the end, the Soviet Union sent over 6000 athletes and tourists. Seoul's success in using sport to facilitate nordpolitik diplomacy was manifested in the flurry of diplomatic activity taking place in the aftermath of the Games. In February 1989, the ROK established diplomatic relations with Hungary. Two months later (April), trade offices were established with the Soviet Union. In November and December 1989, diplomatic relations were established with Poland and Yugoslavia. Czechoslovakia, Bulgaria and Romania followed in March 1990. And in September 1990, the ROK established full diplomatic relations with the Soviet Union. Sport did not cause normalisation in September 1990 between these two longtime adversaries, but it was instrumental in the pace of the diplomacy and as a vehicle for displaying good intentions. Without the Seoul Olympics, normalisation might not have come for quite some time.

The Asian Games and China's Engagement

South Korea's normalisation of relations with China in 1992 is perhaps one of the most understudied but successful cases of engagement.[6] The re-establishment of ties between these estranged countries constituted the second major step ending the Cold War in Asia. And as in the case of the Soviet Union, sport was used very effectively as a tool of diplomacy. In particular, the two countries' interaction over preparation for the 1986 Seoul Asian Games and the 1990 Beijing Asian Games was critical to the diplomatic breakthrough.

Between 1945 and 1980, the relationship between Seoul and Beijing was entirely adversarial. The Chinese intervened in the Korean War in September 1950 and prevented a US-led unification of the peninsula. From that point onward, Sino–ROK relations were characterised by non-dialogue and hostility arguably even more intense than that between the ROK and Soviet Union. China proclaimed a relationship as close as 'lips and teeth' with the communist North Korea and provided a security commitment to the North. The fact that ROK combat forces constituted the second largest ground contingent in the Vietnam War next to the USA only worsened Sino–ROK relations. Despite historical and cultural affinity between the two societies, this was a quintessentially Cold War relationship.

China–South Korea ties started to change from the 1980s. Economics was the primary engine as indirect trade through third countries (e.g. Hong Kong, Japan) steadily inclined. In 1979 trade stood at US$40 million and increased to US$222 million in 1984 and to US$518 million in 1985. An important and unexpected event that contributed to the thaw in relations occurred in May 1983 when a hijacked Chinese civilian airliner was forced to land in South Korea. Seoul and Beijing had to engage in direct negotiations for the return of the crew and aircraft to China. Resolving this incident produced goodwill on both sides that led to an increase in cultural and academic exchanges. Trade saw a big jump in 1986 (US$1.5 billion) that pushed China to 80% of South Korea's total trade with socialist countries. By 1989, total bilateral trade between the ROK and China exceeded by 10 times the total trade volume between China and the DPRK.

After the opening of trade offices, relations were punctuated by a number of cooperative acts. In November 1991, the ROK, as host of that year's APEC meetings, brought China to the meetings despite attendance by Taiwan and Hong Kong. This event enabled meetings between Chinese Foreign Minister Qian Qichen and Trade Minister Li Lanqing with the ROK President Roh. At the same time, China acquiesced in supporting South Korea's bid for UN membership. The two concluded a series of bilateral trade agreements granting the most favoured nation status. Finally, in August 1992, the two formally established diplomatic relations.

What were the determinants of this diplomatic outcome? The permissive condition was the end of the Cold War, but a more specific cause was the desire for both China and

South Korea to alienate rival regimes through normalisation. For Seoul, China was the ultimate prize in the zero-sum diplomatic competition with the DPRK. Having already made substantial inroads with Eastern European countries and the Soviet Union, the ROK viewed China as effectively completing the circle that would isolate the North. Similar incentives existed on the Chinese side. Like Seoul, Beijing saw relations with Seoul as isolating Taiwan. Beijing's required Seoul to adopt a one-China policy, which naturally meant the end of diplomatic relations with Taiwan. Taiwan–ROK relations had a rich history going back to the days of Syngman Rhee and Chiang Kai-shek in the 1950s and 1960s when both leaders supported each other as the first line of defense against Asian communism. Chiang offered to send troops to Korea during the 1950 Korean War. Taiwan was also the first government to recognise the ROK when it was established in 1948. Despite this history, Seoul abruptly and unceremoniously ended relations with Taipei in 1992.

There were also economic incentives for improving relations. China badly needed South Korean capital and technology and was intrigued by the ROK model of economic development which focused on capitalist export-oriented growth, without giving up political control. This 'strong state' model of development practiced by South Korea in the 1970s and 1980s offered much to learn for Deng Xiaoping's modernisation programme. Conversely, the ROK saw in China cheap labour and a large export market, particularly as it faced growing protectionist sentiments in traditional markets like the USA. Improved economic relations would benefit both countries in terms of trade – the ROK benefiting from the import of Chinese mineral resources (coal, petroleum) and agricultural and fishery products; and China benefiting from South Korean electronics, consumer goods and textiles.

In contemplating normalisation with the ROK, Beijing had to consider the impact this would have on relations with its traditional communist ally in the North. The Chinese were comparatively more sensitised to abandoning North Korea, much more so than the Soviets who abruptly did so in 1990. The Chinese would tell the DPRK that they pursued a dual track approach of maintaining old ties with traditional allies, but not restricting the potential for ties with new partners in the region. In typical inscrutable Chinese fashion, foreign ministry diplomats would refer to their position with North Korea as a 'door that is always open', and their position with South Korea as a 'door that is closed … but not locked'.

An important structural factor that prompted Beijing to go ahead with normalising ties with the ROK despite DPRK protests was the end of the Sino–Soviet split. The end of this longstanding conflict reduced the strategic value of the DPRK to both communist powers. The position Pyongyang had previously enjoyed as a country courted by both the Soviets and the Chinese was lost with Sino–Soviet reconciliation. Pyongyang had gone from a valuable ally to a political and economic liability for both communist patrons. China took the step across the Cold War divide with South Korea 2 years later than the Soviets, but it was one with equally devastating impact for the DPRK's bilateral relations as it suspended trade credits and moderated the nature of its defense commitment.

Asian Games Diplomacy

What role did sport play in facilitating Sino–ROK relations? A confluence of structural factors (i.e. end of the Cold War, end of the Sino–Soviet split) and domestic factors (i.e. zero-sum diplomacy with DPRK and Taiwan; economic complementarities) inclined Seoul and Beijing to improve relations. A fortuitous set of events surrounding the 10th

THE ASIAN GAMES: MODERN METAPHOR FOR 'THE MIDDLE KINGDOM' REBORN

(1986) and 11th (1990) Asian Games, however, transformed economic cooperation in the 1980s to political cooperation and eventually normalisation in the 1990s.

The summer Asian Games – a slimmed down regional version of the Olympics – were scheduled to be held in 1986 in Seoul and in 1990 in Beijing. For Seoul, the Games were effectively a dress rehearsal for the 1988 Seoul Olympics and planners worked feverishly to complete construction for the Olympic venues in time for the 1986 Asian Games. As noted above, Seoul wanted to ensure maximum participation for the Olympics, so the effort started with ensuring maximum participation at the 1986 Asian Games from countries across the Cold War divide. The organising committee lobbied China to send a large delegation. They wanted Chinese officials and athletes to come to Seoul, perform well in the competitions and generally have a good time. Through this experience, which would be broadcasted throughout Asia, the Games could build goodwill and change Chinese and South Korean perceptions.

The plan worked. China ended up having the largest delegation at the Games. The Chinese team tallied the most gold medals (94) and came in second in the total medal count (to the ROK hosts). Visiting athletes and officials praised the Korean hosts' hospitality and friendliness. Visiting dignitaries, moreover, returned to China with a newfound respect and interest in South Korea's modernisation. Chinese government-run media outlets ran glowing commentary on the way South Korea had combined Western modernity with Confucian traditions. The communist party journal *Hongqi* (Red Flag) and the prestigious literary journal *Renmin Wenxue* (People's literature) were awash with lengthy observations of the Seoul Asiad (Asian Games). As Chae-jin Lee noted, these reports:

> praised the neatness and modernity of Seoul, the bustling South Gate market, the majesty of the Kyungbok Palace, the modern facility of *Chungang Ilbo* (a major South Korean newspaper), and the beautiful students at Ewha Women's University. [The article] observed that Korean girls always smiled and wore modern dress but observed traditional customs ... [the Chinese author] was impressed that many South Koreans volunteered to work for the Asian Games. He vividly described the opening and closing ceremonies that emphasized Korean traditions.[7]

Because of the superior performance of their own athletes, the Chinese had every incentive to broadcast the Seoul games widely at home. This had the effect of conveying to a wider Chinese audience images of a cosmopolitan Seoul, which starkly contrasted with the destitute and poverty-stricken picture of the DPRK.[8] The overall experience was an important step in building goodwill to complement the burgeoning economic interactions at the time.

Fours years later, China found itself in frantic preparations for hosting the Asian Games, its first major international sport event. A great deal was at stake. In 1978 Deng Xiaoping stated that as China modernised, it would one day host the Olympics, and Chinese officials believed that time had come. They believed a strong showing as the hosts of the 1990 Asian Games would be their prelude to an Olympics bid. The problem faced by the Chinese, however, was that they received minimal support from countries in the world because of international outrage over the Tiananmen Square massacre in June 1989.

The ROK went against the climate of international opinion to help support Beijing's preparations. While the USA, Japan, and the European Union imposed sanctions, the Roh government used the opportunity to expand political and economic cooperation. In a memorable statement, then-foreign minister Choi Ho-joong announced that the ROK and China ' ... [o]ut of political consideration for social stability, China will leave open the possibility for improvement of relations with us. We will also continue to exert efforts to improve relations with China both on governmental and private levels'.[9] Having just hosted the 1986 Asian Games and the 1988 Seoul Olympics, Seoul lavished every manner of assistance on Beijing. This included political support, technical support, logistics and financial assistance. President Roh personally lobbied Asian leaders, many of whom he had just hosted for the Seoul Olympics, to avoid a boycott of Beijing's Asian Games. Over 22,000 South Korean sports fans flowed into Beijing, assisting a Chinese tourist industry decimated by Tiananmen. South Korean conglomerate Hyundai and other carmakers donated over 400 vehicles to China for the transport of athletes and officials at the Games, and with other South Korean companies provided over US$15 million in advertising revenues.[10] Three Korean chaebol conglomerates, Samsung, Lucky-Goldstar and Daewoo, each spent between US$3 and US$5 million on advertising in China, and one estimate put total ROK government and private sector support of the Beijing Asian Games at about US$100 million.[11] A newspaper report captured the phenomenon: 'a flood of South Korean advertising and contributions for the Asian Games is intended to promote Beijing–Seoul ties that could benefit the economies of both nations and contribute to peace on the Korean Peninsula'.[12] ROK President Roh dispatched his relative to lead the presidential delegation to Beijing which conveyed a personal commitment to improve political relations. Key government officials held low-profile, high-level talks on the establishment of trade offices and normalisation of relations.

The North protested to China about South Korea's assistance, but Beijing gladly accepted it. Jiang Zemin, Chinese Communist Party General Secretary, also reportedly rejected DPRK leader Kim Il-sung's requests to limit the size of the South Korean delegation, to not fly the ROK flag at the Games and to reduce the prominence of ROK company advertising billboards at the Games.[13] In the end, China hosted a successful Asiad. Their athletes excelled in the competition, winning the total gold, silver and overall medal counts. Now, because of Seoul's help, the Chinese could set their sights on the next stage – during the closing ceremonies of the Asiad, Chinese President Yang Shangkun met with the International Olympic Committee chairman Juan Antonio Samaranch and informed him of China's intention to bid for the 2000 Olympics. The ROK and China established trade offices shortly after the conclusion of the 1990 games, which then made normalisation a foregone conclusion less than 2 years later.

The Guangzhou Games

Countries and cities in Asia that covet international sporting events do so because they constitute benchmarks of national identity and development. The 1964 Tokyo Olympics, 1988 Seoul Olympics and 2008 Beijing Olympics constituted 'coming-out' parties for these nations to mark their auspicious arrival on the world stage. The games become a political statement to the world about a country's worthiness, refracted through the prisms of performance and preparations.

Bidding for and hosting the games, therefore, is a calculated risk. A poorly run and ill-prepared Olympics could embarrass a country during its moment in the sun. In 1970, for example, South Korea won the bid to host the Asian Games, but then in embarrassment, it cancelled for reasons of finances (Thailand, the previous host, stepped in at the last minute to host in Seoul's place). City officials bid when they believe the nation is on the cusp of greatness, or near it such that hosting an Olympics can propel them over the line. Thus, when an Asian city like Seoul or Beijing prepares to host the world, it does so with almost panic-like frenzy, sparing no expense to ensure a prideful display of advanced industrial and global prowess.

According to the Global Cities Index, 5 out of the world's top 10 global cities are in Asia and by 2025, well over 40% of the world's 75 most dynamic cities (measured in terms of contribution to overall global GDP growth) will be in Asia versus only 13 US cities.[14] It is no wonder, therefore, that we see more cities in Asia now bidding for the Olympics and using the Asian Games as preparation. Following a model set by Seoul (1986 Asian Games and 1988 Olympics) and Beijing (1990 Asian Games and 2008 Olympics), these cities are in search of their moment in the sun. Each of these games becomes a metaphor for Asia's rise in the international system.

The Asian Games is the largest multi-sport competition in the world other than the Olympics. They were first held in 1951 and have grown from 489 athletes and 11 countries at the inaugural games to 9704 competitors from 45 territories and regions in the recent 2010 games in Guangzhou (see Table 1).

The 2010 Guangzhou Asian Games, which took place in Guangzhou, Guangdong Province, China, in November 2010, was the largest international sporting event held in China since the 2008 Beijing Olympics. In one sense, these games represented a new beginning for China in international sport after the climatic 2008 Games. In another, it represented a continuation of China's rise in international sport as another city stepped up to the plate to host the world. The Guangzhou Games was a relatively large gathering, with over 14,500 athletes and officials from 45 Asian countries.[15]

The Guangzhou Asian Games became a vehicle for projecting Chinese diplomacy and identity. The theme of the Games, 'Thrilling Games, Harmonious Asia', suggested the priority was placed on the promotion of congenial regional relations, and to foster economic cooperation and diplomacy. Sister city diplomacy was practiced between China and Southeast Asia by the mayor of Guangzhou, Wan Qingliang, who presented Sanan Kachornprasart, Deputy Prime Minister of Thailand, with a souvenir of the Games' mascot (Bangkok had previously hosted four Asian Games). During Wan's visit, both parties reached the consensus that Thailand would provide free Thai fruits to the Asian Games. Meanwhile, Guangdong would provide 20 stands for Thailand at the Small- and Medium-

Table 1.   Asian Games 1951–2019.[20]

Year	Site	Participating territories
1951	New Delhi, India	11
1954	Manila, Philippines	19
1958	Tokyo, Japan	16
1962	Jakarta, Indonesia	12
1966	Bangkok, Thailand	16
1970	Bangkok, Thailand (South Korea cancelled)	16
1974	Tehran, Iran	19
1978	Bangkok, Thailand	19
1982	New Delhi, India	23
1986	Seoul, South Korea	25
1990	Beijing, China	36
1994	Hiroshima, Japan	42
1998	Bangkok, Thailand	44
2002	Busan, South Korea	45
2006	Doha, Qatar	45
2010	Guangzhou, China	45
2014	Incheon, South Korea	n/a
2019	Hanoi, Vietnam	n/a

Sized Enterprises Expo and promote the popularity of Thai fruits through sale exhibitions.[16]

The Guangzhou Games also acted as a vehicle for promoting tourism and economic diplomacy with China's neighbours. There is a cache associated with being a city that hosts the Asiad, and this attracts visitors. After the Games Cao Jianliao, the vice mayor of Guangzhou, visited Seoul and Pusan to promote tourism in Guangzhou.[17] Statistics from Guangzhou Tourism Bureau show that between November 12th and November 27th, Guangzhou received a total of 8.66 million tourists, up by 42.10% over the same period of last year. Of those tourists, 3.8619 million stayed in hotels, up by 32.22%. As a result, 7 billion Yuan (US$112,070,000) of tourism revenues were generated during the Guangzhou Asian Games.[18]

Finally, the promotional videos and materials associated with the Asian and Olympic Games provided a well-publicised platform to generate soft power for China. Guangzhou's contribution to this was its official video, 'Fate Brings us to Guangzhou', which depicted the Games as the confluence of different traditions in Asia coming together in Guangzhou. The traditions included a Chinese dragon boat team, an Indian Kabaddi team, Iraqi track and field athletes, equestrians from the UAE, weightlifters from Central Asia and footballers from Japan. The video won awards, but more importantly, it conveyed the message that the disparate and diverse traditions of Asia came together in harmony in China.[19] The latter may seem minor to Westerners, precisely because Western media attention to the Games is fairly minor. In Asia, by contrast, the Asian Games is widely reported in the press and media. While eight major Western press (*CNN, AP, New York Times, Washington Post, AFP, Reuters*, etc.) published only 10 articles on the Guangzhou Games, Japanese media published over 50 articles. In general, the Asian Games has promoted the city image and publicity of Guangzhou in Asia and worldwide. It also provided a useful vehicle for China to promote diplomacy aimed at engaging regional powers, all with very little Western attention. Given the growing affluence and productivity of Chinese cities that will make up close to 40% of the world's most dynamic metropolises, we should expect to see many more Asian Games, and perhaps more Olympics emanating from China.

Notes on Contributor

Victor Cha is D.S. Song-KF Professor of Government and International Affairs and Director of Asian Studies, Georgetown University, and Senior Adviser at the Center for International and Strategic Studies (CSIS) in Washington, DC. He is the author of *Beyond the Final Score: The Politics of Sport in Asia* (Columbia University Press, 2009). The author thanks Tianyi Wang for research assistance on this article.

Notes

1. Kissinger, *White House Years*, 710.
2. Cha, *Beyond the Final Score*.
3. Izumikawa, "South Korea's Nordpolitik," 605–642.
4. Soviet opposition was even more important to overcome than Chinese opposition since achievement of the seat came in 1991, before Sino-South Korean normalization the following year.
5. Izumikawa, "South Korea's Nordpolitik," 622–623.
6. Portions of this section are based on Victor Cha, "Engaging China," 32–56.
7. Lee, *China and Korea*, 145 and 146.
8. Ibid., 112.
9. Izumikawa, "South Korea's Nordpolitik," 629.

THE ASIAN GAMES: MODERN METAPHOR FOR 'THE MIDDLE KINGDOM' REBORN

10. Lee, *China and Korea*, 150.
11. Shim, "Diplomatic Games," 26.
12. *Los Angeles Times*, September 21, 1990.
13. Shim, "Diplomatic Games," 26.
14. Foreign Policy 2010 Global Cities Index, as reported on *CNN*. http://travel.cnn.com/shanghai/life/shanghai-most-global-city-china-think-again-692243
15. Guoping He and Ruiying Wang, "Guangzhou Yayunhui Yu Guangzhou Chengshi Xingxiang Duiwai Chuanbo" (Guangzhou Asian Games and the Publicity of the City Image of Guangzhou) (*Duiwai Chuanbo (Overseas Publicity)*, November 1, 2010: 40). Liu He, "Yayunhui Cansaiguo Sulan" (An Overview of the Guangzhou Asian Games partic ipating countries Guangzhou) (*China Reports*, November 1, 2010: 32).
16. "Wan Qingliang Led Delegation to Thailand, Promoting the Guangzhou Asian Games," (*Guangzhou Daily*, July 20, 2010). http://www.gz.gov.cn/publicfiles/business/htmlfiles/gzgov/s2342/201007/554396.html
17. "First Tourism Promotion Meeting after the Asian Games Held in Korea," (*Guangzhou Daily*, December 28, 2010). http://www.gz.gov.cn/publicfiles/business/htmlfiles/gzgov/s2342/201012/716584.html
18. "Seven Billion Yuan of Tourism Revenues during Asian Games," (*Guangzhou International*, December 6, 2010). http://english.gz.gov.cn/publicfiles/business/htmlfiles/gzgoven/s4171/201105/808814.html
19. "Guangzhou Asian Games Official Film Wins Distinction," (*Guangzhou International*, November 7, 2011). http://english.gz.gov.cn/publicfiles/business/htmlfiles/gzgoven/s4171/201111/870422.html
20. "Guangzhou Yayunhui De Duiwai."

References

Cha, Victor. "Engaging China: The View from Korea." In *Engaging China*, edited by Alastair Johnston, and Robert Ross, 32–56. New York: Routledge, 1999.

Cha, Victor. *Beyond the Final Score: The Politics of Sport in Asia*. New York, NY: Columbia University Press, 2009.

"Guangzhou Yayunhui De Duiwai Zhuanbo Celiu Fenxi" (Overseas publicity strategy of Guangzhou Asian Games), *Media Practice Research*, no. 2 (2010): 59.

Izumikawa, Yasuhiro. "South Korea's Nordpolitik and the Efficacy of Asymmetric Positive Sanctions." *Korea Observer* 37, no. 4 (2006): 605–642.

Kissinger, Henry. *White House Years*. Boston, MA: Little, Brown & Company, 1979.

Lee, Chae-jin. *China and Korea*. Stanford: Hoover Press, 1996.

Shim, Jae-hoon. "Diplomatic Games: South Korea Uses Asian Sports to Boost China Ties." *Far Eastern Economic Review*, October 4, 1990, 26.

Index

Note:
Page numbers in **bold** type refer to figures
Page numbers in *italic* type refer to tables
Page numbers followed by 'n' refer to notes

advertising: revenues 99–100
Ali, S.W. 31
alienation 16
All-China Sports Federation 16, 17
Althusser, L. 82–3
America's Pacific Century (Clinton) 68
analogy 8–10
Apple Daily **83**, **84**, **87**
Asada, M. **115**
Asian Football Confederation (AFC) 149
Asian Games Federation (AGF) 16, 17, 18, 144
Asian Games Town Gymnasium **56**
Asian Taekwondo Union (ATU) 80, **81**
Asian Winter Games (AWG) 26–7, 32–3
athletes 78–9
attitudes 5
Australia 143, 147–51; future 150–1; geography 149–51; geopolitics 149–51; government 148

badminton 120
Bairner, A.: and Hwang, D.J. 78
Bang-Chool Kim: Mangan, J.A. and Sun-Yong Kwon 91–102
baseball 65–6; flags 70–2; Major League (MLB) 66, 67, 71, 73; World Classic (WBC) 71, **112**
basketball 117
Beer, D. 49
Beijing Asian Games (1990) 20, 92–3, 144, 145–6, 161; bid 29; gold medals 145; success 146
Beijing Olympic Games (2008) 2, 26, 58, 109, 146; gold medals 65; opening ceremony 100–1; slogan 70; volunteers 101
Benedict, R. 70
bids 26–33, 37–44; Beijing Asian Games (1990) 29; Changchun (China) 31; Harbin (China) 30–1; IMSEs *28*; international 38, 44; process 38, *see also* Guangzhou (China) bid for Asian Games;
Bokhorrst-Heng, W. 131

Bong-Ju, L. 113, **114**
Bonian, S. 42
Brajnath, R. 135
Brand China 134
Bridges, B. 12
bus rapid transit (BRT) 55

Cao Jianliao 164
carmakers 162
Cha, V.D. 92–3, 103n, 110, 112, 125–6, 144–5, 154–64
Chan, C. 137, 141n
Changchun Asian Winter Games (China) 27, 31; bid 31; residents 31
Chen Hsian-zong 85
Chen Shui-bian 78
Cheonan 97–8, 104n; China's response 98
Chiang Kai-shek's clique 17–18
China General Sports Association (CGSA) 29–30
China (People's Republic of) 143, 144, 145, 164; athletes 3; Brand China 134; domination 5; dream 7–8; economy 37; energy 67–70; geography 50; geopolitics 26–33; gold medals 101–2, 145; government 44; Harbin 27, 30–1; international power 21, 143, 148; -Japan relations 119–22, **121**, **122**, **123**; map of provinces **51**; military 126; modern 4; motives 50; new 16; Olympic sport domination 66; Politburo (PB) 148; Politburo Standing Committee (PBSC) 148; politics 37, 143; Sino-American relations 154; Sino-South Korea relations 96, 98, 104n; soft power 94, 147, 148; soldiers 96; status 95; superpower 37, 59, 148; USA relations 68–9, *see also* Beijing; Changchun Asian Winter Games; Guangdong Province; Guangzhou Asian Games (2010); South Korea and China relations
Chinese Communist Party (CCP) 27
Chosun Sports Council 109
Chowdhry, K.A. 41

INDEX

Chu, M.P. 26–33, 37–44
Clausewitz, C. von 67
Clinton, H. 21, 68
communities: international 44; Internet 85–6
competition 18–20; tripartite 19–20
complex: concept 110–11; sport 110–11
Cooper, R. 119
cosmology 10–11
cricket 66
Cruz, A.: *et al* 108–27
Cui Tiankai 98
culture 10–11, 22–3, 37

Dahlgren, P. 85–6
Darwin, J. 10–11
Dayrit, C. 40, 42
Debord, G. 66–7
Deleuze, G. 67, 69
Democratic People's Republic of Korea (DPRK) 145, 159–61
Democratic Progressive Party (DPP) 85
Deng Xiaoping 78, 103n
diplomacy: ping-pong 155; sport 154–5, 160–2
displacement 10
Djakarta Asian Games 16–17
Dokdo (Korea) 113
dominance 4
domination: Chinese Olympic sport 66
Dong Jinxia 3, 53; Lu Di and Mangan, J.A. 49–62

East Asia Institute survey 99
Ebrey, P.B. 49
energy: China 67–70
enmity 120
European historical accounts 10–11
Ever Onward motto 144–5

Farman, H. 81
Farrer, J. 70
Fate Brings us to Guangzhou 164
Faust, G. 70
Fenby, J. 6–7
Ferguson, N. 127
Fitzgerald, S. 135
flags 70–2
football *see* soccer
friendship 18–19, 20–1
Fu Manchu 5

geopolitical hegemony 26
geopolitics: Australia 149–51; China 26–33
George, C. 132
Gi-Heun Kang: *et al* 108–27
Gitlin, T. 83
Global Cities Index 163

Goh Chok Tong 132, 135
gold medals 65, 145, 147; China 101–2, 145
Gorbachev, M. 156–7
governments 44, 131–2, 148, 158, 162
Gramsci 82
Gray, J. 10, 126–7
gross domestic product (GDP) 50, 57
Gross, J. 7
Guangdong Province (China) 50–2, **51**, 53, 58; inter/national profile 58
Guangning, Z. 32, 40, 42, 43
Guangzhou Asian Games (2010) 7, 21–2, 27, 49, 65–7, 72–3, 99–101, 118, 126, 133, 143, 147, 151n, 152n, 162–4; analogy 8–10; Asian Games Town Gymnasium **56**; bus rapid transit (BRT) 55; central business districts 54; China's efforts 66; city transformation 52–3; economic development 52; environment 57; *Fate Brings us to Guangzhou* 164; feat 9; games city **61**; glittering 9–10, **53**, **54**; Huadu Stadium **56**; Huangpu Centre Gymnasium **55**; international modern city 61; investment and construction 53, 55, 57; map **52**; medal table *50*; metaphor and analogy 8–10; migrant workers 57; new 57; night **61**; Pearl River **54**, **55**; political ambitions 58–9; political and geopolitical ambitions 58–9; politics 60–2; praise 60–1; provincial and city project 54–8; regional harmony and disharmony 59–60; residents 32; theme 163; tourism 164; transformation 52–3; transportation system 55; University Town Sports Centre **56**; venues 53–4
Guangzhou Asian Games Organizing Committee 53
Guangzhou Baiyun International Airport 55
Guangzhou (China) bid for Asian Games 32, 37–44; advantages 40; Candidature File 41; City Work Committee 42; division of labour 44; documents 41; inspectors 42–3; Letter of Intent 41; lobbying 39–40; officials 39–44; preparation 43–4; publicise 40–1; tasks 39
Guangzhou Tower 57
Guangzhou University Town Sports Centre **56**
Gyehyun, K. 100

Habermas, J. 87
Hak-Rae, L. 109
Hall, D. 71
Hall, S. 83
Han, I. 99
Harbin (China) 27, 30–1; bid 30–1; residents 30
Hatchten, W.A. 138

INDEX

Hatoyama, Y. 104n
hegemony 82; geopolitical 26
Hiroshima (Japan) 29
history 126
Holloway, S. 41
Hong, Fan: and Lu Zhouxiang 143
Honour of Taiwan 77
Horton, P. 131–9, 143–51
Hu Jintao 27, 59, 98, 148
Huadu Stadium **56**
Huangpu Centre Gymnasium **55**
Hurwitz 86
Hwang, D.J.: and Bairner, A. 78
Hwang Young-Cho 113, **114**

Ikenberry, J. 3, 62
imperialism 16–18
Incheon (Korea) 149, 152n
Incheon Organising Committee 101
Indonesia 16–17
international community 44
international multi-sport events (IMSEs) 28–9, 37; bids *28*; held in China *38*
International Olympic Committee (IOC) 2, 77
Internet communities 85–6

Jacobs, A. 132
Jacques, M. 60, 62, 117
Japan 19, 95; -China relations 119–22, **121, 122, 123**; Cycling Team 120; Figure Skating Team 120; occupation of Korea 109; -South Korea relations 111–13
Jardine, W.: and Matheson, J. 5
Jiang Zemin 27, 162
Jin Gee, O. 138
Joseph, N. 77
journalism 139; Third World development 131–2
judo 113

KAL-007 156
Kelly, J.D. 65–74
Kelly, W. 2
Kim Dae-jung 96, 104n
Kim, Hyun-Duck: *et al* 108–27
Kim Jang-Hwan 100
Kim, N. 158
Kin Yu Na **115**
Kissinger, H. 6, 8
Kok Hua, Loh 136–7, 141n
Korea *see* North Korea; South Korea
Korea Times 96–7
Korean War (1950–3) 104n
Kuomintang (KMT) 85
Kurlantzick, J. 132
Kyunghyang Shinmun 99

Lee, C.J. 161
Lee Hsien Loong 132, 139n
Lee Kuan Yew 131, 132, 138
Lee Myung-bak 94, 96, 98, 103n, 104n
Lee, P.C.: Mangan, J.A. and Liu, C.L. 77–88
Lei, H. 98
Lei, Z. 79
Li, F. 52
Li Menghua 29
Li, T. 135–6, 138
Li Xiannian 29
Li Yongning, 147
Li Zhuobin 39, 40, 41, 42
Lim Fah Kiong 135
Lim, L. 133, 135, 136, 137
Lim Say Heng 133–4, 136, 137
Lin Xinyi 134
Ling Chan Hong 133
Lingle, C. 131
Lingnan culture 58
Liu, C.L.: Lee, P.C. and Mangan, J.A. 77–88
Liu Peng 148
lobbying 39–40
London Olympics (2012) 146
Lovell, J. 5, 10
Low Teo Ping 133, 135–6, 137
Lu Di: Mangan, J.A. and Dong Jinxia 49–62
Luo Jingjun 22

MacAloon, J. 1
Macleod, C. 146
Major League Baseball (MLB) 66, 67, 71; league model 73; Players Association 71
Malabar war games 68
Mandela, N. 15
Mangan, J.A. 2, 4–12, 26, 44, 139; Dong Jinxia and Lu Di 49–62; *et al* 108–27; Kwon Sun-Yong and Bang-Chool Kim 91–102; Liu, C.L. and Lee, P.C. 77–88; memory 123–4; and Ok, G. 117, 125; sport as a mirror 111
Mao Zedong 103n
Matheson, J.: and Jardine, W. 5
Matsudaira, Y. 30
medals *50*, *118*; gold 65, 101–2, 145, 147
media 100–1, 131; Taiwan 78–9, 81–4, **83, 84, 87**
media coverage 15, 22–4
memory 123–4
metaphor 8–10
Middle Kingdom (Zhongguo) 1
migrant workers 57
Military Museum (Beijing) 96
military training **110**
Min, G.S. 99
modernisation 11

INDEX

Multi-Million Dollar Award Programme
(MAP) 134–5, 138
Al-Musallam, H. 146

narration 16–24; political 16–21; tripartite
competition 19–20
National Olympic Committee (NOC) 38–9,
40
nationalism 108
Neitzsche, F. 69
New Delhi Asian Games 144
New Paper, The 133–4, 139
New Zealand: All Blacks 72–3; rugby 72–3
news 23–4
News Chonji 102
newspapers 131–4, 139
Ng Ser Miang 136
non-Olympic events 23
North Korea (DPRK) 96, 97, 156; attacks 97
Northeast Asian History Foundation survey
99
northern policy (*nordpolitik*) 155–6

Ok, G. 91; and Mangan, J.A. 117, 125
Olympic Charter (UNESCO) 125
Olympic Council of Asia (OCA) 29–31, 33,
38–9, 40; Constitution and Rules 38–9;
Evaluation Committee 42; Executive Board
38–9
Olympic Formula 78
Olympic Games 1–2, *see also* Beijing
Olympic Games (2008); Seoul Olympic
Games (1988)
Olympic movement 71
Olympism 65–6
Opium War 5
Orwell, G. 120
otherness 4–5

Park Jung-woo 112–13
Park, R.J. 1–2
participation 18
Pearl River (Guangzhou) **54**, **55**
Peh Shing Huei 134
People's Action Party (PAP) 131, 139
People's Daily 15–24; highlighting Asia as a
whole 21–2; interviews 21; news 23–4; non-
Olympic events 23; reports *16*, *18–19*, *18*,
20; statistics 20–1
People's Republic of China (PRC) *see* China
ping-pong diplomacy 155
Players Association (MLB) 71–2
political narration 16–21
politics 85; China 37, 143; sport 109, **124**, *see
also* geopolitics
postcolonisation 111
power 4; soft 94, 147, 148

prejudice 5–7

Qi, Haixia: and Yan, Xuetong 68–9
Qing Luo: and Wenting Xue 15–24
Quan Zhezhu 31

racialism 109
racism 5
Ransom, I. 148
regional rivalries 50–2
Republic of Korea (ROK) *see* South Korea
rituals 71–2
Robert, G. 137
Roh Tae Woo 155–6, 158, 162
Roo Moo-hyun 96, 98, 104n
rugby 66, 72–3; New Zealand 72–3

Al-Sabah, A.F. 40, 147
sailing 136
Samaranch, J.A. 77
self-confidence 7
Seoul Asian Games (1986) 92–3, 144–5, 155,
161
Seoul Olympic Games (1988) 155–6, 162
Seung-Akhom, P. 39
Shanghai Expo (2010) 147
Singapore 131–9; government 131–2;
journalism 139; media 131; newspapers
131–4, 139; PAP 131, 139; regime 131;
sailing 136; Sports School 135; Team 132,
136; as top-ten sport nation 135; Yacht
Club 136
Singapore Press Holdings (SPH) 132
sites *163*
situations 66–7
skating **115**
slogan 70
soccer: South Korea-Japan Soccer World Cup
(2002) 112–13, 114, **116**
South China Sea 68
South Korea (ROK) 19, 71, 113, 144–5, 155–
6, 158–60; advertising revenues 99–100;
basketball 117; companies 162; economy
111; gold medals 147; government 158,
162; history 91; -Japan relations 111–13;
medals *118*; media 100–1; memorial service
116; patriotic zeal 111; Seoul Asian Games
(1986) 92–3, 144–5, 155, 161; Seoul
Olympic Games (1988) 112, 155–6, 162;
Taiwan's hostility 86–7; and USA 114–15;
WBC **112**
South Korea (ROK) and China relations 91–
102, 104n, 116–18, *117*, 159–60; assets 95;
Chinese outbursts **120**; cooperation 96;
debits 95; declining 91; economies 92–3;
honeymoon 93–4, 98; mutual accord 92–3;

170

INDEX

mutual benefit 92–3, 96; tourism 95; trading 94–5; views 99

South Korea-Japan Soccer World Cup (2002) 112–13, 114; ceremonial dance **116**

Soviet Union 155–9

sport 8, 108, 110, 124–5; diplomacy 154–5, 160–2; mirror 111; politics 109, **124**

sport complex 110–11

state 108–9

statism 109

Straits Times, The 134, 135, 139

Sun Xiuqing 133

Sun-Yong Kwon: Bang-Chool Kim and Mangan, J.A. 91–102

Sunstein, C.R. 86

superpower: China 37, 59, 148

taekwondo 79, 86; World Federation (WTF) 79, 80, 81, 118

Taiwan 16–17, 77–9, 160; athletes 78–9; DPP 85; economy 78; Honour of Taiwan 77; hostility towards South Korea 86–7; KMT 85; media 78–9, 81–4; media articles **83**, **84**, **87**; Olympic committee 77; politics 85; sporting successes 78; sports development 77–8

Tan, B. 136, 137, 139

Team Singapore 132, 136

Thailand 163–4

Third World development journalism 131–2

Tokyo Bid Committee 121–2

tourism 95, 164

trading 94–5

Tu Qiyu 147

UNESCO 125

United Nations (UN) 77

United States of America (USA) 68, 114–15, 154; -China relations 68–9

unity 18–19

volunteers 101

Voon, T. 138

Wan Qingliang 163

Wang Xiaoling 40–1

Wang Yi 24

Weber, M. 67

Wenting Xue: and Qing Luo 15–24

Western press 164

women 3

World Baseball Classic (WBC) 71, **112**

World Taekwondo Federation (WTF) 79, 80, 81, 118

Wu Jing-yu 82

Wu Xueqian 29

www.yahoo.com 71

Xi Jinping 7

Xinhua News Agency 102

Xu Deli 39, 40

Yan Xuetong 126; and Qi Haixia 68–9

Yang Jin Suk 79, 80, 82

Yang Shu-chun 77, 79–82, 88, 118, **119**; disqualification **80**; sensor socks 79–80

Yeonpyeong 97–8

Yonhap News 103n, 105n

Yu Mengyu 138

Yuan Weimin 31, 41, 43

Zardari, A.A. 147

Zhou En-Lai 19, 154

Zhouxiang, Lu and Hong Fan 143

Zweig, D. 68, 70

www.routledge.com/9780415644952

Related titles from Routledge

The Politicisation of Sport in Modern China
Communists and Champions

Fan Hong and Lu Zhouxiang

The Politicisation of Sport in Modern China: Communist and Champions is the first book in English which examines in chronological order key issues in sport in the People's Republic of China from 1949 to 2012 in the context of Chinese history, politics and society.

It explores the complexity of Chinese sport including the sovietisation of Chinese sports policy and practice; the emergence of the 'two Chinas' issue; the Cold War, the Cultural Revolution, sports diplomacy and sports militarism; China's turbulent journey of participation in the Asian Games and in the Olympics; the politics and policy of doping and anti-doping in Chinese sport; and China's sport in the post-Beijing Olympics era.

This book was published as a special issue of the *International Journal of the History of Sport*.

Fan Hong is the Head of the School of Asian Studies at University College Cork.

Lu Zhouxiong is Lecturer of Contemporary Chinese Studies in the School of Languages and Cultures at the National University Ireland Maynooth.

Feb 2013: 246 x 174: 224pp
Hb: 978-0-415-64495-2
£85 / $145

For more information and to order a copy visit
www.routledge.com/9780415644952

Available from all good bookshops

www.routledge.com/9780415529884

Related titles from Routledge

The Triple Asian Olympics - Asia Rising
The Pursuit of National Identity, International Recognition and Global Esteem

Edited by J. A. Mangan, Sandra Collins and Gwang Ok

The Triple Asian Olympics: Asia Rising explores the realities of global transformation, regional ascendancy and metaphorical modernity of the East Asian Olympics and, by extension, East Asia. As the axis of global geo-political and economic power shifts to the East, analyzing the significance of the Olympic Games in East Asia becomes significant to an understanding the shifting nature of the nations of East Asia. The Triple Asian Games are harbingers of dramatic geopolitical change.

This book was originally published as a special issue of *The International Journal of the History of Sport*.

J.A.Mangan, FRHS, FRAI, D. Litt is emeritus Professor, Strathclyde University, UK

Sandra Collins is an Assistant Professor of History of California State University-Chico, USA.

Gwang Ok is a professor of Exercise Science at Chungbuk National University in South Korea.

Sep 2012: 246 x 174: 216pp
Hb: 978-0-415-52988-4
£85 / $140

For more information and to order a copy visit
www.routledge.com/9780415529884

Available from all good bookshops